A Grace Ca[...]
A Story for the World

Fr. Jean Jaouen, M.S.
Translated from the French by Fr. Normand Theroux, M.S.

Missionaries of La Salette Corporation
915 Maple Avenue
Hartford, CT 06114-2330, USA
www.lasalette.org

First English Edition by Grassroots Publishing International, Enfield, N.H. copyright 1991, Normand Theroux, M.S.

Second English Edition by Missionaries of La Salette Corporation, 915 Maple Avenue Hartford, CT 06114-2330, USA February 2nd, 2019

Original Copyright: September 19, 1936, printed by The La Salette Press, Altamont, New York

Imprimi Potest: Rev. Fr. René J. Butler, M.S., Provincial Superior Missionaries of Our Lady of La Salette, Province of Mary, Mother of the Americas 915 Maple Avenue Hartford, CT 06106-2330 USA

Editor: Fr. Ron Gagne, M.S.

Booklet design and formatting: Jack Battersby and Fr. Ron Gagne, M.S.

Bible version: NABR version (United States Catholic Conference of Bishops), used with permission.

Visuals: Most have been used with permission from our La Salette Archives in our Generalate in Rome, Italy, as well as from the visuals library of the Diocese of Grenoble. Other visuals are taken from Wikipedia and are in the public domain with proper attributions as noted.

This and other La Salette titles in digital form can be read on most digital readers and are available at: www.lasalette.org, www.amazon.com and www.itunes.apple.com

Cover design: by Jack Battersby, using a hand-colorized Archive photo from 1900 of the Holy Mountain of La Salette

IBSN: 978-1-946956-24-8

Contents

Acknowledgments

This printing of "A Grace Called La Salette" offers me an opportunity to thank my valued collaborators: Fr. Roland S. Nadeau, M.S., Fr. Donald Paradis, M.S., Lucille Thibodeau, P.M., Ph.D, Roger Chauvette, Fr. Roger Plante, M.S., and Fr. Gilles Genest, M.S.

Normand Theroux M.S.

To all the men and woman,
lay and religious, who have become
missionaries of La Salette,
this book is gratefully dedicated

Preface (1981)

Books whose purpose is to make known the story of the apparition of La Salette are not lacking. This one has the good fortune of having been written by a scholarly man. Its presentation as an honest, unassuming effort, with footnotes reduced to a minimum, should not mislead anyone. Jean Jaouen (1898-1975) possessed an exceptionally broad mastery of documentary sources. When this book first appeared in 1946 he remained steadfast in spite of the criticisms to which he was subjected for having dared publish a critical work on La Salette. But H. I. Marrou, the noted professor of the history of Christian origins at the Sorbonne, observed that Father Jaouen succeeded in situating "the debate outside the impassioned and uncritical atmosphere in which partisans and adversaries of La Salette had been entrenched for a century."

In addition to the presentation of the facts, *A Grace Called La Salette: a story for the world*, contains outstanding pages—probably the best ever written—on the spirituality of La Salette and the religious meaning of the apparition. Father Jaouen ably demonstrates the coherence of the various elements of the discourse and of the vision reported by the witnesses, as well as their agreement with the Gospel taught by the Church.

He had been trained for this task at the theological school of the Saulchoir, an institution directed by French Dominicans. Thanks to that training he gave an accurate and balanced interpretation of the warnings voiced by the Lady of the apparition, warnings which have deeply scandalized so many people. According to them, the apparition reflects an unbiblical understanding of God and Christ in presenting the image of a vengeful Christ while reserving for Mary the exercise of mercy.

Such objections reflect a radical misunderstanding of the message of La Salette. La Salette does not place the origin of Mary's mercy in herself but in the God who mandated her to pray for us without ceasing. More so, other objections raised against the Christology of the message do not stem solely from a superficial reading of that message reported by Maximin and Melanie. Their roots go deeper. They arise from a view of Christ's work which reduces his role to that of prophet of the philosophers. According to the New Testament, Jesus is in reality the Messiah of Israel who accomplishes the mission his Father has given Him not simply by teaching, exhorting, protesting against abuses, but also by offering Himself for people and incorporating them into His body. This process necessarily demands from us a response which in the final analysis consists in taking this word of Jesus seriously: "If any want to become my followers, let them deny themselves and take up their cross and follow me" (Matt 16:24). (1) The mercy of Jesus must be read in the light of the cross which, unfortunately, we too easily dismiss.

The message of La Salette can only be grasped in this light. As Father Jaouen points out, the tears shed by the "beautiful Lady" of the apparition place before us the tragic situation of a people who, forgetting Christ and his cross, loses its identity, wastes away and becomes prey to the powers of darkness, not by virtue of an arbitrary decree, but by the nature of things. When oneness with Christ is lost, the baptized person is delivered up to the forces of evil. "If my Son is not to cast you off, I am obliged to entreat Him without ceasing." Those who look down on this type of language would do well to think of the vomit spewed out by "the faithful and true witness" of the third chapter of the book of Revelation (14-16).

As with other human achievements, Father Jaouen's book has aged in some non-essential aspects. Were he writing today he would probably avoid some references dealing with spirituality. He has already acknowledged these reservations verbally elsewhere. Also, there are occasional inaccuracies in the book. They bear on peripheral points, such as the authorship of the Comte narrative, attributed by Jaouen (following Bossan's lead) to the haberdasher Joseph Laurent; or the religious status of a certain Bonnefous, who had been involved with Maximin's journey to Ars four years before the apparition. The book makes him a Marist brother. In reality, Bonnefous had gone over to the Marianists without ever pronouncing vows there. Finally, many a reader would have liked to find in the book an overview of documentary sources.

The present edition seeks to fulfill this latter wish with a 'Note" dedicated to the sources. But the body of the work, from the foreword to chapter twelve inclusively, reproduces the text of the third edition, the last to appear in Father Jaouen's lifetime and, consequently, the last for which he bears responsibility. We hope that a direct contact with an author who was a master theologian, who had acquired an excellent knowledge of documentary sources, and who was a priest quickened with a deep piety toward Our Lady of La Salette whom he loved to invoke as the Lady of Compassion (2) will help the reader to know better the grace bestowed upon the world on September 19, 1846.

Fr. Jean Stern, M.S.
Archivist, Missionaries of Our Lady of La Salette
Rome, 1981

Notes on the Sources

by Fr. Jean Stem, M.S.

The list presented in this note, taken from the 1988 French edition of this book, follows the chronological order. It contains the main sources of the history of La Salette, both handwritten and printed. This understands also recent works, where one finds reproduced old documents. The titles of the printed matter are indicated by italics. (*All books below are in French, translated in English for your convenience.*)

(1) Pra Account, written in the presence of Melanie (Sept. 20, 1846).

(2) Abbé Perrin Account, Pastor of La Salette : amalgamation of the stories of Maximin and Melanie (October, 1846). The recitation according to Guillaud, known at the Diocese of Grenoble from the beginning of November 1846, is a copy of this relationship.

(3) Account and letters of Abbés Melin, Cat and Maître, Archpriests of Corps, La Mure and Mens (October and November, 1846). Note that this so-called recitation of Abbé Maître is not the copy of the recitation of Abbé Eymery, nephew of Abbé Maître.

(4) Chambon Account (November, 1846). Result of an investigation conducted on the scene by the Abbé Chambon, Superior of the Minor Seminary of Rondeau near Grenoble, and three teachers.

(5) Comte Account, written in the presence of Melanie by Claude Comte, of Corps (November, 1846). Following a misunderstanding, Bossan attributed this recitation to another inhabitant of Corps, named Joseph Laurent.

(6) Recitations and notes of Dausse and Lagier (February-March, 1847). They give separately the stories of Maximin and Melanie, with long passages in patois. The *Lagier Notes* especially are precious, because of the perfect knowledge of patois at Abbé Lagier, a native of Corps, and the meticulousness of his questioning.

(7) Account of Dumanoir, a lawyer (March, 1847 at the latest). The printer Prudhomme used it for his own publications (May, 1847), without mentioning the author.

(8) Accounts of the Abbés Bez and Lambert, the recitation of Long, Justice of the Peace at Corps (May, 1847). All three give the story of Melanie; the first two give also the recitation of Maximin. Lambert reproduces the original patois.

(9) Report of Canon Rousselot, Official Investigator of the Revue de Grenoble (October, 1847). It was published the following year, with additions and some modifications (*The Truth about the Event of La Salette*, Grenoble 1848).

(10) C. Villecourt, Bishop of La Rochelle. *New Recitation of the Apparition... with letters, documents and authentic testimonies,* Lyon-Paris, 1847. Bishop Villecourt went in pilgrimage to La Salette in July, 1847.

(11) Minutes of November-December conferences in 1847 held in the Grenoble diocese.

(12) Letter of Abbé Dupanloup to Albert Du Boÿs, June 11, 1848. The future Bishop of Orléans came to question the two witnesses.

(13) "Memoirs on La Salette" of Abbé J.-P. Cartellier, curate of Saint-Joseph in Grenoble (1849-1857). Abbé Cartellier was one of the main opponents of the apparition.

(14) J. Rousselot. *New documents on the La Salette Event,* Grenoble, 1850.

(15) Bishop Philibert de Bruillard, Bishop of Grenoble. His Mandate of September 19, 1851. It contains the official approval of the apparition.

(16) Marie des Brulais. *The Echo of the Holy Mountain.* Nantes 1852.

(17) J. Rousselot. *A New Sanctuary for Mary.* Grenoble, 1853.

(18) *The Event at La Salette. Note to the pope, by several members of the diocesan clergy of Grenoble.* Grenoble 1854. The Note, of which a manuscript had been sent to Pope Pius IX, has for its principal author, J.-P. Cartellier.

(19) Bishop Ginoulhiac, Bishop of Grenoble. *Pastoral Instruction and Mandate* of Nov. 4, 1854. Bishop Ginoulhiac, who was Bishop of Grenoble since the preceding year and ordered further investigations, responding point by point to the allegations of the *Note*.

(20) Writings of Melanie, after her departure from Corps in 1850. For more details, see the journal *Marianum* (Rome) 1976, p. 484 and the following; *Catholicism*, Paris, Letouzey and Anè, volume 8, col. 1110-1111.

(21) Bossan Manuscripts (1862-1872). They contain the investigation notes of Antoine Bossan.

(22) "Monumental History" by Father Champon (preface, 1870), published partly in the *Annals of Our Lady of La Salette*, between 1881 and 1889. The Abbé Champon indicates unfortunately not always exactly and precisely the origin of the information that he has collected.

(23) L. Nortet. *Our Lady of La Salette*. Paris-Grenoble, 1879.

(24) Joseph Giray, bishop of Cahors. *The Miracles of La Salette*. 2 volumes, Grenoble, 1921. Reprinted many documents.

(25) *The Apparition of La Salette. History—critique—theology.* 3 volumes, Tournai, Missionaries of La Salette, 1932-1935. Reproduces the most important recitations.

(26) Louis Bassette. *The Fact of La Salette*. New expanded edition, Paris (7th district), 1965. Reprinted many documents.

Note: The list given above is necessarily a brief summary. If the reader is looking for additional information or wants to know more about the history of La Salette, we allow ourselves to refer the reader to the chronological file which we have published (Jean Stern's three volumes: *La Salette Authentic documents*: Paris, Desclée De Brouwer, 1988).

Foreword
(Fifth edition, 1988)

This book is a revision of the publication of
1946. The original appeared on the occasion
of the centenary of the Apparition of Our
Lady at La Salette.

Since that time, something has altered the
dialogue between an author and his readers
concerning this subject. Theological works
examining the mystery of Mary have multi-
plied, noting in due course the meaning of
her apparitions for Christians throughout history, and particularly in the
nineteenth century.

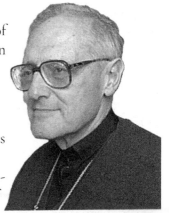

Fr. Jean Stern, M.S. Noted
Newman Scholar and learned
historian and archivist

The apparitions have an "ecclesial purpose"; they add nothing to the
teaching of Christ but urge sinners to be faithful to Him. On these
two points at least, theologians are unanimous. The informed Christian is familiar with the distinction between charismatic grace and
sanctifying grace, which we stressed in the 1946 edition of *La Grâce
de La Salette*. In sum, the Beautiful Lady's discourse and the career
of the two witnesses are no longer the stumbling blocks—if ever
there were—to the Christian people that the learned community
bemoaned in the 1930s. This is why I have focused more closely on
the essentials of the La Salette event. I have eliminated a number of
episodes that are only peripherally related to the approved devotion.

On the other hand, if professional historians are to trust the inquiry
that permitted the Bishop of Grenoble to issue his doctrinal pronouncement in 1851, they need solid proof. To satisfy them we probably would need to gather into one small volume the key historical
sources of La Salette, each one accompanied by a brief critical ap-
praisal. Be that as it may, I believe we can now reconstitute through

reliable and available documents the testimony of the children that served as the basis for the canonical decree.

From the outset, concern for objective truth quickened the quasi-official history that Canon Rousselot drafted for his bishop and for the Christian world. The very titles of his works proclaim it *The Truth Concerning the La Salette Event* and *New Documents*. Cardinal Lambruschini praised him as well as Bishop de Bruillard for the integrity of the inquiry in these simple words: "The doctrinal decree project is proceeding well and I find the wording of it totally acceptable, especially the investigation of the event which was conducted very meticulously." It is unlikely that historical criticism or psychology will one day invalidate the testimony of the two children as Rousselot reported it.

But there is one point that the historian will rightly want to judge on documentary evidence, namely, the continuity of this testimony from the very beginning up to the official inquiry. The importance of proof in such a matter was clear to the Bishop's delegates, and they declared having obtained it by all the methods of an on-the-spot investigation. It is nevertheless better to verify their assertions by all the clues history has left behind.

This is why in this book the presentation of the facts of La Salette is always supported by the first reports and the correspondence of the episcopal commission, both of which have been widely disseminated in recent years. The first were published before World War II by Father Charles Rahier, M.S. in a review entitled *l'Apparition de La Salette*, No. 2, and these texts are accompanied by many studies by the same author or by his confreres, appearing in *l'Apparition de La Salette* (Nos. 1-2), and *Notre Dame de La Salette* (No. 3). The correspondence of the Bishop's Commission has been made available by Louis Bassette in a book published in 1955 at the Editions du Cerf, Le Fait de La Salette, 1846-1854. I prefer referring to these works because they are generally available. Specialists will always find in them references to original documents. The publication of a few documents of marginal interest to the event itself might still be desirable. I allude to them inasmuch as they shed light on the event; the publication of full length, unedited documents was not the purpose of this book.

Evidently, I would hope that the critical apparatus as my study of the pertinent documents do indeed satisfy the requirements of historians. This is not to say that I see the La Salette event and its consequences as a purely historical matter open to endless speculation. By an act of its ordinary magisterium the Church has spoken in favor of the authenticity of the apparition. This means that because the fact appears as morally certain to her, she invites the faithful to commit themselves to it and to receive it as a grace. To what extent can the message of La Salette be considered a sign from heaven? Under what conditions can it change the life and fire the religious spirit of individuals? These are the essential questions to ask on a subject like this one. It is from the Church and through her that answers to these questions must be sought and the grace of La Salette be received. The deep-seated purpose of this entire study is to situate this grace in a vision of faith, in the light of the Church.

The book that was published in 1946 under the title *La Grâce de La Salette* had the very same intention. New perspectives in research, important as they are, have not changed it in this revision. In some instances perhaps, there will be a more attentive concern to the thinking and declarations of the Church; hence the addition to the original title: *La Grâce de La Salette, au regard de l'Eglise*. The journey has followed other paths but has led to the same destination.

References to the earlier work could be of interest to some, but are unnecessary for those who have not read it. The present study is self-explanatory. It is better to approach it directly, in its own structure and movement.

Nor is it directed to any type of specialist. I have kept in mind primarily the many priests, committed lay people, and students who go on pilgrimage to La Salette. I hope they will not object to following a rigorous and exact method which, with prayer, directs the Church when it pronounces itself on miraculous occurrences. In this way perhaps, respect for the Church will be increased. All the pilgrims who come to La Salette because they love the weeping Virgin in a simple way will find enough readable pages, God willing, to give tone to their devotion even if they do not read the book in one sitting or if they omit a few chapters.

Competent people I respect had willingly endorsed *La Grâce de La Salette* when it first appeared. The approval of a bishop or a theologian is certainly valuable to me, but I am reluctant to overemphasize it. What I desire for this book is the acceptance by the Christian heart more than the reactions of critics, rational or impassioned. Of all the opinions that mattered to me at that time, I quote only that of my friend René Nihard, professor of pedagogy at the University of Liége. In a letter written a few months before he died, analyzing the book I had just sent him, he assured me that the psychological arguments in favor of a supernatural interpretation seemed to be particularly compelling. He concluded: 'I confess that I know nothing of the history of the apparition of La Salette. ... Reading your masterful work not only convinced me of the truth of the apparition, but prompted me to pray to the most blessed Virgin under the beautiful title of La Salette, especially for the conversion of sinners and of nations."

Testimonies like this one enlighten and console. By the sign of La Salette may the reader enter into the mystery of Mary. I desire nothing more.

Fr. Jean Stem, M.S.

-1-
Coming to Light

On September 19,1846, at the hour when night falls from the mountains, when the cattle-bells and cries of the shepherds urging their beasts grow quiet, an unaccustomed excitement swept through the hamlet of Les Ablandins. Door to door, people called out to one another and discussed in small groups. Some who had begun eating steaming soup in the glimmer of old lamps affixed to the wall, suddenly saw the door open and, in the shadows, the silhouette of the neighbor asking: "Do you know what they are saying, the strange thing that happened this afternoon to Mémin, Pierre Selme's shepherd and to Mélanie, Pra's little shepherdess?"

Mémin, the young boy Selme had hired eight days before, was the son of Giraud the wheelwright of Corps. He was the first to spread the news. Right after coming down from the Planeau he told Selme. He also told it at Baptiste Pra's. Returning to Selme's in the evening he told it to everyone he met. A beautiful Lady, he said, more brilliant than the sun, had appeared to them, to him and to his companion, near the Sézia Brook. People vouched for the fact that little Mélanie repeated exactly the same story at Pra's.

When they first saw her, the Lady was sitting, her face in her hands, bent over as if by a sorrow too heavy to bear. She rose, called them, and through her tears spoke to them for a long time. Exactly what did she say? The only people who know heard it directly from Mémin and Mélanie. As for these rough mountain folk who found such great pleasure in rushing from neighbor to neighbor, no doubt they distorted the reporting of the children in their retelling. No matter. The village people readily heard the call to conversion in the insistent words of the tearful woman, *"My Son, my people."* She must be the Queen of heaven and of earth, anxious to reconcile the Child of her flesh with the offspring of her charity. "She wept all the while she

1

spoke to us" said Mélanie. Oh! I really saw her tears flow." Finally, after asking the children to make it known to all her people, she rose in the air and dissolved before their eyes.

All this is so very strange! If it is true, changes must take place: no more cursing; attend Mass on Sunday; say your prayers. Otherwise, the harvests will rot, small children will die in the arms of their mothers. Still, is heaven so concerned with earth? Can blasphemy affect the Almighty, weigh down his arm, as this Lady said? Do the sufferings of the poor touch the hearts of the blessed so deeply that they feel the need to appear to them and warn them? Is an apparition, especially to these children, at all likely? Nothing singled them out for celestial favors. They don't know their catechism. They don't go to church, nor do they pray any more than the others. With this background, their account is all the more astonishing. How could they have invented this story which is so far removed from their daily experience? How could they have remembered this long discourse, which they obviously do not understand?

This is what the peasants talked about among themselves, alerted as they were to the nearness of the divine, yet secretly longing for nothing more than to return to their tranquil indifference. At the outset, of course, few admitted being affected by the goings-on. "Most of them made fun of it," Maximin said later. But something had changed in them. That evening, unbeknown to them a breath of fresh air filled the tepid stable where they had hidden from God. Next spring all performed their Easter duty.

What occurred at Pra's is revealing.

After dutifully telling Selme of the happenings on the Planeau, Maximin hurried over to Mélanie's employers, not to see Mélanie—his vitality and exuberance were so different from her unfriendly moods–, but because the Pra household represented for him the entire circle of friends he had at Les Ablandins. His sister Angélique had once worked for them and he felt at ease and at home there. The vision that still dazzled him, the amazing words that continued to burn in his head—all of this he wanted to confide to his friends first. As he approached the house, "Maman" Pra had just come out on the stoop.

"Hey, Mother Caron," (1) he yelled, "didn't you see a beautiful Lady all afire passing through the air above the valley?" "What lady?" "A dazzling Lady who spoke to us on the mountain, to Mélanie and me."

What Lady?

At the startling news people came out of their houses and began to besiege him with questions. Finally, they had him come inside to hear him at greater length. The entire family was gathered together in the semi-darkness and the shimmering light leaping from the hearth: the old grandmother, Baptiste Pra, his wife and two children, his brother Jacques. "We had led our cows to drink," Maximin began, "then we fell asleep. Mélanie woke up first. We climbed up to fetch our cows. Coming down again Mélanie called me: 'Mémin, come see this light! We were frightened and Mélanie dropped her stick. The Lady got up, crossed her arms and said to

French holy card depicting phases of the La Salette Apparition and proposed Basilica

us: *"Come near, my children, do not be afraid. I am here to tell you great news."* And we were no longer the least bit frightened. *"If my people will not obey, I shall be compelled to loose the arm of my Son...."*

All were silent. This last sentence sounded out of place on the lips of the young narrator, since it was spoken with unaccustomed gravity. Was this really Mémin speaking? The beautiful Lady seemed to have inspired him, to have borrowed his voice. A voice with a ring other than his own held sway over these down-to-earth country people-, that of the Unknown Lady who read into their past: *"You swore, you abused my Son's name ..... If the harvest is spoiled, it is your own fault."* They drank these words in, bitter as they might be, like children

3

listening to a marvelous story.

When Maximin was finished, Grandmother Pra dared put into words what everyone felt: " It is the Blessed Virgin," she said, looking into the fireplace. "It is the Blessed Virgin these little ones have seen because she is the only one in heaven whose Son rules." And as she turned toward them, tears streamed down her face.

She ran to the stable and called Mélanie. "Leave the cows," she ordered. "I'll feed them. You come and tell us what you saw with Maximin." "Oh! well," Mélanie replied, happy not to have to come forward first. "I saw what Mémin saw, and since he told you, you know it," she said, pretending to continue her work. "Come this minute," insisted Grandmother Pra. Mélanie followed her into the house. "I wanted to tell you," she said, "but only at supper time, when I had finished my work." Maximin, unable to contain himself, ran off to tell the great news to anyone who wanted to hear it. Pierre Selme had just come in. Maximin's first account had stupefied him and he wanted to know more. Thus, without anyone's planning it, all the elements of an inquest had come together.

Mélanie placed the event in the context described by Maximin. She attributed to the beautiful Lady the same words, the same actions, the same attire. This girl who had never been heard to say two words in French and who never spoke, so timid and withdrawn was she, recited this long discourse partly in French, partly in dialect, with disconcerting ease. She spoke with no less gravity than the boy, but it was tempered by an unaccustomed softness which transformed her unpleasant features. Old mother Pra, more and more convinced, confronted her son Jacques: "You hear what the Blessed Virgin said to this little one? Go ahead and work on Sunday after that." "Bah!" he grumbled. "You're asking me to believe she saw the Blessed Virgin? She doesn't even say her prayers!"

Baptiste Pra, happy not to be involved, reserved his judgment. He was visibly worried. Later, he acknowledged to Father Bossan that he wanted to pick up leaves the next day but did not, "because of what the young girl had told him." For the moment, as head of the household, he decided to give his young employee some practical advice: "If

4

this is true," he said, torn as he was between his peasant distrust and his old Christian stock, "you must tell it to the pastor. It is Sunday tomorrow and he can say it in church."

Selme was of the same opinion. They must neither invite ridicule nor defy heaven. The children seemed sincere. If the Blessed Virgin really entrusted them with a mission, she will not begrudge their master for referring them to the Church. No one could take exception to that. It was therefore agreed that tomorrow Mélanie would meet Maximin and they would go down to the village early before Mass.

What will these poor, innocent children of La Salette meet on the road upon which this first step is taking them? Tomorrow they will feel the Pastor's heartfelt enthusiasm, but tomorrow also they will be the in the public eye and the targets of dull-witted jokes (the Corps dignitaries addressing Maximin "Oh! The Blessed Virgin's son!"). Tomorrow, they will face endless interrogations with the usual traps, threats, and tricks. "Here, take these twenty francs for your relatives; they won't have to beg any more," suggested Peytard to Mélanie, "You can have them if you promise to keep quiet."

Within a few weeks, they would find it impossible to be themselves, to live the lives of children like other boys and girls their age. The curious hordes invading Corps would harass them at the Sister's house where the bishop intended to give them a peaceful hideaway. As adults, they wandered from one place to the next, without resources or steady income, tossed about by the world's harshness as well as by their own weaknesses.

Beneath their unstable lives and their fragile inner equilibrium the underlying hardship that had befallen them was easily recognizable: they had been uprooted. "The apparition has not changed us, it has left us with all our faults," Maximin acknowledged. No doubt. Still, their defects would not have brought on the same consequences and the children would have more easily found their own balance had they remained in their native mountains, yielding only to the laws of the earth and to the ways of a simple life.

Uprooted, they would become defenseless against their own erratic moods, their overwrought imaginations, and the seductions of all sorts that lie in wait for witnesses of a celestial vision. The temporal failure of their lives is one result. Those who sought their welfare and those who exploited them contributed to that failure as much as did their own shortcomings. **(2)** But, at the source of it all, there was the apparition. Without the obligation it placed upon them to bear witness to it, they would have remained what they were: carefree children, inheritors of a peaceful destiny. Should we pity them and ask her to explain why she chose them for such a perilous honor? Let us rather think of the mystery of La Salette. The Virgin who can no longer restrain the arm of her Son had need of the suffering of her young witnesses as a humble complement to her own sorrows and self-offering.

View of Apparition site in 1861 showing pilgrims
climbing mountain with mules

One thing is certain. They were the instruments of a grace which, after a hundred years, is still alive. **(3)** Through them, by the simple account they gave to their masters on the evening of September 19,1846, the Apparition of La Salette passed into history. Henceforth, it will be felt in the lives of people. It will stamp the piety of the Church with apostolic and mystical orientations. It will shape the obscure destinies of humanity. The anxiety of a Baptiste Pra, the muted awakening of conscience and of faith in the first hearers of the Great News were but a hint of the wonders yet to come. They were the imperceptible fissure hollowed out by the stream of grace that would one day flood the world.

Valley of La Salette and Les Ablandins; inset:
Residence of Saint Joseph House

-2-
From Popular Hearsay to Official Hearing

entlemen, would there be someone among you who might know what the pastor meant in the sermon this morning? asked the Mayor on September 20, as he opened a session of the municipal council. **(1)** No one had understood anything except Jean Moussier of the village of Les Ablandins, who referred to the rumor begun by Maximin the night before, and the Mayor himself, who declared having gotten wind of "this idiocy" from a report of the rural policeman. None of these rough-hewn men would have wanted to pass for a child by appearing to be interested in it. They immediately turned their attention to more serious matters.

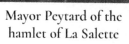

Nevertheless, the great news of the beautiful Lady was spreading. It addressed all the people. Little folk as well as dignitaries lay hold of it: the rural officer was puzzled by the morning excursion of Selme and the shepherds, and the pastor's housekeeper wanted to know what the children had to say to him before notifying him. The pastor himself pressed his ear to the wall to listen and then could not resist his heart's impulse: he burst into the room and had the boy repeat the whole incredible story from the beginning and tearfully concluded: "Ah! my children, you are blessed, you have seen the most Blessed Virgin!" Then he jotted down a few notes to replace this morning's homily. But, at the Mass, when time came to read them, sobs choked his voice

Mayor Peytard of the hamlet of La Salette

and only a few words reached the already informed congregation. No matter. What he wanted to announce, the two shepherds would do for him. He had designated them as the center of attention.

The first to allow himself to intrude on the event was precisely the man who had scolded his guard that very morning for accepting this childish stupidity so eagerly. After Vespers, Monsieur Peytard, Mayor of La Salette, a man who always kept his own counsel slipped four écus (écus were the currency replaced by the Euro) into his pocket and started toward Ablandins. There, he found only Mélanie, since Maximin, after his visit to the pastor, had gone with Selme, had breakfast, and returned to Corps, always in the company of his master.

For three consecutive hours, the mayor conducted his interrogation with cruel skill and persistence. He let her speak without interruption, then began to play cat and mouse with her, watching for the slightest contradiction, pressing her with questions in an attempt to provoke her. He had recourse to threats, hinting about prison and the police. Then he took another tack: Mélanie is young, Mélanie is poor, he could help her. The four écus suddenly flashed on Baptiste Pra's table. "Stop talking about these things, Mélanie, and your future is assured." She wasn't even looking at the coins, so the mayor forced them into her hand. At this, she became indignant. The poor girl, whose younger sister even now begged in the streets of Corps, recoiled from this fortune as from treason. "I threw them back at him," she would later tell Mademoiselle des Brulais.

This particular evening is of crucial importance in the history of La Salette. His skepticism shaken, the mayor made his way back to the village. Of course, he felt the need for a more thorough examination. He advised Pra not to let the shepherdess go down to Corps to meet Maximin. With the boy, he repeated the same tactics that had previously failed with Mélanie. (2) The following Sunday he brought both of them up on the mountain of the apparition to hear them separately once again. He had each one re-enact his/her behavior during the event. Finally, he confronted them with all the thoroughness he could muster. (3) Even if he could not be positively sure, still there was a glimmer of certainty that night as he won over Maximin's employer. And when his critical demands had been met, he would be the first to assure the bishop's investigators that Mélanie and Maximin, although separated one from the other, said the same things from the very beginning. "The following Sunday, September 27, their detailed account was identical to the one they had given me the previous Sunday, and the same one they give me to this day." (4) Monsieur Peytard was an educated and judicious man. His testimony must be duly weighed if we wish to grasp the event of La Salette from its origins. (5)

After the mayor's departure, Baptiste Pra made his own significant contribution to the history of La Salette. Struck by all he had seen and heard, he found his neighbors Selme and Moussier at nightfall and shared his impressions with them. All three agreed that the event called for closer scrutiny and they decided to draft a written account of it for their own use. To include every detail would have been too long, perhaps even beyond their ability. They limited their effort to writing the words of the Lady and the answers the children gave to her questions. Since the meeting with the mayor had lasted until approximately seven o'clock, one cannot blame these men unfamiliar with writing for not having prolonged their vigil until morning to provide us with a more complete account. Besides, they were not at all concerned with posterity. They focused on what they considered to be essential: the complaints and the threats directed at them. They naively entitled their report as a message addressed to them: *A Letter Dictated by the Blessed Virgin to Two Children on the Mountain of La Salette-Fallavaux.*

In these circumstances, this document has incomparable critical value. It was dictated by Mélanie to a man who hardly knew how to hold a pen and who, like a school boy, had to have every word repeated to him. "she had to start over and repeat each sentence," said Pra of Selme. The other two read over his shoulder and assisted him. These simple folk had no scruple for precision or refinement. They made no attempt at style. They had no ambition but to reproduce faithfully the words their repentant hearts heard. Because it was so artless and so totally eclipsed by its subject, the Pra account ranks as the witness text on the La Salette discourse. **(6)**

This same Sunday, at Corps, Maximin, with Selme's approval, was subjected to questioning by the entire village. The little scatterbrain would have liked nothing better than to rejoin his playmates, but Selme, not having found Giraud at home, could not resist telling the news to the wheelwright's wife. The child was thus obliged to give his stepmother a detailed account. Thereafter, he was led to his maternal grandmother to repeat it. There, the busybodies and the idle came and went until nightfall. "A child besieged by a swarm of bees": this is how Maximin remembered, at age twenty, this turning point in his life. He had already confided to Father Champon, who was his tutor at the rectory of Seyssins, **(7)** many a remembrance by which one can assess whether he or anyone else had anything to gain in claiming to have seen an apparition.

He noted quite frankly that the moment they turned into the road to Corps the faithful were coming out of high Mass. Neither of them, therefore, had observed the Sunday obligation since at La Salette they had not waited for Mass before returning to Les Ablandins. What a faint impression the Lady's reproaches made on them! Had they in any way conspired in a false miracle, would they not have felt the need to abet it by their example? The answer Maximin gave to Peytard the next day would seem to be natural to us: "Maximin," said the Mayor, "I would not want to be in your place. I would rather have killed someone than to have invented what you have said in agreement with Mélanie." "Invented!" replied the boy. "How would you want to invent such things?"

Maximin's Father

Then we come to Selme's meeting with Giraud senior. He found him in a tavern. He told him that his son had had a rare good fortune. Giraud mistook the good news for bad and looked worried. The other reassured him. "He has seen the Blessed Virgin!" The man broke into a fit of laughter and all the tipplers joined him in waves of mirth. No conspiracy here. Giraud prattled and drank on in the tobacco smoke until nightfall and promptly forgot the whole story.

Giraud returned to the house so late that the boy was already in bed. The father woke him. He wanted to know what Selme spoke of this morning. Maximin spiritedly told his story. With stupefying ease he repeated the words of the Beautiful Lady. "What person would be clever enough to put so many things in your head in so little time?" asked the father. "For three years now I have been trying to teach you the Our Father and the Hail Mary and you still can't recite them!" Then, without waiting for the end of the story, he went to bed in a very bad mood.

Maximin with his father

The next day the wheelwright's workshop was filled with the curious. Maximin good-naturedly tried to satisfy them all, but as one group followed upon another, Giraud, finding a moment alone with his child, told him not to talk about this any longer and punctuated his order with a sharp reprimand. It was of no use. The news had reached the town on the wings of the wind. That very afternoon, a group went up to explore the miracle mountain and noticed that a normally dry brook had begun to flow. Curiosity then became concern. Mayor Peytard managed to see Maximin, and during the evening the bailiff's wife had him summoned by her husband. While the latter entertained Giraud with a jug of wine, Madame received the small boy and invited him to speak in the presence of the doctor, the notary, and other dignitaries. At this point Maximin learned for the first time that the establishment does not take well to being disturbed by messages from heaven. "Little Jesus" and "Son of the Blessed Virgin" are a few of the jeers that the distinguished panel aimed at the defenseless boy.

Nevertheless, a few days later, Giraud the wheelwright himself rose to the boy's defense. One evening, although now annoyed by the story, he asked his son to relate it to him once more. Exasperated again by the droning of the well-learned lesson, he was about to interrupt him when the boy quickly said, "But father, the Lady also spoke about you!" "About me?"asked the wheelwright. "And what did she tell you?" Giraud learned then that the Lady, having spoken of the spoiled wheat, had reminded Maximin that he had already seen some with his father in the direction of the farm of Coin. When the child recalled his own words to him— *"Here, my son, eat some bread again this year because I don't know who will eat some next year, if the wheat continues like this"*—, the father, better acquainted than anyone with Maximin's personality, never again doubted that an extraordinary power had helped him retain things far removed from his carefree and unstable world. From that moment on, Maximin could freely serve his beautiful Lady's mission: *"You will make this known to all my people."*

The field of Coin mentioned by Mary during her apparition

Maximin obviously played the leading role in spreading the message. Nothing could have been more natural, given Mélanie's isolation in her village. Still, there is one person to whom the little scatterbrain could have deferred more quickly: Father Mélin, the parish priest of Corps. Maximin saw him only on the 26th, eight days after the apparition. This fact, as well as the pastor's negative attitude at Maximin's first disclosure, are worth noting. A vociferous opposition would one day denounce the parish priest of Corps who had been a courageous servant of La Salette.

"On Saturday, September 26, eight days after the apparition, I visited Father Mélin for the first time. He could no longer ignore the stir about the great news at home and throughout the countryside. He appeared cold and uninterested: everyone had run after me but he had remained in his rectory. I must say I didn't think of the parish priest either. Saturday, as he was saying Mass, my sister went to tell him: 'Did you know that my brother saw the Blessed Virgin?' 'Well! Tell him to see me after Mass.' Mélanie had come to see her parents. The parish priest asked to see both of us. He separated us, left Mélanie in the kitchen and had me go into the parlor. There, I told him my story, which made little impression on him. When I had finished, he said to me 'Is that all?' 'No,' I answered, 'there is still something more, but the blessed Virgin forbade me to say it.' He had Mélanie come in, listened to her, and asked her the same question. Mélanie having answered as I did, he understood that the blessed Virgin had given us each a secret. He questioned us with his usual gravity and then dismissed us." **(8)**

Fr. Melin,
parish priest of Corps

Father Mélin was in fact, the first to inform the bishop about the topic that fascinated his parish as well as the whole township. It was his duty. In his letter, **(9)** he stated that his conviction did not differ from that of the faithful. However, he could not be accused of haste as was his colleague of La Salette, Father Jacques Perrin. "I proceeded deliberately in the information that I gathered," he wrote. "I could find nothing that might in the least way possible point to a hoax." Still less could he be suspected of deception. According to witnesses, signs of his progressive adherence to the phenomenon of La Salette came to light. On Monday, September 28, he subjected himself to "four hours of difficult climbing," and went up the mountain. He questioned the children on the site of the apparition. At the end of the examination, his religious spirit showed through. Father Blanc, a sacristan who later became a priest, remembered years later "the deep emotion that welled up within Father Mélin. He maintained an outward calm, but one could see that the account of the two children, as well as his visit to the mountain, impressed him deeply." **(10)**

Bishop Philbert de Bruillard, Bishop of Grenoble during the Apparition

Writing to his bishop, Father Mélin submitted La Salette to its natural tribunal. Fortunately, this authority could obtain some general but objective information, since already, in early October, the news bandied about gave rise to distortions capable of producing anxiety. Bishop de Bruillard's immediate reaction was to warn his clergy against any improper action. On October 9, he addressed the following circular letter to each one of his parish priests:

> *Father, you are no doubt acquainted with the extraordinary events that are said to have taken place in the parish of La Salette, near Corps. I invite you to refer to the Synodal Statutes that I gave my diocese in 1829. This is what is contained on page 94: "We prohibit under the penalty of ipso facto suspension the declaration and publication by printing of any new miracle, under whatever pretext except by the authority of the Holy See or our own, after a thorough and rigid inquiry.*

> *We have given no pronouncement on the events in question. Wisdom and duty therefore prescribe the greatest reserve and above all absolute silence relative to this matter in the pulpit.*

> *Nevertheless, a lithographed drawing accompanied by stanzas in verse has been allowed to appear. I am making you aware, Father, that this publication not only lacks my approbation, but that it has offended me in the extreme and that I have formally and severely*

condemned it. *Be on your guard, therefore, and give an example of the prudent reserve that you will not fail to recommend to others....*"

This was a necessary precaution but not one dictated by a basic hostility. In fact, the bishop intended to pursue the informational process already begun. By return mail he asked Father Mélin a first series of questions: "Have these two children been interrogated separately? Are they devious? Did they have anything to gain by inventing their recital?" Thus was initiated a correspondence between the bishop and the parish priest, increasing in volume each time new facts and new doubts arose.

Furthermore, before this matter could be concluded, more than one voice had to be heard. In the nearby village of La Mure lived an archpriest assisted by two curates who was sufficiently experienced to temper the enthusiastic young Father Mélin. Having been told of the visit the archpriest had made to La Salette around mid-October, the bishop asked him what he had learned. The archpriest answered by sending a neutral account of what the children said, but pointed out that he did not guarantee the absolute accuracy of his report. "Bishop, I thought my trip to Corps was a well-kept secret and already Your Grace is informed of it. I would like to provide you with more precise details than those I have already gathered and which do not satisfy me. Still, I have found in the children's deposition all that I had heard. With their help I was able to rectify many distorted facts." Concluding his report, he wrote: "Here, Bishop, is what I have been able to gather hurriedly." **(11)**

The Bishop appealed to other sources. He instructed a few young priests from his minor seminary, under the guidance of Father Chambon, the superior, to visit the site in his name, and to report to him. He even released for discussion some unsolicited material, such as the report submitted by Father Maître, archpriest of Mens, an obscure account of an expedition to La Salette by the latter's vicar and nephew Eymery. Also, he released the letter from Monsieur Giraud, clerk of Corps, reporting the healing of a Madame Laurent and which the editor of the *Courier de l'Isère* thought would be of no interest to his readers. Finally, he corresponded with Father Rabilloud, first vicar of La Mure, who had been to the mountain himself, as had both his pastor and his colleague Father Verdon before him. Through these intermediaries as if through a telephone switchboard, the bishop received all the news floating through the region of Corps: the children's answers to questions ("When they speak of their Lady, they are little doctors"); a pilgrimage numbering 1,400 people (Father Mélin counted 1,023, others, over 2,000); the striking details of cures embellished by rumor.

All this provided a slim dossier favorable on the whole to the apparition, but whose inadequacy becomes immediately evident upon perusal. Reporters were only scratching the surface of the event. Father Berthier, the Vicar General of the diocese, carefully examined the dossier and strongly objected to the omission by Father Mélin of certain comments against the "strange language" ascribed to the "white lady... by priests who are completely credible." Silence and prudent reserve characterized the prescribed attitude regarding "this singular apparition of which too much has already been said." On the other hand, Bishop de Bruillard felt obliged to consult with his Cathedral Chapter and the professors of his major seminary on such an important matter. The two commissions reported to him on December 15.

The seminary professors evidently shared the Chambon report's favorable opinion of the children of La Salette. They acknowledged that the apparition, true or false, had produced startling and sustained results. The miracle was "very plausible." Still, if there was to be a doctrinal decree, they considered it prudent and necessary to wait until complete certainty had been reached because "certain points raise some questions about the truth of the Lady's words." These matters had to be carefully identified and weighed before a credible document could be drawn up. **(12)**

The canons, for their part, were not looking this far ahead. They did not discuss documents or theological likelihoods. They believed that in the present state of affairs, nothing required the authorities to intervene because the incident, regardless of its nature, was producing nothing but good results. There was no danger in delay. If the account was true, the children were fulfilling their mission in spreading it and, in any case, "the person in the apparition had not even told them to reveal it to the authorities more than to anyone else." Nevertheless, they expressed the wish for a juridical inquiry that would provide a better understanding of the facts.

An apparently negative balance sheet concluded this first phase of the diocesan inquiry. Could it have been otherwise? How could anyone discern anything from heaven in this Maître-Eymery report, estimated to be the most complete account of the incident?

> At this sight, they were still frozen in fright. "Do not be afraid, my children, come forward, I am here to tell you great news." To them, this was as comprehensible as Greek. "What she say?" whispered the boy. "I don't know what she said," answered the girl. "You do not understand, my children? Well, come closer, I will speak to you in patois."

> At these words, a deep happiness flooded their spirit and filled them with unspeakable joy. They came down, crossed the brook, and stood near the Lady at the respectful distance of four meters. The Lady then took three steps forward and spoke to them in something like these words: "If the people do not repent, my Son is so angry that he will release on them the thunderbolts of his vengeance. ..."

A few comments are necessary here in order to pursue the La Salette event with the objective eye of the historian.

Other Witnesses to the Effects of the Apparition

We should be aware that, at the outset, our knowledge of the event does not rest on documents but on witnesses. Men whose name, condition, and character we know have seen and heard the children. From Pierre Selme to Bishop de Bruillard, including Lagier and Dupanloup, a long line of intermediaries links us with the testimony of Maximin and Mélanie. From the starting point of the children themselves, we must critically compare the accounts of these several reporters.

Among the intermediaries mentioned above, some have gathered their facts directly from the children, others have not. The latter, even if they do not reveal the substance of the La Salette event, are nevertheless useful inasmuch as they can inform our judgment. Thus, Jean-Baptiste Pra and Pierre Selme presented evidence before counsel Dumanoir on the circumstances in which the shepherds had become acquainted, had spent the day of September 19, and had given their first account. (13)

They confirmed this deposition at the diocesan office. Also, Mayor Peytard pronounced the two children incapable of lying, (14) and he himself stated that ever since their first interrogation he had "found no variation whatsoever in the account they have been repeating now for almost 15 months." (15) The historian must attach the greatest importance to this unrehearsed agreement. It forbids him to suggest without proof that the La Salette event could have its source other than in these two well-known and illiterate children. It is gratuitous and pointless to liken the discourse they ascribe to their beautiful Lady to a text coming anonymously from somewhere else. To suggest such a thing requires that one demonstrate by what pedagogical methods such words could have been instilled in such unschooled minds. By what right can anyone who has not provided such a demonstration object to an entire historical tradition? Why cast doubt on the good faith of these first-hour witnesses and all those who followed them? They and the entire population of Corps and La Salette, with the priests leading the way, react spontaneously and naturally before the event. One step, one act brings on another in an unbroken chain. It is a solid and intelligible explanation. Does not the real myth, if there be one, consist in the attempt to enlighten us by eliminating the witnesses?

From those who have gathered their facts directly from the children, we require more than merely the appearance of honesty. When they give their impression of the children, we believe them inasmuch as they appear to be objective. When they pass on the accounts of these children, we likewise are mindful that subjective elements could have come between what they heard and what they wrote. We must therefore examine the characteristics of their composition, the circum-

Text of the La Salette Apparition with
the defenders of La Salette Apparition

stances of time, their intention as well as their attention, in order to grant greater credibility to those who come closest to the ideal of pure transcription which is here the golden rule. In this respect the account written by Pra on the night of September 20 is infinitely superior to that of Father Eymery who was satisfied with the following kind of approximation: "the Lady speaks roughly in these words," and to that of "these priests commendable in every respect"—Father Chambon and his companions—, who, having been up to La Salette on October 20, waited until November 10 to sign their account.

Father Bossan, a scrupulous annalist if ever there was one, had an opinion of the diocesan report which we can now readily understand. "The documents we submitted to the two commissions for examination did not contain enough proof to make an airtight case. The only description of the event the members of the commission had in hand was both incomplete and inaccurate in certain respects. The other accounts were simply ordinary letters written to convey news. They were not papers written after a thorough examination, formal interrogations, and serious inquiry." **(16)**

The time for this hoped-for inquiry would soon come. When on the first sunny days of spring the lines of pilgrims began to move up the mountain, the authorities needed to assume their responsibilities. Their delegates then had to select among the already numerous written accounts those in which the testimony of the children was most transparent. They compared them with each other as well as with their own observations.

Meanwhile, the snows of December enshrouded the Corps countryside in relative calm. Roads were blocked. The swarms of the curious had disappeared. Mélanie's contract with the Pra's expired and she joined Maximin at the house of the Sisters of Providence. Both learned the alphabet, not at all regretting the noisy fame that had surrounded them for a while, and unconcerned about what they would say should the turmoil one day resume. Father Mélin and the Sisters alone observed them and told the bishop of their good behavior.

While the mountain slept, news of La Salette swept through France.

Early in 1847, the press entered the fray, sensitive to the influence these rumors would have on the economy. The rising cost of living was already overwhelming: what would happen if the farmers decided to follow the Lady's advice and not sow? Anticlericalism, of course, entered the scene and the occasion was ready-made for Louis Veuillot to cross swords with *Le Siècle, Le National, Le Constitutionel.* Muting his sarcasm, he accused his adversaries of already confusing the miraculous with the absurd and reminded them that in Grenoble, the bishop's administration was demonstrating more tact and wisdom.

> It is sad that we cannot prove the existence of a cost of-living crisis in Nineveh, when the prophet marched through the streets crying out: "Forty more days and Nineveh will be destroyed" This could be one more convenient crime to put up against the authority of Holy Scripture. To bring back to God, that is to say, to resignation, to courage, to charity, and to hope entire nations threatened or afflicted with great disasters; to provide them with the only human means of enduring these calamities, and perhaps, of preventing them—what a crime! We are surprised that "Le Constitutionel" did not make a lead article of it and did not ask Mister Dupin if it were not possible to prevent such horrors by a few arrests. Don't we have any law, any decree in France that would save us from miracles? Or from believing in them? Why shouldn't it be forbidden to discuss such miracles before they are approved by the Council of State? **(17)**

Pressure from civil authority echoed mounting opposition in the Parisian press. The mayor of Morestel, in the department of Isère, obtained one of the accounts criticized in the newspapers. He passed it on to the assistant-commissioner and asked the top-ranking civil authority to prohibit the circulation of "such absurdities." The assistant commissioner went further. "These sinister rumors can have deplorable consequences in the countryside, where they are shared by people of good character, which strengthens their influence." All of this was relayed to the commissioner, the Baron Pellenc, who passed it on to Bishop de Bruillard, "who, in his superior discretion, was to find some way of avoiding the evil brought on by exaggerated fears." An appeal was also made, it would seem, to the Minister of the

Interior. One appeal led to another until finally, on June 12,1847, the Minister of Justice and of Worship, Mister Hébert, wrote to Bishop de Bruillard. The atmosphere of a whole era pervades this document. One must read it to see how the government of Louis Philippe managed to insulate itself from the miraculous.

Paris, June 12, 1847

RE: See books. Publication and diffusion of a picture representing the Apparition of the Virgin to two children and accounts of this Apparition.

Bishop,

I have been made aware of the diffusion, in many departments, of a picture showing the Apparition of the Virgin to two children on a mountain of La Salette in the township of Corps, near Grenoble, and of various accounts of it printed either together with the picture or separately, containing details of this alleged apparition and the forecast of a great famine, as well as of a serious illness in children.

Farmers are warned against sowing wheat. Such passages are apt to cause panic, particularly among the rural population; in a time of food shortages, they could even threaten the public peace.

One of these reports, printed in Angers, by the widow Piguet-Chateau, at 14 Saint-Gilles Street, reveals that one archbishop and two bishops have assumed responsibility for this affair and have informed the Roman Curia.

You are identified, Bishop, as being one of the prelates whose authority is used the better to disseminate the above mentioned picture and reports.

You will appreciate, as I do, Bishop, the dangerous nature of these publications and you will not allow them to be placed under your sponsorship, in whatever manner. Moreover, you will readily see the importance of halting the progress of this evil by promptly causing the truth to be known among the people and by foiling such devious schemes whose success is all the more assured because they are directed at religious sentiment.

I pray you, Bishop, to please inform me of the manner in which you will implement the present communication.

Please accept... **(18)**

Bishop de Bruillard replied to this challenge with a quiet defense of his clergy, referring the minister to his circular letter of October 9 of the previous year, and, by the whole tone of his letter, reserving to a bishop the right to take cognizance of a supernatural event. "My ears and eyes are open to all that is said, is done, and happens."

"Food crisis... the danger of sinister rumors"—it is evident from these hostile phrases that the attention of the crowds had been focused on the news of La Salette by the famine of 1846-47. The pangs of need made it difficult for the poor to face the threats of the unknown Lady with the same equanimity as that shown by the wealthy. Nowhere in the rural areas do we see the prediction of the fruitless sowing taken as advice. Still, in her book *l'Echo de la sainte montagne*, Mademoiselle des Brulais reports an enlightening conversation she had with a resident of Corps in September 1847.

"Have you had any famine here?" asked the schoolteacher from Nantes.

"Yes, Madame. The poor folk died of hunger on the mountain; they didn't even have as much as a potato to eat."

"The potatoes were bad here as elsewhere?"

"Of course, Madame, and for three francs you couldn't have bought as many as you can now for eight pennies; fifteen days before Christmas there was not one good one left. The Blessed Virgin had said that too."

"This is so true," adds the author, who was then lodging in the convent of the Sisters of Providence, "that in order to share their bread with the poor, these good religious of Corps used the flour just as it came out of the mill without even taking out the bran. They still continue today to bake this coarse bread in order to ration their small supply of wheat and to share it again with the poor if this winter proves to be as severe as last year's."

Anxious as they were about their daily bread, the ordinary people lived in confidence and gratitude. The region visited by the beautiful Lady was gradually returning to the practice of religion. Many cures were rumored to have taken place and the people gave simple thanks by means of pilgrimages, holy cards, lamentations, and verse.

Cures Begin

Thus, a haberdasher of Corps, Joseph Laurent, has left us one of the best accounts we have of the event prior to the official inquiry. Marie Gaillard, wife of Francois Laurent, crippled with chronic rheumatism, had been cured on November 24 through the intercession of Our Lady of La Salette. Her brother-in-law took it upon himself to repay this family debt. He wrote an account of the apparition under Mélanie's dictation (but not without adding a few embellishments of his own) **(19)**, and accompanied it with a lamentation which was sung the next day, November 28, on the mountain of La Salette, during the pilgrimage alluded to by Father Rabilloud in his letter to Bishop de Bruillard. At the beginning of December, both the account and the lamentation were published in Grenoble by Barnel. Street singers had gotten hold of a copy and had simply taken it to the printer.

A similar deed by the printer Prudhomme gives us an idea of the enthusiasm surrounding the message that the establishment disliked so much. The first day Maximin and Mélanie were together once again at Corps (Saturday, September 26), Mister Gueydan had heard each one of them. He pointed out to Father Bossan **(20)** that he did not take down their words in dictation. He began by "fabricating" stanzas of a lament that two minstrels from Corps wanted to sing while traveling through the countryside selling medals from La Salette. He then repeated the details learned from the children to Monsieur Prudhomme. The latter wrote his own version of the matter and published it with Mister Gueydan's stanzas in April 1847. This pamphlet, adorned with simple prints, carried a lengthy title revealing its reading audience: "Tribute to Our Lady of La Salette, followed by a very detailed account of the Apparition of the Most Blessed Virgin on the mountain of La Salette, near Corps, Isere, on September 19, 1846, and of extraordinary happenings that have followed this event." According to Father Bossan, 300,000 copies were sold.

At the same time, people from all parts of France were writing to Father Mélin for information about the water from the fountain. He also received reports of cures which he forwarded to the diocesan bureau. A particularly noteworthy cure was that of Sister Saint-Charles which took place at the convent of the Sacred Heart in Avignon on Passion Sunday, 1847, at the conclusion of a novena accompanied by the use of water from La Salette. A board of examiners established by the diocesan bureau at the close of this same year called the cure miraculous.

Not surprisingly, come early May, the curious, the investigative, and the praying crowds filed up the mountain as soon as the snow cleared. While at Corps the substitute justice of the peace interrogated the two witnesses of the apparition by order of the Royal Procurator, Father Bez toured the mountainside, gathered up all he heard on the event and its setting, and before the month was out published the first book on the subject. *Le Pelerinage de La Salette ou Examen critique de l'Apparition de La Salette a' deux bergers.* (21)

He was followed closely by Father Laurent Hecht, Prior of the Abbey of Einsiedeln in Switzerland (June 1847). Published in German, with a printing of 120,000 copies, *L'Histoire de l'Apparition de la Très Sainte Vierge à deux bergers...* bore witness to the interest generated by the event outside France. However, it should be read with caution.

Father Lambert, of Beaucaire, a more perceptive observer, began a week's investigation in Corps by recording with the wariness of a notary the recital of the two children. "Account of Maximin Giraud, written verbatim under his dictation, in the presence of six witnesses, May 29, 1847, from nine o'clock in the morning until noon." "Account of Mélanie Mathieu-Calvat, written verbatim under her dictation, in the presence of six witnesses, May 29,1847, from four o'clock in the afternoon to six-thirty." In deference to the Bishop of Grenoble, he did not publish his work, but communicated it to the diocesan investigators as soon as their names were known. In this case, because of the flawless method used, the official recorder adopted this text as the most dependable one he could present to the bishop and to the commission assisting him.

Many Pilgrims Arrived

Those with an instinctive trust in the maternal Virgin flocked to this high place in ever-increasing waves. Under the observant eye of Father Mélin, the number of daily arrivals increased from a few isolated groups in early May to five thousand by the end of the month. They came from Paris and Marseilles, from Bourges and Briancon, from the city and from the countryside. Priests came with their flocks and so Father Mélin had to provide for many Masses each day. This movement was sustained throughout the month of June, and, finally overwhelmed, the hapless parish priest admitted to his bishop that "the high cost of living added to further expenses that were forced on him by his many visitors made his position untenable." He was nevertheless cheered by all that he saw. He discreetly pressed the bishop for a decision by extolling the faith of the crowds.

> *The labor of the fields had not stopped the pilgrimages to La Salette. I do not believe there are such throngs in any shrine to Mary, neither in the diocese, nor in the vicinity. Every day this ravine is crisscrossed by large numbers of people coming from all directions. They come to pray, to sing, to weep, every hour of the day...* **(22)**.

This grassroots movement of the Christian people was becoming irresistible. It reached its high point in the extraordinary pilgrimage of September 19, 1847. That day, without cue, solely on the invitation of the beautiful Lady, 50,000 at the lowest estimate (some have said 100,000) gathered on the plateau of the Mont-sous-les-Baisses. Many witnesses assiduously reported the enthusiasm of this crowd gathered under night storm and midday sun.

> *It would be difficult, Bishop, to imagine the size of such a crowd. It would have taken a half-hour merely to walk around it. It was so*

pressed that one did not walk in it but was carried forward, as upon the waves of the sea, especially around the little chapel.... This whole gathering of people was pious and recollected; torrential rains fell from five o'clock in the afternoon until midnight, but not a word of grumbling or complaint was heard. The chanting of the litanies, the Salve Regina, and the Ave Maria went on without let up through the night. Priests celebrated Mass from three in the morning until eleven. Since communion could be distributed only in the small makeshift chapel no more than 25 people at a time could receive.... Communion could be given only to 1,000 people in all. The others were simply unable to reach the communion rail. **(23)**

Pilgrims climb the Holy Mountain by mule; collection: Victor Bettega

Thus did the parish priest of La Salette report to his bishop. His impressions corroborated those of all the other witnesses: Father Arbaud, **(24)** Father Sibillat, Father Gerin, pastor of the Cathedral of Grenoble. This latter searched his memory and could find nothing to compare with what he had seen. "Never," he wrote to Father Desgenettes, parish priest of Notre-Dame des Victoires, "have I seen a spectacle like this, neither in Lyons when the Bourbons returned from exile; neither at Bonaparte's return from Elba; neither at Notre Dame des Ermites on the anniversary of the miraculous consecration of this chapel; neither in Rome, when Pius IX regained possession of Saint-Peter's; yet here, there were only two-thirds the number of pilgrims..." **(25)**

The Bishop of Grenoble already knew where his duty lay: either his silence would abet an error or the Church had to intervene to legitimize such manifestations of devotion. On July 19 he issued a decree establishing a commission of inquiry.

> *Philibert de Bruillard, by divine mercy and the grace of the Apostolic See, Bishop of Grenoble:*
>
> *Given the two reports addressed to us last winter by the commissions appointed by us for this purpose, on the Apparition of the Blessed Virgin to two young shepherds of the parish of La Salette, in the township of Corps;*
>
> *Given the immense impact this event has had on the population, be it in the environs of the place in question, be it the neighboring dioceses and in a large part of France;*
>
> *Given the official reports handed to us regarding the many cures, either astonishing or miraculous, which occurred either on the mountain, or elsewhere, through the use of the waters that flow there;*
>
> *Given the requests we receive each day from every quarter urging us to come to a decision on the event;*
>
> *Given the firm belief experienced by a great number of persons, priests and laypeople, who have come to share it with us after having visited the site and heard the children, not counting thousands of pilgrims we have not seen and who share the same opinion;*
>
> *Given that it is our duty to gather juridical information at Corps as well as at La Salette and in those places where there are reports of marvelous cures;*
>
> *We have appointed Father Rousselot, professor of theology at our diocesan major seminary, honorary Canon of our cathedral and*

*honorary vicar-general as well as Father Orcel, honorary Canon
and superior of said seminary, as delegate commissioners to pre-
pare an inquiry and to gather information pertaining to the fact in
question. We invite them to join with priests and lay persons whose
presence they deem useful in arriving at the truth. In a very special
way will they seek the counsel of medical doctors who have treated
the sick who attribute their cure to the invocation of Our Lady of
La Salette or to the use of the miraculous water.* **(26)**

Seeking Verifications of Cures

The appointed investigators were far from converted to the cause of
La Salette. Father Rousselot, in the preceding month of December,
signed the two reports directed to the bishop, that of the canons and
that of the professors. Father Orcel himself had written the second in
which we recall, "certain items raising some suspicion about the truth
of the words of the Lady" were closely scrutinized. Both of them, in
fact, were suspending judgment as they accepted their mandate to
shed light on the event that fascinated all of France.

In the agenda drawn up for them, there was a marked insistence by
the bishop to seek out the proofs of cures attributed to the invocation to Our Lady of La Salette. As early as December, the commission
of professors had indicated this path of inquiry as the most fruitful,
declaring that the testimony of the children "could be confirmed and
made impregnable by the intrinsic examination of what they said, or
better still, by miracles, genuine indications of divine action."

Bishop de Bruillard's delegates left Grenoble on July 27, and traveled
through some ten dioceses in search of testimonies and documents
capable of producing serious evidence of miracles. Father Rousselot,
author of the official report, wrote: "We have been greeted favorably
everywhere; people spoke of nothing but this famous apparition, of
the water from the marvelous fountain, of pilgrimages made or to be
made to the holy mountain, of miracles wrought or graces received
by the intercession of Our Lady of La Salette and by the use of water
from La Salette."

Can we conclude from this that the investigators had not been demanding enough relative to the event itself, to the sincerity of the children, and to the authenticity of the texts they sought to establish? Emphatically not.

The investigators became acquainted with Lambert's double report while in Nimes in early August. Reaching Corps on August 25, they interrogated the two shepherds separately. The next day, by trails that are narrow, difficult, and steep, they climbed to the site of the apparition in the company of the two children, the parish priests of Corps and La Salette, other ecclesiastics and thirty to forty pilgrims. There, they carefully examined the site. They asked to hear once again, in greatest detail, the story of the apparition.

They returned to Grenoble only after having heard on the spot all the witnesses who could inform them of the shepherd's consistent telling of the same story from the very first day. We can believe them when they state in the first chapter of their report: "All those who, from the very first days after the apparition, had interrogated the children and had taken notes, did indeed attest to the children's fidelity in giving to all to whom they spoke the very same account, without variation either in form or in substance."

Examining Accounts of the Apparition

To support this statement they could have produced the signed testimonies of Selme and Pra, of Peytard and Mélin, and of many others. They had read and had in hand many written reports from priests who had briefly visited the mountain in October of 1846. At first reading, these reports (Cat, Eymery, Chambon, Guillard) deviated, at least in the wording, from the text they themselves submitted. They did not draw from them the objections that later opponents would attempt to exploit in bad faith. The reason for this is that they had received from their authors the assurance that their writing was not an official report.

Present among them was the very person who, though being unaware of it, was at the source of all the erroneous reports, the parish priest of La Salette, Father Louis Perrin. **(27)** This good priest did not in the least realize that the comments he had once recorded differed considerably from what the children said. If his writing contained enigmas that detractors would use one day for their own purposes, why should the investigators worry? Had he even told them of this paper tucked away in some drawer? In any case, he himself was convinced that he was hearing what he had always heard since his arrival in the parish.

The investigators were coming to realize that in this account they were compiling, the children were "repeating the words today like a lesson learned by rote." **(28)** The best transcriptions of the account provided them with the best tangible proof that it had never changed from the very beginning. From the Pra report to that of Lambert, the path of their research was marked by two documents of unequal value, but sufficient upon which to base conviction: the Laurent account which was in the public domain, and Lagier's notes, which the official reporter attests to having read. "His manuscript contains some forty pages. We have had it in hand."

The Lagier Notes deserve the historian's special consideration. They were taken, pencil in hand, by a priest native of Corps, who chatted with the children in their own dialect and who conducted an inquiry which would be the envy of today's best psychologists.

It was the end of February 1847 and the mountains were quiet. Father Lagier, parish priest of Saint-Pierre de Chérennes, was called to his family by his father's final illness. Finding himself with forced leisure on his hands, he decided to spend it attempting to unravel this mysterious phenomenon. The undertaking was not in-

Fr. Lagier, parish priest in the Isère region, interviewing Maximin about the Apparition

spired by concern for posterity or for the glory of the Blessed Virgin, but by an aggressive skepticism. "I don't mind saying that I began my interviews with the shepherdess hoping to uncover some hoax... I wanted to reach a conclusion that would match my first impressions." He interrogated Mélanie three times for a total of fifteen hours, using methods we will describe and evaluate later.

Maximin was down with smallpox for a few days, and could give only one interview. Nevertheless, the initial experiment was conclusive. Whenever he found an objective scribe for his narrative, Maximin clearly said the same thing as his companion, gave the same description of circumstances, of the phases of the apparition, of their own actions, repeated the same discourse given in the same order with only a few variations in expression. The description of the beautiful Lady was also the same, albeit shorter in Maximin's case because of a briefer interview.

That the two witnesses should agree on such details as the length of the cross hanging from the Lady's neck, or the color of the buckles on her shoes was astonishing. Lagier's swift pen missed nothing, recording the spontaneous dialogue as it came. "Her shoes were white (Maximin's words): on the instep of the foot there was a buckle like that of old Prudhomme, if you know him.—Yes. They were reddish like that" (points to a statue of Napoleon, to his yellowish epaulette and to the pommel of his sword). **(29)**

The investigators sought out Lagier's notes for no other reason than to make sure that the first accounts were identical to those they were now hearing. Having done this, they then chose the versions established by Lambert and presented them to the bishop's commission. Their choice was explained by the semi-official character of this deposition recorded verbatim in the presence of six witnesses. They rightfully congratulated themselves on the results obtained. The stateliness of the narrative, veiled in the first accounts, where the writers felt obliged to alter certain expressions and eliminate certain words that offended them, emerged whole once again in the austere beauty of the discourse as it is seen word for word in its simplicity and its purity...."

But today's critics generally hold that the nearer to its source a written testimony is, objectivity of course being safeguarded, the better the chances that truth will come down to us in its original purity.

In order, then, to reconstruct the event the two shepherds experienced, inasmuch as history can do this, we would need to focus more directly on Lagier's notes.

These notes, written in the give-and-take of casual conversation, had the advantage of scaling down to acceptable limits Rousselot's categorical statement: "The children have always maintained the same wording, without variation of any kind, neither in form nor in substance." Where substance is concerned, one can agree with him completely. But to insist that the words, the expressions, never vary from one report to another is quite another matter. Divine assistance, even in the case of the Gospel writers, never so constrained the workings of the human brain as to transform it into a recording machine. Fortunately, Lagier's notes show that, before becoming stereotyped by repetition, each child's account went through a normal intervening phase of creation. This is especially true of the actions they narrate: their own comings and goings, their personal reactions, the appearance and the attitudes of the beautiful Lady. Details of this sort are always colored by the curiosity of the witness.

Lagier, in his own unique way, elicited many such details that had gone as yet unnoticed. This is also true, to a certain degree, of their account of the beautiful Lady's words. Mélanie is older and also more wary of the subjective distortion she might be tempted to give them. Moreover, because she is less familiar with French than Maximin, she repeats the French part of the discourse verbatim. When she is speaking in dialect she is freer, as is Maximin, in the use of expressions. With the simplicity of an eleven-year-old, Maximin sometimes adds his own comment: "The cart drivers who go on the road," says he, using a familiar image. Mélanie says: "Those who drive carts." Further on when he tells Lagier about the promise of blessings attached to conversion he explains candidly: "It will be found that the potatoes have sown themselves, but have not spoiled."

Rousselot must have noticed, as Lambert had, that Maximin had his narrative and Mélanie her own, and that slight variations in the reports resulted from psychological differences. From the very beginning when the girl said, "the hand," the boy would say "the arm." Still, according to Maximin, recalling the Coin episode, the Lady addressed him in the familiar second person singular (tu) pronoun, while Mélanie quoted her as using the more formal and reverential second person plural (vous). The familiarity seemed quite simple and natural to the boy when the Virgin spoke to him. Mélanie's version was colored by the natural reserve of a young girl when describing events in which men are involved.

A solid inquiry did not require that these variants be studied scrupulously. Basically, what the official report stated still holds true: the children always used the same language. But the contemporary reader can only rejoice in seeing the children describe what they alone saw in words that reveal their own frame of mind. It is a proof that heavenly assistance was given them as it is always given to people chosen to convey a supernatural message. Above all, it is a proof of the absence of collusion. They were not reciting a well-learned lesson, taught them by a conspirator with enough time, patience, and pedagogical acumen to triumph over their childlike ignorance.

We now know what intermediaries would be most capable of passing on to us, at each stage of the testimony, the message of La Salette as well as its context.

The official investigation took it for granted that in the better accounts, differences in the discourse itself were minimal and purely verbal, except for Laurent's festoons. The best way to clear this underbrush and obtain the wording heard simultaneously by the two children was to adopt Pra's key witness account. It is the oldest and surely one of the most dependable of all. Certain of Maximin's expressions could be adopted from other texts, especially when they concern him personally. A combination of Lagier's pen and the work of the assigned investigators gives us the most thorough and fruitful inquiry, and thus, the best report of the event and of the descriptions of the beautiful Lady that one could possibly hope for.

-3-
The Apparition

Pierre Selme was a fatherly employer. He had promised Giraud the wheelwright, when he hired his son for eight days, that he would never lose sight of the hyperactive boy. This Thursday, as Maximin watched his cows and his goat in the field of Babou, Selme's benevolent eye had noticed the boy's loneliness. Coming home to Les Ablandins that night, he had suggested: "There is a little girl who brings her cows up the mountain. Why don't you go up with her?" The children exchanged greetings that night, but their encounter must have been brief. There was the evening meal to eat and, for Mélanie, chores to be done in the stable.

The next day they drove their small herds up the mountain together on the Planeau hillside, as Selme had ordered, but they did not speak or play together until the afternoon. As they returned to the village that evening they were happy with this first attempt at camaraderie

Alpine mountaintop field and valley before the La Salette apparition

and they parted with a challenge: "We'll see who gets up first."

Young children like Maximin take such challenges seriously. Mélanie had forgotten about it when, early that Saturday morning, she heard Maximin's ringing laughter stirring up the entire Pra household and making her feel lazy.

They milked the cows, had breakfast, and met on the road above the village. The first rays of sunlight were playing on the Obiou. The two shepherds prodded the animals on. Maximin had just won his wager and he was in a happy mood, yelling and jumping, teasing his dog Loulou. The lunch basket he had carried on the previous days had been cumbersome. This morning, his meager lunch tucked into his jacket, he was so wonderfully and completely free that he felt he could go to the ends of the world.

Selme, several yards behind, kept a close watch on the little caravan.

Turning right at Les Ablandins, the path runs up the side of the Babou. The dry Sézia stream did not tempt the animals as they walked by. Soon, Maximin's carefree and irrepressible shouts reverberated through the alleys of Dorsières. The children took a side path toward the Chamoux valley to avoid the thin flat land grasses that would lure their flocks to a stop. Meanwhile, Selme's long strides took him rapidly up the slopes of the Planeau. Negotiating numerous trails up the mountain, the children finally came within Selme's view. He had lost no time. The long swaths of freshly mown, sweet-smelling hay showed that he had lost no time getting to work.

Maximin and Mélanie prodded their flocks toward their master's fields, Maximin atop the Planeau, Mélanie some 130 feet below. The long climb had tempered Maximin's boisterous mood. Watching his small flock, and watched in turn by Selme, playing with grasshoppers and hacking lumps of turf with his knife, Maximin enjoyed every moment.

Selme's practical sense interrupted Maximin's peace: "Mémin," he cried, "quick now, lead your cows to drink." "I will call Mélanie Mathieu and we'll go together," replied Maximin, his clear child's voice straining to be heard. Mélanie clearly heard!

Hurriedly rounded up, the two flocks made their way instinctively to the watering place. This was a natural pool in the Sézia ravine, surrounded with stones and earth and fed by the last trickling of a drying brook. It was called the fountain of the animals.

The two shepherds chatted lightheartedly. After each cow had drunk they chased it away with stones and dumps of earth to the bottom of the gully at the foot of Mount Gargas. Then came time to rest, a good time of day for the two little shepherds because all the herds of the mountain were plunged into a communal drowsiness.

They returned now to the bottom of the ravine in a calmer mood. Near the brook there was the small, clear, cold spring gushing out of the earth, where shepherds drank. It wasn't difficult to find, since generations of shepherds had sheltered it with a ring of flat stones.

Sitting on the rustic benches, the children happily savored their pieces of local cheese and bread, washing them down with spring water. The sky was blue and the mountainside was alive with light and flower-scented air. They ate peacefully, their innocent banter blending with the innocence of nature around them.

Then they noticed people coming up along the dry bed of the Sézia. It was a shepherd from the Chabannerie and one from the Bertineaux, also Rosette de la Minouna, also from Corps. All morning long they watched their flocks on the mountainside below Maximin and Mélanie who could not recognize them from their higher position. It was delightful to meet on the mountain this way, especially when a new shepherd was just arriving from Corps and was returning home soon. Quickly, the young friends drank the cool water and sat down to ply the young Maximin with questions about the village. They would also like to have him relay bits of news for the people back home, but will he remember? At least, mother Minouna will be happy to hear that he has seen her daughter.

The visitors left and our frugal diners gathered up the leftovers, Mélanie in her lunch basket, Maximin in his jacket.

Crossing the brook, they found a place to rest farther down the hill, near another spring also surrounded with flat stones. It ran intermittently and, at the end of this scorching summer, not a drop oozed out of the earth. Dropping basket and jacket on the stones, the two children stretched out on the grass.

Why was it that, on this day, contrary to habit, they slipped into sleep? Were there certain things their hearts must forget? Must their eyes recover a newness before contemplating a light more exquisite than that of the sun?

How long did this unwonted siesta last? They would later say one hour, one hour and a half. Awaking, Mélanie did not think so much of lost time but of the cows she could no longer see. Seven years of bondage and scoldings made fear well up quickly in her chafed spirit: "Mémin, Mémin," she cried, rousing her sleepy companion; "let's go find our cows. I don't know where they are." Maximin quickly rose. Taking his stick, he ran down the ravine behind Mélanie.

Relief! From the hillock above the dry spring they turned and saw their flocks lying down in the grasses where they had herded them before. Maximin jumped with glee. Quickly recovering her professional tone, Mélanie said: "Let's go pick up our things and feed the cows." But instead of coming straight down, she went slightly to the left by a path leading from the mound to the shepherds spring. Halfway down, the path turned, revealing the bottom of the ravine and the dried-up spring .

The Beautiful Lady

Suddenly,—look!—On the stone where Maximin had thrown his jacket, a light shone and shimmered, as if a sun had fallen there.

"Mémin, come quickly. See that light over there!"

"Where? Where is it?" Maximin cried as he came on the dead run.

"Look, over there!" The light they saw was so bright and strong that the dazzled children rubbed their eyes. Slowly the globe of light

39

opened and they discerned the subtle outline of a woman sitting and weeping, her head in her hands, her elbows on her knees. They could hardly believe their eyes, so bright was she, her body, her hands so drenched with light. "O moun Diou!" exclaimed Mélanie in her native dialect. The warnings of grandmother Caron rushed to her mind in a flash: "Little one, you laugh at those who pray, do you? Well, some day you'll see something!" Frightened, she let her stick fall to the ground. No less fearful, Maximin still found the strength to reassure her. "Keep your stick, Mélanie, I'm keeping mine. If she does something to you, I'll give her a good whack!" Still dazed, Mélanie picked up her stick.

First Phase of Apparition: Weeping Mother

Together they stared transfixed as the Lady stood up in the oval of light, her face visible now, her hands in her long sleeves crossed in front of her. Immediately they heard a voice as of a mother calling: *"Come, my children. Do not be afraid. I am here to tell you great news."*

Their fear vanished then and there. Her voice penetrated them like music. They ran to the bottom of the ravine, crossing the brook. With sovereign grace the Lady took a few steps toward them. The boy at her left, the girl at her right, they were so close that they almost touched. A person could not have passed between them and the Lady. The same circle of light enveloped them all, in which all shadows disappeared.

The shepherds immediately felt that a tender gaze had settled upon them, but the face was so dazzling that they were unable to react to its gaze. Never once was Maximin able to see her face clearly. Two or three times during the apparition, however, Mélanie was able to discern a white, slender, and very pretty face in the light. (How does

40

one describe in human terms what is not of this earth?) The Lady lowered her eyes and leaned slightly toward them, her tears falling all the while and disappearing in the light. She said:

If my people do not obey, I shall be compelled to loose my Son's arm. It is so heavy that I can no longer restrain it.

Mélanie thought: her husband wants to beat her children. Maximin imagined that her son had beaten her. He felt sorry for her and was about to say "Don't cry, Madame, I will help you," but did not dare interrupt her. The unknown Lady continued:

How long have I suffered for you! If my Son is not to abandon you, I am obliged to entreat Him without ceasing. But you take no heed of that. No matter how well you pray in the future, no matter how well you act, you will never be able to make up to me what I have endured on your behalf.

I have given you six days to work. The seventh I have reserved for myself, yet no one will give it to me. This is what causes the weight of my Son's arm to be so crushing.

The cart drivers cannot swear without bringing in my Son's name. These are the two things which make my Son's arm so heavy.

If the harvest is spoiled, it is your own fault. I warned you last year by means of the potatoes. You paid no heed. Quite the contrary, when you discovered that the potatoes had rotted, you swore, you abused my Son's name. They will continue to be spoiled, and by Christmas time this year there will be none left.

What does she mean? Maximin asked himself no questions. He stood before her, drinking in her words, totally absorbed in her. Mélanie wondered what the expression "pommes de terre" meant ("potatoes," in French; literally, "earth apples"). She turned toward Maximin to ask him. The beautiful Lady anticipated her question.

Ah! You do not understand French, my children. Well then, listen. I shall put it differently.

And she spoke to them in their own dialect. "Si la recolta se gasta...."

With the ease of one born and bred in Corps she expressed herself in the local patois. The children were not even surprised at this. Was it more difficult for them to believe their eyes, looking on the regal splendor of her servant's dress, these pearls, the gold, the roses on her apron and on her shawl? Or was it harder to believe what their ears heard when she spoke as a queen: *"If my people will not obey,"* as she told them in their own language how the realities of earth are linked with those of heaven?

> *Si ava di bla... If you have wheat, it will do no good to sow it, for what you sow the beasts will eat, and whatever part of it springs up will crumble into dust when you thresh it.*

A great famine is coming. But before that happens, children under seven years of age will be seized with trembling and die in the arms of those holding them. The others will pay for their sins by hunger. The grapes will rot and the nuts will be worm-eaten.

Suddenly, Mélanie no longer heard the Lady's voice although her lips were still moving. She was aware that Maximin was listening very attentively. Then she, in turn, was able to hear words that Maximin could not hear. Maximin's restlessness won out over his effort to behave. He toyed with his hat, taking it off, putting it on again, and with the tip of his walking stick he poked at the pebbles. Finally, they both heard the Lady's voice again.

If people are converted, the stones will become mounds of wheat and it will be found that the potatoes have sown themselves.

Do you say your prayers well, my children?

Second Phase of Apparition: Conversation

Spontaneously, the children answered with

one voice: "Not too well Madame, hardly at all."

Ah! my children, it is very important to do so, at night and in the morning. When you don't have time, at least say an "Our Father" and a "Hail Mary," and when you can, say more.

Only a few rather old women go to Mass in the summer. Everyone else works every Sunday all summer long. And in winter, when they don't know what else to do, they go to Mass only to scoff at religion. During Lent, they go to the butcher shop like dogs.

My children, haven't you ever seen spoiled wheat?

"No, Madame," declared Maximin, quick to speak for Mélanie as well as for himself.

Turning toward Maximin, the Lady replied:

But you, my child, must have seen it once near Coin with your papa. The owner of the field said to your papa, "Come and see my spoiled wheat." The two of you went. You took two or three ears of wheat in your hands. You rubbed them, and they crumbled to dust. Then you came back from Coin. When you were only a half-hour away from Corps, your papa gave you a bit of bread and said: "Here, my son, eat some bread, this year anyhow. I don't know who will be eating any next year if the wheat continues to spoil like that."

"It's very true, Madame. Now I remember it. Until now I didn't," admitted the little scatterbrain as he remembered feeling his father's sadness on the road to Corps the day they had gone to buy an ash tree from the owner of the farm of Coin.

"Well my children, you will make this known to all my people," the beautiful Lady concluded in French.

That was all. What she had come to do in this place, with these children, was now done. She added nothing. No comment. There was no advice about the mission she had just confided to them. They should make it known and that would be enough. They were to tell people what they had seen, heard, and felt during that half-hour. In

43

this coming together of the marvelous and the ordinary, in the contrast between their simplicity and the sublime things they saw and heard, her people would discern whether or not the beautiful Lady of the Sézia was reality or fantasy. Why instruct the children? Why transform them? The truth of the message would show through their ignorance as through sheer crystal.

The beautiful Lady's visit had come to an end. Maximin drew back as she walked past him. She crossed the Sézia, skimming the stream bed. How sad that she should ruin the roses on her shoes by walking on them! thought Maximin. But no, she does not touch the ground as she walks. She glides over the grass without ever treading on it. When she was about ten feet past the spring, without turning back she spoke to them again: "Now, my children, be sure to make this known to all my people." **(1)**

Third Phase of Apparition: Mary's Assumption

Perhaps she would begin speaking to them again? Was it her gentleness that drew them to her so irresistibly? She had no sooner spoken her last words than that the two children rushed after the amazing visitor. Step by step Maximin followed her. Mélanie ran straight up ahead of her as she went up the steep, winding grade. From each spring two parallel paths ran up to the top of the hillock. Halfway up, a third path crossed them horizontally. Following one of these paths then the other, the Lady traced a wide open "S" as she glided up the side of the ravine. This was later interpreted to be the pattern, in miniature, of the Via Dolorosa, or Way of the Cross, going from the Pretorium to Calvary and fourteen stations were erected along the path the Lady walked that day.

Near the top, the Lady stopped. Slowly, she

44

rose to a height of about five feet, and remained there for approximately thirty seconds. Standing before her, Mélanie saw her raise her eyes to heaven, then lower them to the far horizon toward the southeast, in the direction of Italy and Rome. Her tears no longer flowed but an infinite sadness lingered on her face. And then, slowly, the head, the shoulders, the entire body dissolved in brilliant light.

The little shepherds sadly stared at the indescribable, vanishing splendor. The sense of loss they felt revealed the depth of their attachment. As long as she was with them their only thought was of her. Through her they had lived and breathed. In her presence they had experienced the most perfect happiness they had ever enjoyed. They would have followed her to the ends of the earth and now her glory was slipping away. They understood that she was different from other women. The little roadside chapels showed saints surrounded by rays and halos. Could she be one of those? "Perhaps she was a great saint," ventured Mélanie.

"If we had known she was a great saint," quickly rejoined Maximin, "we would have told her to take us with her." A few minutes earlier, as the Lady vanished, he had leaped up with all his strength to grasp one of the roses on her shoes, the last, vestige of their dear and gentle Lady. But the roses had vanished too, absorbed in the blinding light. "If only she were still here," sighed Mélanie. "She doesn't want to be seen so we won't know where she is going." Their eyes and their hearts were still held by the oval light. Could it possibly open up again and reveal some trace of the majestic, fleeing Lady? Maybe some final secrets? In a few more seconds of anxious hope that glorious brightness too was gone. There was nothing more than the nostalgic light of September shimmering in the air and on the hill.

Slowly, the shepherds returned to the actual world. It was at least three o'clock according to the sun. Time to feed the animals before returning to the village. Maximin retrieved his jacket, Mélanie her lunch basket. Their hearts were filled with a gladness and a gravity they could not define. Their childlike minds teemed with questions. Loulou, Maximin's dog, was still there, lying down by the spring, sleeping. With a playful tap, Maximin awakened him. With a start, the boy realized that his normally cantankerous pet had not barked at the Stranger, that he had slept as if nothing had happened. It was one more reason for Mélanie to think that the Lady was certainly a saint from heaven. She reviewed in her mind all the saints she had seen in the roadside shrines and wondered which one most resembled the Lady. Her Lady was weeping, and yet none of the saints she had seen was as beautiful as she. How could she ever look so stately, so dignified? How could she speak with a voice so gentle and so soft? Little girls who cry make such faces! Who could she be?

At this very moment the entire praying Church was pronouncing with tenderness the name of the Unknown Lady. Of course, the children did not, could not know this. The first vespers of the Feast of Our Lady of Seven Dolors, celebrated then on the third Sunday of September, began with a hymn recalling the divine tragedy which brought tears to the most beautiful woman who ever was. From convent chapel to rectory garden, to the ends of the earth, a single prayer arose: "Queen of Martyrs, pray for us." But also at this same moment came another cry: "Get rich! Acquire and hoard!" This cry had so dominated people's lives that the divine tragedy was in a mysterious way being played anew. And so, the Queen of Martyrs came again to the world. She spoke to these children about the arm of her Son, about spoiled harvests, about her suffering and her prayer.

All of this obviously went beyond the children's comprehension, but the vague notion of having been in contact with something heavenly made them walk on air.

The cows and the goat were still grazing peacefully at the foot of Mount Gargas. Herded by the children, they came to drink again at the spring. Later, skirting the summit of the Planeau, the children spied at the bottom of the ravine the three other shepherds they had seen previously at the fountain. But this time they did not speak to them. They could think of nothing else but the marvelous Lady, and, besides, Maximin and Mélanie instinctively felt that such things were not to be confided to children.

Maximin suddenly exclaimed: "Hey! She stopped speaking even though she was still moving her lips. What was she saying?" "She told me something," replied Mélanie, "but I don't want to tell you. She forbade me to say it." "Oh! You know, Mélanie, I'm so glad. She told me something and I don't want to tell you either." Thus, they discovered that they had each been told a secret.

Having reached their employer's fields they felt freer to share impressions. Their long delay had been made up now, and no one could scold them. Selme was no longer around. His work done, he had left the fields after lunch, trusting Mélanie's know-how and vigilance.

"When I first saw her," Maximin said, "I thought she was a woman from Valjoufrey who wanted to steal our lunch. But when she spoke of the arm of her Son, I thought it was some lady whose son had beaten her and who had run away. I felt like telling her to be quiet, to stop weeping, that we would help her."

"Did you notice," said Mélanie, "that she cast no shadow, nor did we when we were with her? How bright she was!"

"How beautiful she was! For me, the prettiest thing was her cross!"

"Her shawl, her chain, and her cross, those were the brightest. If she had given me a dress like hers, even less pretty, I would have taken it."

And so, while running after their animals, picking up a flower here and there, they shared their impressions very freely. Later, while answering exacting questions, they supplied many other details, enabling us to have a clear description of the beautiful Lady who enraptured them.

Her Appearance

She was tall and slender. No woman they knew appeared as tall as she. We might perhaps remember that throughout the conversation the children were standing close to her. Their short stature, the sloping terrain, her high headdress can explain, at least in part, the children's impression of her height.

Her whole bearing and attire can be understood as a lesson in modesty. She wore a white dress that covered her whole body from the throat to the top of her shoes. Her hands were crossed inside long and ample sleeves. A shawl knotted in the back covered her breast and her waist. A bright yellow apron hung from her waist to her feet. Her white headdress, about eight inches high and in the form of a cone rounded at the crown, framed her face and joined the collar of her dress at the back, hiding her hair and ears. White shoes, decorated with a square reddish buckle and gold-colored stockings completed her servant's dress.

One thing was clear: this was a servant of the Lord, living in glory. A lavishness never seen on earth heightened her servant's reserve. A double wreath of light shone around her: the first, extremely bright and narrow, closely enveloped her while the second extended three or four yards around her and encompassed the two children themselves and erased all shadows. The dress and the shoes were spangled with light.

On her breast two chains of sparkling gold drew the children's eyes. The first was large and flat, made of links placed side by side along the edge of the shawl. The second, much thinner, hung from her neck and held a cross with a corpus. The crucified Christ was incandescent and seemed the center of all her glory. Near the crossbeams, but detached from them and held by nothing, were the instruments of the Passion: a hammer on the left and tongs on the right, as if she were offering the world the choice of nailing or of releasing her Son. Then a garland of many-colored roses encircled her feet, another ran along the chain around her shawl, and a third crowned her head, clearly symbolizing the joyful, sorrowful, and glorious

Our Weeping Mother

48

mysteries of the rosary.

The floral crown on her forehead was the brightest: stars shimmered between the roses and there was a diamond at the center of each flower. Their combined font of light created a crown of brightness around her white headdress.

The expression on her face was at once heart-rending and beatific. "She wept all the time she spoke to us," asserted Mélanie in Lagier's notes. "I really saw her tears flowing. They flowed and flowed!" These mysterious tears never reached the ground, but disappeared in the light as they fell. Mélanie noted that the tears never prevented the Lady's face from radiating an immense kindness. Though the part of her face between the lips and the forehead so dazzled Maximin that he could not behold it, the voice of the Lady, according to him, revealed the depth of her sadness. Still, the voice remained clear. It poured into them with the softness of a melody and filled them with a joy they had never known. "We were so happy," they kept repeating in their simple words. One day Maximin would find a new way of expressing his feeling: "We seemed to be eating her words."

The children had seen heaven open and their pure hearts met the ever-pure Lady. No cultural background, no strength of mind could have brought them the joy they were now experiencing. The name of their "great saint" and the meaning of her message eluded them. A few words grasped here and there, a few simple responses could not have signaled their comprehension of the Lady's discourse, nor even of its real purpose. They readily admitted having repeated the words of the discourse for a long time without understanding them. "About as much as we understand Latin at Vespers, for example." **(2)** No matter. As long as the Lady enabled them by the sweetness of her presence and her ways to make known to all her people the message that concerned them rather than the children.

Recalling the vision, sharing new-found happiness, they saw that time had fled quickly, as in a dream. When the shadows from Boutières covered La Salette and began climbing the Planeau, they knew it was time to go down the mountain again. The little shepherds had a timepiece all their own, as simple as their very existence.

They may have been a little earlier than usual today, but how could they keep the secret of this wonderful meeting any longer? The whole village certainly saw the beautiful Lady all afire when she rose above the Collet. Their elders would tell them what to think of all this. They would know the name of the "great saint" and the meaning of her words: *You will make this known to all my people.*

They started down toward Les Ablandins, their hearts moved by the sadness of the mysterious visitor and filled with the premonition that something strange had entered their lives.

Pierre Selme was worried. He was standing on his stoop, waiting for his shepherd. He had not seen Maximin since the Angelus and now he heard the approaching cow bells. As they brought in the cows together, Selme in his fatherly manner gently reproached the shepherd: "Well Mémin, you didn't come to see me in my field as I had told you?"

"Oh! Don't you know what happened?" replied Maximin.

"Well, what happened?"

"We found a beautiful Lady by the spring who entertained us and spoke to us a long time. I was afraid at first. I didn't dare fetch my bread, which was near her. Then she told us: "Come near, my children, be not afraid. I am here to tell you great news." The restless Maximin suddenly became serious as he spoke for the first time what the Lady had told him, in French and in his own dialect. He described her disappearance, her sadness, her glorious beauty. Selme was stupefied. In silence, he listened to the shepherd who seemed to be returning from another world.

We know the sequel and how at the end of the evening the fear of God overcame all attempts at mockery. Pra and Selme concluded that the pastor had to be told. In all probability, and unwittingly, they were deciding what would become of the apparition.

Three phases of the Apparition at the Mountain of La Salette

-4-
The Verdict

*I*t is the Virgin that these children have seen, exclaimed Mother Pra as she heard the story of the apparition for the first time. "My children, you are blessed, you have seen the Blessed Virgin," Father Jacques Perrin said to the two children the next day. On the spot and on impulse, he shared the "great news" with his parishioners. Two weeks later, the parish priest of Corps, Father Mélin, reporting on the event to Bishop de Bruillard, also attested his own belief. "The people naturally understood that it was the Blessed Mother who has come to warn the world before her Son comes to punish it. My personal conviction after gathering every proof I could is the same as that of the faithful. I believe that this warning is a tremendous grace. I don't need another miracle to believe. But my very sincere wish is that God would, in his mercy, bring about another miracle to confirm the first."

Such eagerness to believe may come as a surprise to some. But there is probably more wisdom in this spontaneous adherence than is at first apparent. These first-hour believers saw and heard the witnesses of the apparition. They possessed a vivid and concrete notion of the witnesses' capabilities; they knew how limited were the children's memory and power of fabrication and how ignorant and uninterested they were in all matters of religion. All other moral consideration aside, the very idea that these two children would have taken on the role of inspired seers must have seemed utterly preposterous to them. Nothing in their behavior or aptitudes pointed to that. Moreover, their story was coherent. Whatever negative traits can be attributed to them, could their hoax have achieved this amazing degree of authenticity, that intangible quality we could call Our Lady's very own "presence"? These reasons were more or less clearly perceived, and undergirded the simple folk's decision to believe after listening to the children.

The official Church, however, could not give such a prompt verdict. A certain delay seemed important to determine if the children would hold to their story. Then, from the considerable accumulation of documents that all claimed veracity, the exact tenor of the story had to be retrieved. We already know that one of the major goals of the investigators was to present an authentic version of the story to their bishop. The fact having been duly established, there remained to be seen whether it was in accordance with Revelation as held by the Church for eighteen hundred years.

The message, of course, had to be worthy of its origin, God himself. All other hypotheses had to be eliminated before arriving at a supernatural conclusion. Still, in such matters, the human spirit is fragile and can be easily seduced by appearances. That is why the Church traditionally grants a decisive importance to miracles, conversions, and all the fruits of salvation that one could legitimately connect to an apparition. Hence, people already open to the grace of La Salette had no greater wish than to see "one miracle confirmed by another," as Father Mélin was fond of saying. Bishop de Bruillard's delegates conducted inquiries in many dioceses in order to ultimately rest his verdict on undeniably true miracles.

The path the Church was to follow was thus set: God's blessing would uphold the proofs centered on the apparition. Only a long and mature inquiry would allow the Church to decide whether or not the intuition of the people of God held all the criteria of certainty required by the examiners.

Bishop de Bruillard now had the report of his two delegates.

La Salette Icon with the three phases of the Apparition

He proceeded to establish a Commission that he would himself chair. The choice of members was not arbitrary, nor did he fear objections to his opinion. Aside from the investigators we already know, he designated his two other vicars general, the members of his chapter, and the five parish priests of the episcopal city.

This Commission met for the first time on November 8, 1847, at the bishop's residence. Normally, it was to meet every Monday. But at the second meeting (November 15), the children appeared before the Commission and consultations were held with Father Mélin and Mother Sainte-Thècle, superior of the convent where the children were staying. Taking advantage of the children's presence in Grenoble, the Commission decided to extend this session through November 17. After the eighth session, held on December 13, the bishop pronounced the Commission's work concluded.

Reading the minutes of these sessions, one is amazed by the openness of the discussions. This openness was complete and applied to any questions relevant to the report. Members were even allowed to wander far afield to broach, for example, the topic of money-making in relation to the new shrine, or to linger more than necessary on unimportant remarks attributed to the children.

The Bishop intervened only in the fifth session to bring the debate back on course. "It seemed to me that much time was lost when many topics not relevant to the apparition, and of no help in deciding for or against it, were allowed into the discussion." At this point he considered the issue of the children's story as having been sufficiently discussed and asked the members to give their opinions by answering *yes* or *no* to seven specific questions. The Assembly also voted by article on the section of the report reserved to miracles and other spectacular occurrences of a moral order resulting from the apparition. The bishop's delegate, for his part, strove in every way to highlight his colleague's good will. He pleaded in favor of the supernatural origin of the event, bringing forth objections without underrating them, gathering and presenting documents relevant to the debate.

Bishop de Bruillard's Decree appeared only four years later, but he revealed herein that "as early as the close of the Commission's sessions" he was completely convinced. In fact, twelve of the sixteen members of the Commission had responded affirmatively to the question: Did this event really take place, or, are the children either deceived or deceiving? The minority opinion was still divided on a rather important point: three dissenters said they did not have enough proof to assent to the fact and only one felt he was justified in rejecting it. Almost unanimously, the Commission, beginning with the bishop, felt that there was a clear case in favor of the supernatural interpretation.

Without going into every detail of the debate and without neglecting the critical approach so essential in such a case, it can still be affirmed that the objections, taken singly, had little consistency. If we attempt to gather them up into a whole, we discover a basic flaw: they do not focus light, they diffuse it. They do not clarify the mystery, they bring confusion.

One case in point. At the first session, Maximin is said to be a liar. The implication was that his story of the apparition was just one more lie. This assumption naturally brought Mélanie into the liar's circle and efforts were made to prove it. According to one Commission member, "she told certain people that she had seen a mysterious light long before the apparition. To others, she said that she had seen this light only after." These statements were contradictory. In one case or the other, she lied.

This logician was told that circumstances have to be taken into account. It was difficult for mountain children to respond to a barrage of questions they did not understand. It was more expedient to question Mélanie then, because she was present. She entered the room and the report notes: "Upon questioning, the child affirmed that she had never seen a light before the event, only at the moment of the apparition, and that she had never said otherwise. The one who had reported the incident originally asserted that he knew differently, and this from credible witnesses. The discussion was not pursued." This last sentence is admirably discreet. No one wanted to follow the dissenter on indefensible ground.

The dissenter came upon a better argument relative to a variation found in a few earlier narratives and which has since disappeared from the approved text.

Excitement ran through the Corps countryside in the fall of 1846 and many priests made trips up the mountain to see and to question the children. Many of them sent more or less accurate reports to the chancery (Cat, Eymery). The first consultants found more than one stumbling block in these reports. Others kept personal notes, but quite likely had them read by certain members of the present Commission. Practically all of these reports written by priests between mid-October and November 9 contain this sentence attributed to the beautiful Lady: "In winter, they go to Mass when they don't know what else to do, but they fill their pockets with stones to throw at the girls."

These writings may have been hasty and confused, but their agreement on this point is revealing the sentence must have been spoken by the children. They stopped saying it, but what are we to think of this variation? Does it not place their sincerity in doubt? And what about the majesty of the Discourse, that the Advocate held as such a powerful argument?

The town of Corps, below the hamlet of La Salette

The Commission had to come to grips with this problem. No one could justify the presumption that the children were liars. On the contrary, after a time of doubt, their credibility became all the more obvious once the tangle of textual criticism was unraveled.

As soon as the problem surfaced, Father Rousselot had contacted the people better able to solve it. Father Louis Perrin, the parish priest of La Salette, was the first to communicate the results of his investigation to him. Perrin had questioned the children's employers. They had never known lying to be one of the children's prevailing faults. About the troublesome sentence, Baptiste Pra could no longer consult his own notes since they had been taken from him at Corps, but he believed the troublesome sentence to be part of the story. **(1)**

The fourth conference concluded without solving the problem. The elements of a simple solution appeared suddenly during the fifth conference. From his parish at Saint-Pierre de Cherennes, Father Lagier wrote to Rousselot. During his stay in Corps the preceding winter, Lagier had done more than interrogate the shepherds. He had ventured as far as Les Ablandins and he still had in his possession a copy he had made of Pra's report. There is nothing in it, he assured Rousselot, of stones thrown at girls. He adds: "Neither Mélanie nor Maximin mentioned this to me, but having heard from other people about their having said it, I brought it up with Mélanie. Here is her answer: "I have never personally spoken of that. Maximin said it because he was told to say it. I told him that the Lady had never told us that and he hasn't mentioned it since."

In the course of his investigation, the Advocate had sought out Maximin for an explanation of his childish remark. He chose to see him again during the days when the children were appearing at the bishop's residence. At the last session he could more properly gauge the meaning of the incident because concrete details were added to Lagier's basic explanation: Maximin had said it because he had been told to say it.

"Asked why he had added this remark, Maximin gave two answers. The first is that while giving the account in the early days, he was more taken up with the thought and the image of the beautiful Lady

57

than with what he was saying. (2) Maximin's second answer was that he had heard many comments and applications made on this part of the story and people were pressing him to approve them with a simple yes. Hence, the innocent accretion of *stones thrown at girls* slipped carelessly into his account. The young people guilty of this behavior must have felt implicated in the complaints of the Virgin. From that time on, these disturbances have ceased completely."

This explanation gains new strength from Maximin's answers to the Advocate during the commission's sessions.

The Advocate asked him: "Didn't people want you to add things to your account that the Blessed Virgin had not said?"

Maximin answered: "Yes, sir. In a meeting of women and girls, I was told that the Blessed Virgin had spoken of dances and bad confessions."

The Advocate pressed on: "So! What did you answer to these women?" Maximin said: "I said that the Blessed Virgin never mentioned that. And since they absolutely insisted that the Blessed Virgin had said this, I left them, saying: "As you wish." (3)

The Advocate might have dropped the subject if the stakes had merely been a remark contradictory to Maximin's account. It is clear from his exposition that neither the addition nor the retraction of the unfortunate remark makes Maximin a false witness and that the remainder of the discourse—the substance of it—bears the stamp of dignity and grandeur. That, in fact, is precisely the problem. Considering Maximin's ignorance and the suggestibility of an eleven year old boy, it is amazing that the changes in the message were not more serious, given the number of biased interpreters involved. But in this incident, he is formally accused of lying. Rousselot attempts to deal with the difficulty.

"There is more: some people, having questioned Maximin on this "throwing stones" incident, observed that he no longer mentioned it. They asked him if he had included it in past accounts. Maximin answered that he had not. Therefore, he had lied."

The Advocate reviewed the theological definition of falsehood with the priests. Lying, he reminded them, is speaking contrary to one's mind, and he warned all accusers against the presumption of reading another's mind to know what is really there. Then, politely but firmly, he taught them a lesson on the art of interrogating children to learn the truth from them.

"We say these same people have only themselves to blame if they have not obtained the truth. Prejudiced against the children as well as the event, they have been too severe. They have interrogated them not like people who deserve compassion, but like deceitful criminals. At that moment, at least, they forgot that truth is attained by the wisdom of the seeker."

The Children's Advocate spoke of their accusers indirectly, but it is not unlikely that the accusers were themselves present in the audience. The Gospel exhortation in psychological dress points to this. Not wanting to belabor the issue, he observed that this point, even if agreed upon, was still not inherent to the truth of the apparition.

The accusation of lying viewed in the light of the children's general behavior is reduced to a few unsubstantiated peccadillos. Seen against their overall witness to La Salette, it disappears completely. Even after this refutation by the Advocate, a minority still held their ground. By way of explanation they said that the children had been duped by an impostor. Every subsequent attempt at explanation brought out inconsistent allegations and gratuitous suppositions.

The Advocate also had his own observations to make about the charge of fabrication. "Attempting to explain away La Salette in this manner means running away from a miracle with the help of another. It is combating reality with fantasy. It is being unreasonable in order to appear demanding." The lying children hypothesis led to the same impasse. It would have been miraculous indeed to have consistency in testimonies emerge from a story concocted within an hour with such poor talent.

To suggest that an impostor had mystified the children meant denying eyewitness testimony for those who had closely examined the site of the apparition. Above all it meant denying La Salette by refusing to see what is essential in it, because the manner of the children's testimony is secondary to what they are in fact saying. The apparition itself, apart from its heralds, shows us its divine signature. The scene and the words that the two ignorant children attribute to their beautiful Lady together fashion a harmony so complex and so faultless that it reduces to naught any suspicion of trickery.

But a minority in the Commission remained in opposition, even in the face of such arguments. Obviously, only absolute proof and evidence can change the human mind. While Father Rousselot spoke of the Discourse's biblical style and tone, others could find only coarseness in the message. Three nays opposed the approval of the majority in the matter of miracles even though these cures had been called naturally inexplicable by medical doctors. Could these priests really have benefited more from their theological studies than had their brother priests?

At this stage, it would be premature to speak of bad faith. One member of the commission, Father Cartellier, pastor of Saint Joseph

The village of La Salette-Fallavaux; artist: E. Dardelet

Parish in Grenoble, would later lead a coalition against the bishop's doctrinal decree. For the moment he stayed in the minority with a vicar general, Father Berthier, and with two other parish priests of the city, Fathers de Lemps and Genevey. He differed from his minority companions only in obstinacy. Their excessive severity with regard to the supernatural was really based on a confusion of levels, that of moral and that of physical certainty. They dreaded the proclamation of a new miracle in a faithless society. They were thus led to exact proofs that would meet the demands of a positivistic methodology. They were insensitive to the finer-meshed demonstrations of the spirit. This is, at least, the impression one derives from their general attitude as well as from a lengthy technical discussion wherein one of their spokespersons maintained that moral certainty has no margin of probability.

Whatever their motivation might have been, their failure is clear. They never succeeded in explaining away La Salette through the simple interplay of natural causes. They attempted it, they perhaps believed it. They had recourse to many contradictory hypotheses simply because none of them fully embraced all the facets of the problem. It is always such with miracles, and so it will be tomorrow with La Salette as it was during the first days of the opposition. A totally rational solution is apparently found, one unknown to the believers. But then another aspect of the problem, more important than the one supposedly being clarified, goes unnoticed and forgotten. What is explained, then, is not the event as reality presents it. It is a travesty of the event as one would have wanted it to be.

Controversies Arise

The opposition of 1847 surely deserves more respect than one would give the Lamerlière caper of 1854. In a well known decree, Bishop Ginoulhiac directed a withering condemnation of it, but did not hesitate to highlight in transparent terms the weaknesses of the first. "It is quite remarkable and not without importance for the reality of the apparition, that during eight years of wonder and awe on the part of some and opposition on the part of others, no one has yet been able to find, outside supernatural interpretation, one theory able to withstand the slightest test, one theory whose futility is not immediately evident and worthy of nothing but ridicule."

This had been Bishop de Bruillard's own conclusion as the inquiry he had launched now came to an end. He had so wanted to respond to "the voice from heaven" and proclaim the apparition a reality and thus grant to so many faithful the comfort of praying to Our Lady of La Salette in sure harmony with the Church. He felt designated for that very task, because the event had taken place in his own diocese. Such a proclamation by him would have been in accord with the universal Church's long-standing legislation. But the petty opposition that had arisen under his very eyes had made him understand that by dint of intrigue and confusion, it could stop him from performing his duty.

While the Commission was still in session, an eminent patron unexpectedly covered the minority's retreat. Cardinal de Bonald, archbishop of Lyons and metropolitan of Grenoble, had written three times to his suffragan bishop to dissuade him from pronouncing on La Salette a judgment engaging the Church. The Commission had been dissolved and the opponent's feared that the venerable bishop might pronounce himself as he had intimated. The cardinal shared the opponents apprehension and apprised the bishop of it on January 10, 1848, in an attempt to discourage such a step. There was a strange association here. How did it begin? Toward what end was it moving?

It is unlikely that the archbishop had initiated such tactics. His correspondence had begun only on November 19, after the Commission's fourth session and the testimony of the children at the bishop's residence. His objections were merely the ones the opponents had brought before the assembly and which had prompted Bishop de Bruillard to remark that "the progress of the discussions, although unimpeded, was prodigiously delayed." One cannot help think that these same opponents, hardened in their hostility, had appealed over the bishop to the metropolitan. For what purpose? Under normal conditions, the cardinal could not assume responsibility in the matter, but the Council of Trent recommended that the bishop, "In difficult and perplexing cases," have recourse to the provincial council. Arguing from this clause, the opponents could cause an endless number of problems for the Bishop of Grenoble.

The bishop's first concern was to provide the cardinal with the findings the advocate had brought before the Commission. His eminence's objections, like those of the informers, were external to the fact (What will unbelievers, Protestants, say? What an opening for all types of speculation!) Or else, they approached it superficially, pointing to irrelevant detail (the dress is strange, the prophecies have not been realized). There was only one attempt at an explanation, but it betrayed a complete ignorance of the facts of the case. "The dialogue between the Blessed Virgin and the two children was not involved enough, nor long enough not to have been taught to the children with purposes of financial advantage for the area. The attempt has been quite successful." One had to disregard all that the inquiry had revealed about the natural abilities of Maximin and Mélanie. Three years later, the cardinal would write of them in a letter to Father Rousselot and would call them "Marcellin and his sister." It was even more regrettable to see the religious meaning of the message escape him. He might have given it one hour's careful reading and have asked himself one question: "What if it were true?"

Fr. Joseph Rousselot, Professor of Theology at Major Seminary in Grenoble

Father Rousselot's reply, revised by Bishop de Bruillard, in no way convinced the archbishop. He did not respond but withdrew into a kind of reticence that the opponents in Grenoble exploited as they did everything damaging to La Salette.

The Ars incident to come shows this well. It was awkward for the diocesan bishop to proclaim his conviction. A few rough-hewn hypotheses had muddled what was originally so clear, and his decision would be contested. There was no alternative other than to wait for providential signs.

In all likelihood, the bishop perceived such a sign in Father Dupanloup's thoughtful adherence to the cause of La Salette. The future bishop of Orléans (he would be named the following year), had come in early June 1848 to relax with his friend Albert du Boys, Lord of Combe-de-Lancey, in the Isère. At that time and in this area, the La Salette question became an immediate concern. He made the trip, and spent three days visiting Corps and La Salette. He questioned the children, especially Maximin. From Laus, where he was staying, he sent his friend a letter which is a model of the most objective and most penetrating psychological analysis, of which the conclusion expressed the same verdict as that reached by Bishop de Bruillard and his commission: "If I were obliged to pronounce myself and to say "yes" or "no" to this revelation, and if I were to be judged on the strict sincerity of my conscience on this matter, I would say "yes" rather than "no" and I would not fear being condemned before the judgment seat of God as guilty of imprudence or superficiality."

This is a celebrated letter, well known in the history of La Salette. On the subject of the children's testimony it is one of the important sources. The public did not learn of it until 1849 when Father Dupanloup included it in his journal *L'Ami de la Religion*. Bishop de Bruillard may have read it soon after its original recipient did. In any event, the author obviously had communicated with him, since he had obtained the files from the bishop's residence. From that time on, Father Dupanloup provided the bishop with the wise and judicious counsel he needed to deprive the opposition of any further advantage. He promptly read the Rousselot-Orcel report and was pleased with it. (4) He points out a contradiction in which it is said that Maximin had returned to Corps on Sunday morning, September 20. But it also included Peytard's assertion that he had interrogated the two children at Les Ablandins in the evening of that same day. (5) Rousselot immediately asked the parish priest of La Salette to clarify this point with the mayor. The answer confirmed the report's accuracy. "On the following Monday, the mayor tells me, September 21, 1846, I went down to my vineyard to pick a few ripening grapes. As I returned from the vineyard, I was completely taken up with what Mélanie had told me the night before, so I stopped at Giraud's house and had Maximin come to me...."

We can only imagine the joy the good bishop must have felt in meeting the visiting priest. Father Dupanloup was a demanding person in the service of truth. A few months earlier Bishop de Bruillard had written to Cardinal de Bonald in terms that were amply justified by Dupanloup's own approach: "I don't know if the situation is the same in Lyons as it is here. I'm amazed to see that here the fiercest opponents are precisely those who have refused to see, to interrogate, to confront the children, to visit the site, to question the people, to notice what is happening among the crowds of pilgrims. On the contrary, those who believe have taken every precaution not to be deceived."

The truth has power over those who love it! Bishop de Bruillard decided to place all his confidence in the truth as he responded to the call of Providence. Four days after Dupanloup's letter, on June 15, 1848, Bishop de Bruillard authorized the publication of his investigative report. In this context, we can better understand its title, revealing firmness and hope: *The Truth Concerning the Event of La Salette.* (6)

This publication enriched the original report with new facts, new written testimony, and much clarification of details. The Bishop of Grenoble was actually offering the Catholic world the state of the question. In his preface, after having stated his own opinion, Bishop de Bruillard plainly expressed his expectations:

This report, much desired and long awaited, seems to have done away with many a prejudice, to have enlightened public opinion, and convinced open minds. Those who believed, those who did not, and those who doubted will read it with interest and, we hope, with profit. Those who have believed will know that they have not been rash and naive for having done so. Those who saw fit to suspend judgment will be impressed by the many proofs accompa-

nying the extraordinary occurrence. Those who are influenced by prejudice, who stand against everything that is outside the natural and all that is extraordinary, will surely recall that the truth can sometimes appear unlikely, and that an event that has resounded throughout the Catholic world for twenty months cannot be dismissed out of hand.

The bishop's hopes were not in vain. Pope Pius IX kindly accepted the gift of Rousselot's report. With the plaudits of eight archbishops and bishops, the book was immediately translated into German, English, and Italian.

Bishop de Bruillard was able to express his hopes and purposes even more firmly with the publication, early in 1850, of Rousselot's *New Documents Concerning the Event of La Salette*. **(7)**

These documents are an important sequel to the Report discussed with us, adopted by a large commission convoked by us, and published with our authorization.

Mary is the Patroness of France and of our diocese. We have been pleased during these three years to see a new pilgrimage established in her honor. Our hopes will have been fulfilled, however, when, with the collaboration of everyone, from this diocese and elsewhere, we see a shrine worthy of Her who appeared on the holy mountain, large enough to receive eager crowds and beautiful enough to satisfy the loving devotion of the pilgrims of Our Lady of La Salette.

From a historical point of view, the substance of *New Documents* is slighter than that of the preceding volume. There was no need to explain La Salette once again, but rather to clear a path for the doctrinal decree. *New Documents* contains a theological dissertation on miracles, accompanied by a shrine chronicle covering 1848-1849, meant to show that the apparition had remained a source of grace. There was also a refutation of more recent objections drawn especially from a rash of visions said to have occurred since La Salette. The author responded that there were ways of telling true money from counterfeit.

In mid-1850 it looked like the most rabid opponents of La Salette had pinned their hopes on a renewed scrutiny of the event. On June 30, under the presidency of Cardinal de Bonald, a provincial council was convoked in Lyons. Father Cartellier, who had been a member of the Commission in 1847, had written a statement for the occasion. He had promoted it widely. The press had taken it up. Father Berthier, who had scolded Father Mélin by mail in the early days, represented the bishop by proxy vote and could have effectively used this power to expose the opponent's position. Father Rousselot was also present, but with a consultative voice only. Bishop de Bruillard had hoped that the council would place La Salette on its agenda. He later regretted this lack of decisive action when the cardinal complained about the bishop's doctrinal pronouncement. Cardinal de Bonald categorically refused the proposal of Bishop Parisis of Langres to examine the question. Did he deem this kind of discussion inappropriate for such an important gathering? Cartellier smugly thought so. More reasonably, we can assume that the cardinal did not find enough grounds to interfere with the internal affairs of another diocese.

The Incident at Ars

And then came September 1850 and the unfortunate incident at Ars. The flighty Maximin had run away from Corps and did not know where he was going. "Anywhere, but far from here" was all he had in mind. By so doing he embroiled La Salette in its most critical predicament.

The Ars incident set off an uproar. Maximin has recanted, claimed the opponents gleefully. The saintly Curé misunderstood him, replied those who believed, not without some anxiety. Bishop de Bruillard tried to clear up the matter as soon as he learned of it. He interrogated Maximin, wrote to the Curé of Ars, and sent emissaries. He even considered a confrontation between Maximin and Father Vianney, but the latter's ordinary,

Philibert de Bruillard (1765-1860), bishop of Grenoble

67

Bishop Devie, opposed it. "The good priest is not competent to deal with this matter," said the bishop. For three months Bishop de Bruillard had been gathering documentation on this question which he forwarded to the Bishop of Belley, asking for his opinion.

Bishop Devie received this file on the eve of the consecration of his coadjutor, Bishop Chalandon. Bishop Chatrousse of Valence and Bishop Guibert of Viviers, the future Cardinal Archbishop of Paris, were also present on this occasion. The four bishops discussed the question. The curate, Father Raymond, was interrogated at length. According to Bishop Chalandon they concluded that this incident left La Salette unchanged. After the departure of the bishops, Bishop Devie communicated the substance of these consultations to Bishop de Bruillard.

"We consider it certain," he wrote on January 15, "that the children were not in collusion to mislead the public and that they really saw a person who spoke to them. Was it the Blessed Virgin? Everything points to that conclusion, but this cannot be established except by 'the miracles of the apparition.'"

Having before them every kind of evidence capable of enlightening them, testimonies coming from Ars as well as from Grenoble, these serious and competent men recognized that this incident in no way crippled Bishop de Bruillard's canonical investigation. Whatever the externals may have been, in the presence of evidence they agreed that the boy never intended to recant. There was no reason to make this incident public. Wisdom would have suggested referring everything to the competent authority, the Bishop of Grenoble. But, for three years, the opposition had grown in bitterness and obstinacy. Cartellier seemed to nourish a personal antagonism toward La Salette. He exploited every resource of argumentation and intrigue at his command.

Cartellier had won over the Cardinal of Lyons and he recruited the brilliant and acerbic pen of one Father Claude Déléon, a man already in trouble with the Bishop of Grenoble, in the crusade to demolish La Salette. He was well aware that Déléon's talent was superficial yet dangerous. In addition, he risked inciting him to open revolt. But obsession won out and he gained an ally, however mutinous, to his everlasting discredit. Cartellier journeyed to Ars, not so much to pray nor to commiserate with the holy Curé, but to scoop up from Father Raymond all that could buttress Maximin's so-called retraction.

The Ars incident was plundered by the press and anonymous writers because of such men. It provided material for a tract entitled *Mémoire au Pape* (*A Report to the Pope*), wherein truth is inextricably enmeshed with falsehood. Exaggerated and disfigured, the Ars incident remained for generations the first stumbling block on people's journey to La Salette. It warrants careful study, and we will return to it later. Suffice it here to note its influence on canonical procedure. What we are about to witness is an amazing example of providential paradoxes.

Pope Pius IX (1792-1873)

Father Raymond, who was actually responsible for the Ars disturbance, had given Cardinal de Bonald a version of the facts highly unfavorable to Maximin and La Salette. The cardinal then decided to intervene with the full weight of his authority. From the children's zealously guarded secret he developed a clever attack. Either the children would have nothing to say or the secrets would reveal the hoax. To demand them himself from the children would be untactful within the jurisdiction of his suffragan bishop. He decided to veil the request behind an order from Pius IX. On March 21, 1851, he wrote Rousselot this strange note:

> *I have not concerned myself with La Salette, Father, other than to send to the bishop the respectful comments you have already seen. Today, as counsellor to the Pope, I must concern myself with it. I would ask you to tell me if Marcellin and his sister [sic] would confide their famous secret to me, so that I may communicate it to His Holiness.* **(8)**

Cardinal Gousset, the Archbishop of Reims, stopped by Lyons a few days later on his way to Rome. Cardinal de Bonald told him of this note and asked Gousset to seek the Holy Father's approval for such a request.

In Grenoble, a request in the name of the Pope suffered no delay. On March 23, Canon Auvergne went to the minor seminary at Rondeau where Maximin had been staying for five months.

Canon Auvergne: Maximin, I have come to speak to you about something very important. You promise not to repeat what I am going to say to you?
Maximin: Yes, sir.

Canon Auvergne: Can the Church be in error?
Maximin: No, sir.

Canon Auvergne: If the Pope were to ask you for your secret, you would tell him, wouldn't you?
Maximin: I am not yet before the Pope. When I am, I will see.

Canon Auvergne: How is that?
Maximin: What I tell him would depend on what he tells me.

Canon Auvergne: If he orders you to reveal your secret, you will not tell him?
Maximin: If he orders me, I will tell him.

Canon Auvergne: There, child, I am happy to see you so well disposed. I will go quickly to Corenc to see if Mélanie would be as willing as you are to tell her secret at the Pope's command.
Maximin: If Mélanie does not want to obey, then I will think that perhaps we have been tricked by the devil or by some magic. But as for what I said I saw and heard, I will stand by until I die.

From Rondeau, Auvergne went to the "Providence" of Corenc He found Mélanie more hesitant. "The Blessed Virgin forbade me to say it," she kept insisting. "To know the truth," the canon said, "the Church needs to know your secret. You will say it if the Pope orders you, won't you?" "I will tell him and only him." This was all anyone

70

could obtain from her that day. She obstinately refused to communicate her secret through the intermediary of a bishop, archbishop, or prince of the Church, as the bishop's secretary had suggested.

On March 26, Rousselot went to Corenc himself. The superior told him how disturbed Mélanie has been since Father Auvergne's visit. During the night, she speaks in her sleep. Her roommate has heard her saying "They are asking for my secret. I must tell the Pope my secret or I will be separated from the Church." Over forty times she repeated, "separated from the Church."

After a few encouraging words to Mélanie, Rousselot came to the point:

Abbé Rousselot: If the Pope asks you to tell him your secret, will you tell him?
Mélanie: Yes, sir.

Abbé Rousselot: Will you tell him willingly?
Mélanie: Yes, sir.

Abbé Rousselot: And will you tell him without fear of offending the Blessed Virgin?
Mélanie: Yes, sir.

Abbé Rousselot: If the Pope orders you to tell your secret to someone designated by him to receive it and to communicate it to him, would you tell it to this designated person?
Mélanie: No, sir. I will tell only the Pope and only when he commands it.

Abbé Rousselot: And if the Pope gives you this order, how will you make your secret known to him?
Mélanie: I will tell him myself, or I will write it and put it in a sealed envelope.

Abbé Rousselot: And this sealed envelope, to whom will you give it for remitting to the Pope?
Mélanie: To the bishop.

Abbé Rousselot: Would you give it to someone else?

71

Mélanie: I would give it to the bishop or to you.

Abbé Rousselot: Would you confide it to Father Gérente (the convent chaplain)?
Mélanie: No, sir.

Abbé Rousselot: Would you pass it on to the Pope through the Cardinal Archbishop of Lyons?
Mélanie: No, sir.

Abbé Rousselot: Nor through another priest?
Mélanie: No, sir.

Abbé Rousselot: Why not?
Mélanie: Because in Lyons people don't believe much in La Salette. And then, I don't want them to open my letter.

Abbé Rousselot: When the Pope knows your secret, will it offend you if he publishes it?
Mélanie: No, sir. That will concern him. It will be up to him.

Abbé Rousselot: Good-bye, my child. Always pray to the Blessed Virgin, and love her. **(9)**

A report of these meetings was immediately sent to Cardinal de Bonald. Two months elapsed. With no word from Lyons, Bishop de Bruillard decided to write to the Pope himself. In his letter dated June 4, he asked if the cardinal's wish had been satisfied. He included for his Holiness the report which the cardinal had not even acknowledged. He gave a summary of the La Salette question and the present situation of the children, including the Ars incident. He spoke respectfully of the cardinal's intervention in the La Salette inquiry, citing the lack of information revealed by the "Marcellin and his sister" passage. And he offered to answer any of the Pope's questions addressed directly to him con-

Cardinal Bonald, archbishop of Lyon, circa 1860.

cerning the secrets.

The Secrets

Fifteen days after this letter was off to Rome, the cardinal again requested, not only minutes of conversations, but the "famous secret of La Salette... the secret and nothing else, the secret purely and simply." This long, enigmatic silence is easily explained by the fact that the mandate, so distastefully solicited from the Pope, had just reached him via the nunciature. In any event, Bishop de Bruillard had explained the situation to Rome. Caught between the demands of the cardinal and Mélanie's insistence on having her secret pass through the diocesan bishop, de Bruillard chose the path he was already following and assumed the responsibility himself of communicating the secrets to the Pope.

On July 2, Mr. Dausse, a devout Christian who had earned the bishop's trust during the Ars incident, brought Maximin from the minor seminary to the bishop's residence. On the way, the schoolboy chattered as if he were in recess with his playmates. "But Maximin," said Mr. Dausse, "you must reflect on what you will write. You must recall your secret well, so as not to forget anything." "I don't have to worry," said Maximin, "I remember it well. You will see how I will write quickly, without hesitation, when we get there." Without further ado, he resumed his endless chatter.

At the bishop's residence, Maximin was brought to a second-story room with a window above Notre Dame Square. He was seated at a desk. The bishop left Mr. Dausse with Canon de Taxis to help monitor the boy. He asked his assistants to ring for him when the secret was written.

Maximin sat at the desk, placed his head in his hands, dipped his pen, and shook it on the floor. "Do you think you're in some kind of cabin," scolded Canon de Taxis. Casting a distracted look on the stained floor, Maximin began to write. First there was a reflection on what he had seen. "On September 19, 1846, I saw a Lady, brilliant as the sun, whom I believe to be the Blessed Virgin, though I never said it was the Blessed Virgin. I always said that I saw a Lady, not that I saw the Blessed Virgin. It is up to the Church to judge whether it really is the Blessed Virgin or another person, according to what I will say further. She told it to me in the middle of the discourse after "the grapes will rot and the nuts will go bad." "She began by telling me..." **(10)**

Maximin showed this preamble to Mr. Dausse who said: "Good. Now you must write the secret. This is not the secret" He returned to the desk and wrote rapidly as if inspired by an inner voice. Suddenly, his copy finished, he rose and threw the paper in the air, saying, "Now I am like everyone else. From now on, no one can ask me about it. They can always ask the Pope. He will tell it if he wants to." He ran to the window. The two monitors pounced on the paper and saw that it was covered with blots. "Is this how you write to the Holy Father?" asked Canon de Taxis rudely. The guilty schoolboy grumbled but returned to the task. This time he did it correctly. The bishop was called. Mr. Dausse urged him to read Maximin's paper to avoid sending a document that might be embarrassing to his Holiness. Maximin then placed his secret in the envelope to which was affixed the Episcopal seal. A witness certificate accompanied the secret.

That evening, the two men went to Corenc to get Mélanie's secret. Brought to the chaplain's quarters, the girl listened to Mr. Dausse's recommendations and began to cry. As with Canon Auvergne, she hesitated, promised, then changed her mind. Night finally came. She told them she would write it on the following day.

On July 3, at eight o'clock in the morning, Mélanie came to the parlor of the chaplain's quarters. The bishop's delegates and Father Gérente, the chaplain, were present. Mélanie wrote calmly and without hesitation. She finished her account at nine o'clock. Mr. Dausse was reminded to have her sign her written statement. She then wrote on the envelope: "To his Holiness, Our Holy Father, Pope Pius IX, Rome." The delegates witnessed to the fact that the statement was the work of Mélanie and that she had written it freely. They brought it to Bishop de Bruillard.

But a few hours later, once again gripped with anxiety, Mélanie asked to be taken to Father Rousselot. Her scruple was that she had mentioned only one date for two events that had not occurred at the same time. Father Rousselot calmed her by allowing her to rewrite her secret. She did this at a house of the Sisters of Providence in Grenoble in the presence of Canon Auvergne and Mr. Dausse on July 6. Once again she wrote without hesitation, except to ask for the meaning of the word "infallibly" and the spelling of "soiled" (*souillée*) and "Antichrist" (*antéchrist*). The two witnesses then accompanied the girl to the bishop. He read the secret in the privacy of his own room and then emerged shaken and in tears. Afterward, the two witnesses signed the sealed envelope, adding the usual declarations. **(11)**

On the evening of July 6, Father Rousselot and Father Gérin, pastor of the cathedral, left for Rome as the bishop's emissaries, bearing a letter of accreditation to the Holy Father and the two secrets of La Salette.

"I have entrusted my two envoys," wrote Bishop de Bruillard, "with reporting to me whatever your Holiness sees fit to say about the apparition of the Blessed Virgin. In the case of a favorable response, would your Holiness permit the Bishop of Grenoble to declare, in a doctrinal decree, that he judges the apparition to possess the characteristics of truth and that the faithful are justified in believing it to be true? Whatever the decision of your Holiness may be, I will yield to its word in heart and deed: *Roma locuta est, causa finita est. (Rome has spoken, the cause is ended.)*"

Meanwhile, Cardinal de Bonald stopped in Grenoble while returning from the Grande Chartreuse. On July 14, he had the children brought to him and by every means at his command, tried to get them to reveal their secrets to him. As much as he pressed them and insisted that they failed to recognize his dignity and his mandate, they had no more consideration for him than for so many other obnoxious people they had been turning away daily for four years. Mr. Dausse reports that, as the cardinal kept insisting on the special mission he held from Rome, the children boldly asked him to show them his mandate. There was nothing he could do in the face of the steadfast refusal of these rustic children.

In Rome, Bishop de Bruillard's emissaries were very kindly received by the Pope. When a man like Déléon says that Pope Pius IX had been cold, and that he looked upon the writings presented to him as "massive stupidity," on what evidence does he base himself? We have the written account of the two delegates who were brought alone into the presence of the Holy Father. Afterwards, they spoke openly of the encounter without fear of reprimand by the Holy See. Of course, they wanted to record the tenor of this event for the sake of history. On the other hand, Déléon's sources earned the Vatican's scathing denial through its official, Bishop de Ségur: "The Holy Father never spoke to me of La Salette." **(12)** We can confidently accept the details given to us by those who were the sole witnesses to the interview.

After an extremely cordial introduction, the Pope opened the envelopes presented to him. He read Maximin's letter first without any visible emotion. "Here is the openness and the simplicity of a child," he said as he finished reading it. The delegates answered that the witnesses were young mountain children who had only recently entered an educational institution. As he read Mélanie's statement, they saw the Pope's facial expression change, his lips press together, his cheeks swell as if under the pressure of a powerful emotion. Having finished reading it, he said: "I will have to reread these letters more at leisure. There are scourges threatening France, but Germany, Italy, the whole of Europe are guilty and deserve punishment. I have less to fear from outright godlessness than from indifference and human respect. The Church is not called militant without cause and here you see its leader." As he said these words Pius IX pointed to himself. "I had your book read by Monsignor Frattini, the defender of the faith," he said to Father Rousselot. "He told me he was happy with it, that this is a worthwhile book, in that it exudes truth."

Monsignor Frattini himself repeated this commendation to the champion of La Salette. The promoter added that he saw no reason why the Bishop of Grenoble could not proceed to build a large and beautiful chapel and that as many votive offerings be placed within it as there were ascertained miracles. Other miracles would follow. Cardinal Fornari, former Nuncio to Paris, also assured Father Rousselot that he was reading and enjoying his book. Other eminent churchmen expressed their belief in La Salette. Cardinal Lambruschini, prime minister to Pius IX and prefect of the Congregation of Rites, said to him: "I have known about La Salette for a long time and as a bishop I believe it. I have preached it in my diocese and I noticed that my words made a great impression. I also know the children's secrets: the Pope has communicated them to me."

Father Gerin had left Rome shortly after the papal audience. Father Rousselot remained until August 24. On July 19, he informed Bishop de Bruillard of the success of his mission and added these meaningful words: "His Holiness told me he would answer Your Excellency in a manner that would make you forget the annoyances caused you by the Cardinal of Lyons."

On August 22, Father Rousselot was again ushered into the presence of the Holy Father. The Pope asked him if he liked Rome. "Holy Father," he said, 'I am especially happy to be at

Luigi Lambruschini,
Cardinal Secretary of State
between 1836 and 1846

the feet of Your Holiness." Pius IX warmly blessed him, his bishop, and the entire diocese of Grenoble. Spontaneously he stressed that he was not forgetting the two shepherds of La Salette. He then presented gifts for the Bishop of Grenoble, tokens of a more than ordinary esteem and affection. **(13)**

Insofar as it does in such cases, the Holy See was clearing away all the obstacles to Bishop de Bruillard's cherished dream, which was to proclaim the truth of the apparition and to erect a shrine on the site the Lady had favored with her presence. Confirmed in his competence and in his belief, the diocesan bishop began preparing his official statement. An open-minded correspondence had developed between him and Bishop Villecourt of Larochelle. Since the latter's visit to La

Salette, his book, *Un nouveau récit de l'apparition*, had highly praised Father Rousselot's work. **(14)**

The old bishop had no sooner intimated his need for an outline or a draft for this proclamation than such was sent him by his young colleague. Bishop de Bruillard gratefully received it and made it the foundation of his own statement, giving it his personal precision and firmness. In order not to overlook any of the rules of the Church or of the views of Rome he submitted his final draft to Cardinal Lambruschini. The text was returned on October 7 with an evaluation addressed to Father Rousselot:

> *Father, with your letter of September 17, I received the text of the proposed decree your learned and holy bishop of Grenoble wants to publish on the event that has taken place on one of the mountains of his diocese. As soon as my schedule and my weakened health allowed, I read the decree attentively. Here are my views. The bishop narrates in precise historical detail the extraordinary event of La Salette and does it without bias. This is always recommended in Sacred Scripture and by Church regulations. All is in order and complete, especially the investigation which was conducted with edifying and laudable rigor. I have only one observation to make concerning one of the dispositions prescribed by the venerable prelate, namely number 3. **(15)** I believe that wisdom and prudence suggest that we not attest with such great solemnity in the name of the Church the truth of the event in question.*

In the diocese, however, the news brought from Rome by Rousselot and Gerin spread quickly. The friends of La Salette were elated and some fretted over the bishop's delays. The opponents, on the other hand, unleashed a supreme effort to thwart the decree they thought imminent. The press made much of the Ars incident, presenting it categorically as "an undeniable retraction." With naive treachery, it praised the wisdom of the diocesan administration for having resisted popular pressure, even "urgent requests." The Ars affair, replied Rousselot, was known in Rome and "appreciated at its true worth."

The clergy retreat began in Grenoble on September 24. Opposing factions met and partisans could be counted. On the 25th, a petition containing 240 signatures was handed to the bishop. "Yielding to our own convictions and strengthened in their belief by the encouragements his delegates had received from Rome, they petitioned the bishop "with respectful insistence" to authorize the pilgrimage of La Salette and to have a shrine built. A counter-petition recruited barely 18 names, three of which were fraudulently signed. Furthermore, two printed tracts were widely distributed throughout the seminary. One was signed J. Robert (this was one of Déléon's first pseudonyms, one that was not immediately seen through). The other was anonymous, but was attributed to Jean-Pierre Cartellier, under whose name it appeared a few days later in three city newspapers. "They publish the account of a trip to Rome, why not an account of a trip to Ars?" This was the theme obsessively intoned by the choir-leader and his echo.

The bishop did not want to establish the devotion to the Virgin of La Salette in this climate of division. In a circular letter dated October 10, he reminded his clergy that pastoral care can be accomplished only in unity and peace and that, to end these discussions, he expressly forbade all priests of his diocese to issue any publication on La Salette, directly or indirectly, without his authorization. Yet on the same day, scrupulously careful to listen to opponents in good faith, he had Maximin interrogated again by the panel of questioners most capable of convicting the boy or of convincing his detractors.

> *The Ars incident was re-examined on October 10 at the Grande Chartreuse where Maximin was staying. He underwent a rigorous interrogation at which were present the Bishop of Orléans, a bishop from the mission fields whom I don't know, Father General, and a learned and virtuous lay person. I have received three letters and I have heard the report of one of the witnesses. The Ars incident is to be seen as nothing more than a misunderstanding from which nothing can be concluded against the fact of the apparition. This fact is still maintained with unshakable constancy by the pious novice Mélanie.*

This report of the final act of the official inquisitors was addressed to Father Berthier on the day the decree appeared. The bishop thus deferred to a loyal objector. While expressing firmness in his role as bishop, he still found the words to spare the man's feelings. "The reading of my decree is mandatory. Your sense of duty is too strong to allow you to dissuade anyone from doing so. I greet you with all the esteem and affection you know me to have for you, my dear Vicar General."

From that moment on Father Berthier's attitude never showed the least opposition to his bishop on the subject of La Salette. Fathers Genevey and de Lemps submitted with the same discipline. Father Cartellier, however, was of another spirit.

The Decree of 1851
La Salette is Indubitable and Certain

The long-awaited decree came off the presses on November 10, 1851, but it bore the significant date of "September 19, the fifth anniversary of the famous apparition." It is a masterful work wherein the spirit of faith and the serenity of the shepherd join forces with critical intelligence to relate the history of the event and of its consequences, of the canonical instruction as well as of the reactions of the Christian world.

> While many good people eagerly welcomed the fact, we carefully sought out all the reasons for which we might reject it if it could not be accepted. On the other hand, we were strictly obliged not to consider impossible an event the Lord could have allowed for His greater glory. Indeed, His arm is still strong and His power is the same today as in ages past.

The last page in particular completely dominates the opposition to which the document had to allude. It is clear that in all this trouble, nothing counts more for the saintly old bishop than the will of Providence.

> We know that opponents have not been lacking. What moral truth, what human reality, or even divine, has not encountered any? But to alter our belief in such an extraordinary event, so inexplicable outside divine intervention, whose every circumstance and conse-

quence conspire to show the finger of God, we would have needed a fact contrary to this one, a fact as extraordinary, as inexplicable as that of La Salette itself. At the very least, we would have needed to explain La Salette by natural causes. We have not found this possible, so we now openly proclaim our conviction.

We have redoubled our prayers, begging the Holy Spirit to assist us and to communicate His divine light to us. Confidently we have also asked for the protection of the immaculate Virgin Mary, Mother of God, considering it one of our most pleasant and most sacred duties to omit nothing of what could contribute to the increase of the devotion of the faithful toward her, and to manifest our gratitude to her for the special favor our diocese has been granted. In any event, we have never ceased being disposed to be scrupulously guided by the holy rules the Church has given us through the pen of its doctors, and to revise our judgment on this matter as on all others, if the Chair of Saint Peter, the mother and queen of all the churches, saw fit to deliver a judgment contrary to our own.

We had these dispositions and were animated by these sentiments when Divine Providence allowed us to persuade the two privileged children to communicate their secret to Our Holy Father, Pope Pius IX. In the name of the Vicar of Jesus Christ, the shepherds understood that they had to obey. They decided to reveal to the Sovereign Pontiff a secret they had guarded until then with an unconquerable constancy and that nothing could have taken from them. They wrote it themselves, each one separately. Thus fell the last objection against the apparition, that is, that there was no secret, or that the secret was unimportant, even childish, and that the children would not want to communicate it to the Church.

The judgment was then expressed in canonical form. The principles established by Benedict XIV were recalled, as well as the principal phases of the diocesan inquiry, and the reasons for the judgment and declaration. Even today, in order to situate the event of La Salette in its religious context, we must meditate on at least the following essential paragraphs:

Considering first the impossibility of explaining the fact of La

Salette other than by divine intervention, however we may view it, either in its circumstances, or in its essentially religious meaning;

Considering secondly, that the wonderful consequences of the La Salette event are the testimony of God manifesting Himself through miracles, and that this testimony is superior to that of men and to their objections;

Considering that these two motives, when taken separately and even more so when taken together, must preside over the whole question and completely neutralize all contrary pretensions and suppositions, of which we take full cognizance;

Considering finally that compliance and submission to admonitions can spare us new chastisements that threaten us, while a too-prolonged resistance can expose us to ills without remedy;

On the express request of all the members of our venerable Chapter as well as of the great majority of the clergy of our diocese;

To satisfy the rightful expectation of so great a number of good people, from our own country as well as from abroad, who could accuse us of keeping the truth captive;

Having invoked anew the Holy Spirit and the help of the Immaculate Virgin;

We declare the following:

Article 1 — We judge that the apparition of the Blessed Virgin to two shepherds on September 19, 1846 on a mountain of the Alpine chain, situated in the parish of La Salette, of the archpresbytery of Corps, bears all the characteristics of truth and that the faithful have grounds for believing it indubitable and certain;

Article 2 — We believe that this fact acquires a new degree of certitude from the immense and spontaneous gatherings of the faithful on the site of the apparition as well as from the multitude of wonders that have resulted from the said event, a very great number of which it is impossible to doubt without violating the rules of human testimony;

Article 3 — Wherefore, to show our heartfelt gratitude to God and to the glorious Virgin Mary, we authorize the devotion to Our Lady of La Salette. We permit it to be preached and that practical and moral consequences be drawn from this great event....

Article 7 — *Finally, since the principal purpose of the apparition has been to summon Christians once again to their religious duties, to divine worship, to the observance of the commandments of God and of the Church, to the abhorrence of blasphemy, and to the sanctification of Sunday, we entreat you, our very dear Brothers, in view of your spiritual and even earthly interests, to re-examine yourselves seriously, to do penance for your sins, particularly for those you have committed against the second and the third commandments of God. We entreat you, beloved Brothers, to become submissive to the voice of Mary calling you to penance and who, on behalf of her Son, threatens you with spiritual and temporal ills, if, remaining insensitive to her maternal admonitions, you should harden your hearts....*

Such was Bishop de Bruillard's judgment in 1851, and since that time, his successors in the See of Grenoble have all expressed their agreement with him. Whatever may have been the occasional confusion created by the adversaries of La Salette or by the two children's subsequent behavior, we cannot find a single bishop who has not exhorted the faithful of the diocese, by some decree or pastoral letter, to heed the teachings of the weeping Virgin. No word or act of any episcopal successor has ever hinted at the invalidation of this decree. Bishop de Bruillard was responding to the rules established by the Church, and Rome granted its seal of approval. The decree was and remains the judgment of the Church. But what does this mean for us today?

First, it should be understood that a verdict of this kind does not compel us to theological faith. Neither would an approbation from Rome, assuming it were given. Belief in private revelations belongs to the arena of human faith. It pertains to the prudence of each person to weigh the motives for believing and to judge if they are worthy of assent.

A rescript from the Sacred Congregation of Rites **(16)** taken up again by the 1903 encyclical, *Pascendi Dominici Gregis, #55 (Feeding the Flock)* by Pope Pius X (1835-1914) declared, precisely concerning La Salette, but also concerning Lourdes and the Miraculous Medal.

He said:

> *"Such apparitions or revelations are neither approved nor condemned by the Holy See. It has simply permitted devout persons to believe them on the level of human faith, according to the tradition that hands them down, confirmed by testimonies and conclusive evidence."*

But does it follow that we can view the diocesan bishop's decision as insignificant?

Some would seem to think so. Occasionally we have seen a re-examination of the event conducted in such a way that would imply that the bishop's dossier of the case is no more than a historical curiosity. But such an opinion gives too slight a weight to the charism of governance imparted to bishops and by means of which the Holy Spirit acts on behalf of the Church. A synthesis is always greater than the sum of its parts. We are reminded of this truth in the life of the Church when we read the solemn formula following the preamble in Bishop de Bruillard's pronouncement: "Having invoked anew the Holy Spirit and the assistance of the Immaculate Virgin."

Does not this appeal for providential help, on which he in this instance has the right to count, confer on his judgment something specific and more decisive than the simple power of reason? Does not this decree then occupy a privileged place among the documents and other facts of the La Salette event?

The faithful Christian can indeed believe that such a decree is an endorsement of the fact. In pronouncing himself as he did, the Bishop of Grenoble was performing an act of the Church's ordinary magisterium. His judgment does not compel us to theological faith. But it does express the prudence of the Church and appeals to ours in order to enlighten it, to strengthen it, perhaps to make up for its lack of information. In any case, it helps it overcome the hesitations we always experience in the presence of a phenomenon like La Salette. We almost require the approval of competent authority before assenting to a miraculous event. Our minds and hearts seek the security of such a pronouncement.

But can such a pronouncement compel us to blind obedience if our mind is convinced to the contrary? No, not if we see our objections to be as solid as the assertions in the case, or not if we have based our objections on the scientific methodology of one of the moral sciences, like history, psychology, or theology. Then indeed we have a right to dispute the verdict of the Bishop of Grenoble. What is certain, however, is that the faithful Christian must not see the Church's pronouncement as extraneous to the issue. The native instinct of such a person, an affinity, makes him or her lean toward the Church in an attitude of respect and welcome —that is, if his prudence is quickened by the Holy Spirit. The Christian will always experience more joy in agreeing with the Church than in resisting her. But, even in contradiction, he would proceed soberly and with great circumspection.

La Salette Defies a Natural Explanation

The objections against La Salette are as old as the children's first report. "I am going to believe that this little one has seen the Blessed Virgin? She doesn't even say her prayers!" objects young Pra. "It is well known that we have not lacked for opponents," admitted Bishop de Bruillard, summarizing in a simple statement the minor wars that had harassed his every step for four years. Since then, in the course of a century, La Salette has sustained many other attacks. In sum, the event of La Salette still defies natural explanation, but the smoke of old controversies still wraps this apparition in an aura of suspicion and distrust. Maximin recanted at Ars. An eccentric, Mademoiselle de Lamerlière, was condemned by the courts as the heroine of La Salette. The children turned out badly. The message of La Salette is just one variation on the Letter from heaven.

There are so many stories and controversies that the mind panics and is convinced that behind all the standard objections there are certainly other, more obscure ones that would emerge suddenly from the woodwork were they given a chance. This is a case where the prudence of the Church can buttress our own.

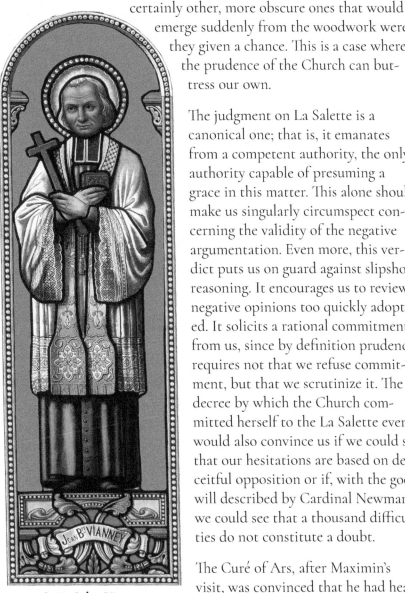

Saint John Vianney:
Curé de Ars at the time
of the Apparitions

The judgment on La Salette is a canonical one; that is, it emanates from a competent authority, the only authority capable of presuming a grace in this matter. This alone should make us singularly circumspect concerning the validity of the negative argumentation. Even more, this verdict puts us on guard against slipshod reasoning. It encourages us to review negative opinions too quickly adopted. It solicits a rational commitment from us, since by definition prudence requires not that we refuse commitment, but that we scrutinize it. The decree by which the Church committed herself to the La Salette event would also convince us if we could see that our hesitations are based on deceitful opposition or if, with the good will described by Cardinal Newman, we could see that a thousand difficulties do not constitute a doubt.

The Curé of Ars, after Maximin's visit, was convinced that he had heard a formal retraction from the child's own mouth. The words of Maximin left him no other conclusion. But he was tortured by the fear of having done something against the Blessed Virgin and by the awareness of being in contradiction with competent Church authority. Hence, one of the signs he petitioned from heaven to escape the dilemma was the visit of a certain person from Grenoble with the news of his return to the faith. And when this happened, he wanted the Bishop of Grenoble to be the first to know about his change of position on La Salette.

Some might be shocked by this need to comply with Church authority. It is, indeed, a sign of holiness. Father Raymond, the holy Curé's assistant, was considerably less concerned with such thoroughness. It is equally noteworthy, that the saint not only safeguarded his fidelity to the Church but also achieved objectivity about the issue at hand. Even before having been miraculously enlightened, he suspected that Maximin's words should be reinserted into their psychological context. "After all," he told Father des Garets, "all this signifies little. The boy might have wanted to mock me as he had mocked the curate before." He was right, and he thus gave us a perfect example of the art of sorting through one's thinking in a delicate conjecture.

If, indeed, a negative stance toward La Salette can be called a doubt, it would be presumptuous to seek a way out of it miraculously as did the Curé of Ars. The exceptional character of his predicament as well as his personal holiness justify the daring means he chose. For the ordinary faithful, struggling with bona fide objections, rational examination remains the normal path to belief. The bishop's preamble is itself the outcome of a lengthy investigation of countless documents and dozens of testimonies. Essentially, this was the journey of his own conviction, and one we would now like to retrace with the reader. We hope the reader will acknowledge, if he or she has not already done so, the "impossibility in which we find ourselves to explain the fact of La Salette other than through divine intervention." **(17)**

-5-
The Children of La Salette

Before the Beautiful Lady drew them out of obscurity, nothing had set Maximin and Mélanie apart from the ordinary.

A little boy whistling to his dog and tending his goat, picking dung on the national highway—this described Maximin for the people of Corps. An adolescent girl, slender, withdrawn, chasing after her cows through roads and fields, morning till night: this is how Pra's little shepherdess Mélanie appeared to the people of Les Ablandins. These children did not stand out in school or in catechism class. And they were poor! Only the tenderness of a mother could have been interested in their small world of thoughts and feelings. But this motherly gaze which can penetrate to the deepest part of a child's heart had long since stopped following them.

Then came September 19, 1846, and people took notice. Their parents and their teachers then began to observe closely what they had seen every day. Learned people came in droves to question the two children.

What struck everyone was the contrast between what the children had experienced and what they still were. The vision they professed to have seen had brought about almost no change in their normal behavior. Those who knew them attested to this. Their character seemed not to have been influenced nor their intelligence developed, at least within the scope of normal living. Only when they repeated the words of the beautiful Lady did an unexpected gravity come over them. Only when they defended their mission could one suspect a divine assistance in their answers. Beyond this, their natural abilities remained most ordinary.

Mélanie was the older of the two. Born on November 7, 1831, she was nearing fifteen. She was small and frail, and had so kept the appearance of a child that one might have thought she was hardly eleven. Her father, Pierre Calvat, surnamed Mathieu, barely managed to feed his large family, although he was alternately a mason and a sawyer and took work necessitating long absences from his family. Mélanie began her life's work in the streets of the town. Since she was eight years old she had worked for various employers in Saint Jean-des-Vertus, at Quet-en-Beaumont, at Sainte-Luce. In the spring of 1846 she was hired by Baptiste Pra in Les Ablandins. She lived with her family in Corps only during the three harshest months of the year, December, January and February, when the snows confined the herds to the stable.

A short statement from Pierre Selme gives an idea of the type of education the children received in such circumstances. Describing a typical week in the lives of Maximin and Mélanie, Selme simply stated: "Early mornings, they walked to their fields and would return only in the evening.

Pra house where the message was first re-counted by the children

Then, they ate their soup and went to bed." The other weeks could not have been much different. In this mountain country, the rights of children never went beyond basic necessities: eating their soup and sleeping. To city-bred philanthropists they would have said: here, work is lord and master. So true was this of the household of Pra, the most humane of Mélanie's masters, that their little shepherdess had been present only twice in six months at the parish services.

The law of work also prevailed under her father's roof when the girl returned home for the winter. She helped her mother and took care of her little brothers and sisters. There could be no question of going to school. Even the parish priest, Father Mélin, seemed never to have seen her at the catechism classes before the apparition. Her mother certainly tried to teach her a few snatches of religion. She would tell Father Arbaud that Mélanie was not intelligent. Her brothers and sisters would learn their catechism lessons well, but Mélanie could retain nothing. She could hardly recite the "Our Father" in French and still did not understand it very well.

"How is it, then," asked Father Arbaud, "that your daughter did not understand French, since, as I can now see, you yourself speak French well enough? Normally, children speak the language of their parents."

To this she answered that Mélanie certainly understood some French words when the Blessed Virgin spoke to her and that she could have known more had she stayed in her own home. She was prevented from doing so when she had to live for the better part of the year with families who normally spoke in dialect. (1)

This statement calls for a few qualifications. Some authors have wanted to make of the acquisition of French by the children a kind of miracle of La Salette. When Father Lagier asked her if she understood what the Lady had said in French, Mélanie answered that she had understood "all in all very little," adding immediately, "I did not know what she wanted to say!" For Mélanie, therefore, French was not an altogether foreign tongue. She understood it badly and could not speak it, but she possessed some elements of it, either because she had heard it spoken around her, or because she was able to grasp some similarities between the patois and the French. That she was able to provide short explanations in French to visitors who questioned her immediately after the apparition is attested to by Baptiste Pra. But from these stammering responses to the easy handling of the language, there was a continuous progress whose stages can be discerned through the testimonies of that time. (2) In all critical rigor, one can attribute Mélanie's knowledge of French to natural causes. It could have been a familiarity already present before the apparition, activated by the pressure of necessity, and improved with normal exercise. What is beyond doubt, as we shall soon see, is that the French part of the discourse constituted one more obstacle for Mélanie's weak intellect and unfaithful memory.

We wonder what she retained from the catechism lessons her mother had apparently tried to give her. She could perhaps add the recitation of the "Hail Mary" to that of the "Our Father." This is stated by

Similien, whose authority is doubtful. (3) But the abstract letter of the catechism and the mother's intermittent lessons, limited to the most mechanical techniques of repetition, must have exercised little hold on Mélanie's unawakened mind. She knew about saints through roadside chapels. (4) But she could not tell one from the other except from the visible traits she saw in the representations. Indeed, on September 19, after her beautiful Lady had disappeared in the sky she could find nothing else to say to Maximin than that this was perhaps a great saint! She had not recognized, even by her words, the Lady who during a half-hour had spoken of her Son and of her people.

Maximin and Mélanie were only allowed to make their first communion eighteen months after the event. The girl is sixteen and a half. Over a century later, and with our present way of thinking, we might easily call Jansenistic a parish priest who would impose so long a delay. Good Father Mélin could not do otherwise. Sister Sainte-Thècle, superior of the convent of Corps, stated before the bishop's commission on November 16, 1847 that "for one year now, Mélanie has not succeeded in reciting by heart the acts of faith, hope, and charity," although she had her say them twice a day. Should we suspect the child of cheating a little, showing herself less talented than she really was? But her mother had noticed the same incapacity. In any event, certain facts learned subsequently shed some light on her poor memory. For example, people always noted that the child could not spell.

About Melanie

Could Mélanie pray, even if she was ignorant of dogmatic formulas? The testimonies here are formal and they confirm her own admissions. When the Lady asked: "Do you pray well, my children?" the two children answered spontaneously: "No Madame, hardly at all." And Lagier, as exact as one would want, insisted that Mélanie be precise on this point. "Both of you?—Yes.—Together?—Yes." We remember young Pra's remark on the night of September 19: "I'm going to believe that this girl saw the Blessed Virgin? She doesn't even say her prayers!" That same night, having learned by experience that there are ties between heaven and earth, Mélanie stayed for a while at the foot of her bed and heard old mother Pra call to her: "Hey, little one, you're still here! You're saying long prayers tonight to make up for all the other times!" More explicit still, the following bit of dialogue between her and Lagier is so ingenuous that it dispels the entire elaborate scaffolding of the *Autobiography*. **(5)** He wanted to know the reason for the fear that made her drop her staff at the first sight of light in the ravine. "Why were you afraid?—Because when I saw this, I remembered my employer's wife scolding me and threatening me, telling me that I would surely see the devil or something one day, because I never said my prayers and I mocked others when they prayed to God before and after meals."—Is that true? –Yes.—

Then you thought you were seeing the devil?—No, I don't remember quite what I thought."

Perceptions of Mélanie's character naturally differed in nuance but agreed on essentials. Bishop Villecourt described it in lyrical tones.

"Bring together in your imagination," he said, "all the traits that can describe the most perfect and the most striking modesty, and you will hardly have an idea of Mélanie's. Her face is regular and delicate. Her eyes are soft and her voice is of angelic charm that immediately inspires you with consideration and esteem. There

Fr. Lagier meets with Melanie

is nothing here of the rustic manner of mountain shepherds. Change her clothing and you will never suspect that she was born in the most miserable hovel, and that her parents, brothers, and sisters depend on alms to relieve their misery. Mélanie is about sixteen years of age, yet you would have trouble believing she is twelve. She speaks little and only when spoken to. Then she speaks with a grace that blends the pleasant tone of her voice with a reserve and an unspeakable charm." (6)

The following year, Father Dupanloup painted a less enthusiastic portrait:

> As for the little girl, she also seemed to me to be very unpleasant in her own way. Her way, I must say, is still better than that of the little boy. The eighteen months she spent with the religious of Corps have, so they say, developed her a little. In spite of that, she seemed to be sulky, peevish, stupidly silent, saying nothing but yes or no when she answers. If she adds anything she does it with a certain stiffness and ill-tempered timidity that does not predispose one in her favor. (7)

Which of the two portraits is correct? The reality they give us is basically the same one, but perceived from different angles. A timid personality will be described by some as modest and reserved and by others as sulky and stupid. It is certain that Mélanie is timid and it is understandable that an early bondage and the obligation to beg have made her withdrawn. Sulkiness is the handy refuge of these little ones who have been deprived of their childhood. Baptiste Pra testified that before the apparition Mélanie was "lazy, disobedient, ill-tempered to the point of refusing sometimes to speak to those who were addressing her." (8) Neither this good man nor Dupanloup seemed to understand that the closed child could have suffered from a lack of understanding on the part of adults as much as from the callousness of greedy masters.

Mademoiselle des Brulais, with deeper intuition, broadened Mélanie's outlook and described more objectively the defect with which she is reproached:

On September 12, 1847, she writes: "I have just conversed for almost an hour with Mélanie Mathieu. Since I have been living in the convent she speaks to me more freely and without fear. In spite of her natural timidity and her withdrawn nature, she answers my questions with remarkable ease, and I take advantage of this good disposition God gives her toward me to invite her to open her heart on the great revelation granted her, a revelation she never speaks about on her own initiative: she must be prodded to do so by questions. But still, she never obstinately refuses to repeat the words she was enjoined to make known to the people. She is silent sometimes, when pointless questions are put to her. Then she will shrug her shoulders and turn away, or will show a little testiness. She is naturally stubborn and moody. Before the apparition she could even be sulky, refusing to answer when spoken to. But since the apparition, there has been a noticeable change in her and she is improving every day." **(9)**

It could be conceded to Dupanloup that Mélanie's attitudes were unpleasant. They could even be embarrassing if we could see in them signs of real selfishness. How could the Blessed Virgin appear to such a child? But these traits are only the reflex actions of a little slave who is protecting herself the only way she knows how. Habit has made those reflexes permanent. What is truly magnificent is that so much hardship has not penetrated that part of her heart reserved for what constitutes the true spirit of childhood: purity, humility, evangelical trust.

It must be understood that when Bishop Villecourt spoke of the softness of her eyes and the angelic charm of her voice, he was impressed, as were many others, by all the innocence radiating from Mélanie. "One notices especially," notes Bez, "in her posture, in the tilt of her head, in her glances a great modesty during conversation. She is neither embarrassed nor shy with strangers." **(10)**

Mademoiselle des Brulais sees Mélanie's modest attitude as a sign of humility:

> She is above all remarkable for her great and rare modesty. Far from being proud of drawing attention, she would like to escape it if her sense of mission did not overcome her natural timidity. This is

*what she means when she says: "I would prefer not to have to say it,
as long as they know." And there is the answer she gives to a member of the clergy who asked her if she was happy and pleased that
the Blessed Virgin had given her this revelation: "Yes," she answered,
"but I would be happier still if she had not told me to say it." "And
why is that?" "It makes me too visible."* **(11)**

This was said on September 18, 1847. To be completely fair, one must
compare the testimony of the Superior of Corps given on November
16 of the same year. In her deposition at the bishop's house, she stated
that for a month she "had begun to fear that Mélanie might become
vain from the renown she had acquired from the apparition." **(12)**

At first sight the witnesses seem to contradict one another. But
let us notice the dates. "For a month," says the superior. What had
happened then between September 18 and mid-October? What had
happened was September 19, the first anniversary of the apparition,
when crowds flocked to the mountain in numbers conservatively
estimated at fifty-thousand people. Mélanie was there. She was asked
questions, admired all day. Someone even shouted: "See all these
crowds! You are really the author of all this!" She shrugged her shoulders as if she thought the statement absurd. **(13)** But from that day,
the rash exclamation could have crept into her soul.

Henceforth, Mélanie's future depended on the clear-sightedness of
her directors and the resistance she herself offered the Tempter who
had just brushed her soul. This sister had understood it and was
alarmed at the first signs of self-satisfied vanity. Her protégée was
safe under her firm guidance. That small cloud she had pointed out
would not appear again until Mélanie's entrance into the novitiate.
The following year, Bishop Dupanloup made no distinction between
the children as he praised their simplicity:

> *The fact is that they do not even understand the honor they have
> received and the celebrity that will henceforth be attached to their
> names. They have seen thousands of pilgrims, sixty-thousand in one
> day, come at their beckoning to the mountain of La Salette. They
> have not become more vain or more studied in their words or their
> attitudes. They view all of this without astonishment, without one*

self-complacent thought. **(14)**

Baptiste Pra is rhapsodic about Mélanie's detachment. "Coming home from the mountain in the evening, drenched from the rain, she would not even ask to change her clothes. Sometimes, and always in character, she would fall asleep in the stable. At other times, had we not been careful, she would have spent the night under the stars." **(15)** We tend to attribute these violations of the most basic rules of hygiene to her lack of education. But there is something beyond that. Most children do not need schooling to learn the consequences of such negligence. Clearly, if an adolescent has not learned this after fourteen years of age, she is not and never will be the scheming type. In fact, restless as Mélanie's life was later to become, at no time can she be accused of this. At this time in her life, her carelessness was recognized as a character trait by all those who saw her at the convent of Corps. "She and Maximin," recorded the investigators in 1847, "give all the money they receive to the Superior and never inquire about the use that is made of it... When one of them is interrogated, the other does not seem worried or anxious about what is being asked of the other. After an interrogation, one never asks the other what was said."

Concerning the goods of this earth, Mélanie had maintained the indifference of little children. We saw this on the day after the apparition, when the mayor thought he would dazzle her by offering her twenty francs. Two years later, we saw it again when Bishop Dupanloup, having tried the same ruse to draw out her secret and having offered to come to the aid of her family, received the answer: "Oh! we have enough. There is no need for so much money." A staggering response when one thinks that at that time her younger sister was still begging in the streets of Corps. Such traits give form and countenance to Gospel entreaties: "Unless you change and become like children...."

Why should this little girl who did not even say her prayers have seen the Blessed Virgin? Jacques Pra demanded to know the answer to this question on that first evening. And this is the question people have been asking for over a century. Reasonable people, respectable peo-

ple, wise people. If there is an answer this is where it will be found:
"Unless you become like little children...."

About Maximin

The gift of childhood was also Maximin's sole recommendation. But he possessed it to such a degree that it was no longer, in his case, a question of spirit, or of something preserved by miracle or effort: childhood was part of his very being. Happier than Mélanie, he could afford to live out a playful and carefree existence. And he had lived it, we would be tempted to say, a bit too much. But was that his fault?

Born in Corps on August 27,1835, he lost his mother while he was still an infant. His father remarried and gave him an insensitive stepmother. He might have gone hungry had it not been for the affection of a younger brother who shared his own bread with him. **(16)**

Giraud the wheelwright, Maximin's father, was a skilled craftsman and basically a good man. He had accomplished his journeyman's circuit of France and he loved his little Mémin. Life might have been more pleasant in his home had he been less a fixture at the local tavern. But what of it! He was drawn there by the same weakness that prevented him from more effectively protecting this child of his first marriage. And with that, he was proud, like a craftsman conscious of his worth and like an extremely sensitive man. When people heard him proclaim in his house and at the tavern that he, having been a wheelwright journeyman through France, could not accept to hire his son out to others, were they hearing the self-assertion of pride or perhaps a more secret feeling, a supreme fidelity to the boy's deceased mother?

In any event, Maximin, contrary to the customs of these mountains, had never been leased out for work. He ran free in the narrow streets of Corps or along the national highway, left to his own devices. He ran along the sides of surrounding mountains where his goat grazed on the sparse grasses hiding among the tufts of lavender. His father went through the motions of sending him to school and to catechism classes. Maximin would stop at the threshold of these tedious "jails" or would run away as soon as he had had enough of them. His family's yen for schooling must have spent itself in the face of this determined craving for freedom. Giraud's wife would bring Maximin to church services, but he would find ways of escaping her vigilance to join his playmates on the square. With this regimen he knew nothing of catechism or of any of the school subjects.

The sum total of his religious knowledge is revealed in his father's astonishment upon hearing the story of the apparition for the first time: "Who could have taught you so many things in an instant? For three years now I've been killing myself trying to teach you the "Our Father" and the "Hail Mary" and you still don't know them." All of eighteen months were needed, in Father Mélin's opinion, to instill in him and in Mélanie the rudiments needed for first communion.

What he had more than Mélanie on September 19, 1846 was an ample supply of French words acquired from frequent contact with the language. Maximin, in fact, frequented the "Café de l'Isère," not for the usual reasons, but because it was next door to his father's house. He found friends there to play with. He also overheard many French conversations since the cafe was the meeting place for coach drivers making the run between Grenoble and Gap. Without his being aware of it, the national tongue became familiar to him, not enough to enable him to speak it fluently, but enough to allow him, on occasion, to join in more elementary conversation. In the children's account of the apparition, Mélanie did not know the meaning of "pommes de terre" and she turned to Maximin for an explanation. She obviously thought he knew more French than she did.

The absence of piety in Maximin is disconcerting. Before the apparition, not only did he avoid Mass, but he did not even go the next day, a Sunday. It is true that on that day his employer took him back to his father, an obligation which superseded that of Mass. It is also true that from another point of view, the children's conduct was delightfully indifferent to apologetic concerns. The fact remains that Maximin's absence from Mass on Sunday, after having heard such a discourse the preceding day, shows that for him religion was a world unknown.

Rousselot, who liked him, and Dupanloup, who did not, agreed two years later that Maximin was not naturally pious. Sister Thècle balanced this view: "But he readily assists at Mass and prays well whenever he is reminded of his obligation." The impression we have of Maximin at this time is that he indeed had good will but no natural inclination to piety. This view is confirmed by an anecdote from Mademoiselle des Brulais.

> A clergyman asked the boy: "Are you better, Maximin, since you have seen the Blessed Virgin?—Yes, sir, one quarter. One quarter? How is that? How do you measure that?—I love God, sir.—You did not love him before?—I did not know him, sir. If I had known him...." Suddenly, Maximin became completely fascinated by the clergyman's breviary. He asked to have the holy cards, took the book in his hands, and leafed through it with his usual restiveness. **(17)**

Mademoiselle des Brulais called it restiveness, other people called it giddiness. Something about Maximin made him constitutionally unable to concentrate. Father Bez saw him serve Mass in the spring of 1847 (one of his first attempts) and said judiciously that he did it "still with a light-headedness inherent to his character and I believe, to his physical makeup." **(18)** It was rare, in fact, to meet a child whose need to fidget was so strong. Whoever questioned him, man or woman, lay person or clergyman or official, Maximin was sure to fidget, to gesticulate, to pry into and examine something belonging to the questioner. He grabbed a bishop's hat or a capuchin's cord, and impishly found a fruit that Mademoiselle des Brulais had stored away. All this was done with the snoopy, prying inquisitiveness of a child and with total indifference to all the conventions of civility. "What do you say, Perpetual Motion?" would tease the kind Sisters of Corps. Of course, the restlessness and indiscretion were not to everyone's liking. Bishop Dupanloup in particular had all the trouble in the world trying to suppress his repugnance for this child who conformed so little to the canons of common politeness.

Félix-Antoine-Philibert Dupanloup (1849-1878), eventual Bishop of Orléans, France, noted psychologist

"Maximin's rudeness," Dupanloup writes, "is uncommon; his agitation is extraordinary. His is a peculiar nature, bizarre, unstable, thoughtless, giddy. But his giddiness is so coarse, his instability sometimes so violent, his bizarre behavior so unbearable, that the first day I saw him, I was not only saddened by the experience but also discouraged. What good is it, I asked myself, to make the trip to see such a child? What a stupid thing I have done! I had all the trouble in the world preventing the most serious suspicions from taking hold of me." **(19)**

We know that these suspicions never took hold. The unpleasant impressions even became one more reason to believe as Bishop Dupanloup's objective mind observed Maximin's prodigious transformation each time he was brought to speak of the apparition. Still, all the witnesses said that this boy was motion personified. As soon as he finished the narrative of the apparition, he passed from inspiring recollection to screaming rowdiness and endless chatter, to all the outbursts of an unchained imp. How was it even possible with such a temperament to concentrate on God? "It is not surprising that he has not learned to serve Mass well after having been trained daily for a year." **(20)** He did not lack intelligence. The Sisters saw him as more alert than Mélanie. But he was dedicated to play, to giving free rein to his quick and wiry energy.

Here he is from head to foot as Father Bez saw him at eleven and a half:

> *He is short, with a wide, round, open face, alive with health. His eyes are attractive and fiery. He looks with gentleness at the people questioning him, without fear or blushing. His arms and hands are always in motion as if by nervous contractions. When he speaks his head leans slightly to his left shoulder. In conversation he gestures naturally and sometimes becomes excited enough to strike the object nearest him, especially when people don't agree with him. He never becomes angry, though, even when his questioners accuse him of lying, or during the long interrogations to which some stranger will subject him through sheer curiosity. He just gives his antagonist a disdainful look, shrugs his shoulders, and turns his head away.* (21)

One finds in this portrait the inevitable instability we already know of. Yet beneath the rough-hewn exterior one discerns a simple and gentle spirit.

Maximin not only never got angry when he was contradicted, he also manifested a feeling of affection that on many an occasion made him quite moving. Bishop Villecourt in his enthusiasm had made much of these signs of affection given him by the open-hearted boy. On occasion, Maximin would urge the bishop to accept a medal from him as a souvenir. Again, along the road to La Salette he dashed to the left and to the right to use up the energy in his little legs, and suddenly threw himself against the bishop in a burst of filial trust. Then, there was a pleasant leave-taking from the bishop, Maximin pressing him to stay on longer, a sudden warm embrace, and then tearful good-byes.

With an aloofness for which the critic will be grateful, Bishop Dupanloup reported that Maximin had given him the cold shoulder throughout the entire journey up the mountain (he probably had his reasons), but upon arriving Maximin thought he recognized him from a picture just given him of a priest helping the wounded at the barricades. "From that moment on," stated the narrator coldly, "he proffered me the most lively and rustic friendship."

At the convent of Corps, Father Arbaud spotted him at the kitchen door one day "telling his story to a beggar who listened to him with delight. As he finished the narrative, he gave him a small coin as a sign of friendship." Such incidents must have been frequent because compassion for the poor was the most lively memory that Mélanie, in her old age, had kept of her little companion of bygone years.

But Maximin's ingenuousness, especially, erased the unpleasantness of his hyperactive nature. Whereas an adult might work hard and long to develop the qualities of purity, simplicity, and humility, to Maximin they come as naturally as does breathing.

"A serious person," writes Father Bez, "asked him one day whether the Blessed Virgin he claimed to have seen had spoken to him about impurity." "I don't understand what you mean, Sir," he answered candidly. "I don't know what that is."

On the other hand, the Superior of Corps, interrogated by Rousselot on what she had observed of Maximin during the preceding ten months, answered without hesitation:

> He has never spoken to us about La Salette and we have avoided having him speak about it so as not to give him any undue importance. When he returns from interrogations people put him through, he never tells us or the other children, or anyone else, who it was that asked to see him or what questions were asked. After his trips to La Salette or after the interrogations, he comes in very simply, as if he had not been involved at all. I do not want him to accept money from pilgrims. When the money is forced upon him he always gives it to me and never worries whether I spend it for him or for his parents. He receives religious articles such as books, crosses, rosaries, medals, holy cards, which he never keeps. He often gives them to the first little friend he meets, or he loses them or absent-mindedly misplaces them. **(22)**

Words like simplicity and humility are inappropriate when applied to Maximin, inasmuch as they imply effort and acquired habit. In his case, there was not a trace of deliberation or effort to overcome an obstacle. He acted this way because this is what he was. He was simply being faithful to his own nature.

"What I will say for having observed it," says Dupanloup, "is that the children, and little Maximin in particular, whom I have observed more closely and at length, seem to have kept a simplicity, I would even say a humility, that are absolute. So absolute, in fact, that the simplicity and the humility do not even appear as virtues at all in them, in spite of the honor and the exposure they have received. This is the way they are, and they seem totally incapable of being otherwise. They remain so with an innocence that is nothing less than amazing when one observes all of this closely and reflects upon it."

The more we listen to the witnesses of Maximin's humble life, the more we observe in him a total incapacity to plan, scheme, or to be self-complacent. This little boy who freely shared or lost what he possessed was very much the same one who, when he led his cows up the mountain the previous year, ate his day's lunch as he went, sharing it generously with his dog. When Pierre Selme asked him: "What will you eat later?" Maximin replied, "But I am not hungry."

This child who knew nothing of his fame, who shared his story with beggars as enthusiastically as with the powerful, was still the same boy described to us by Rousselot:

> Maximin is not conceited. He candidly acknowledges the misery of his condition, the wretchedness of his first jobs. "Where were you, what did you do before being loaned to Pierre Selme?" He answers simply: "I was with my parents and I picked dung on the national highway." He goes further. He admits his faults, his bad inclinations. Twice I had him come to my room. There I said to him: "Maximin, I was told that before the apparition of La Salette you were a bit of a liar." Maximin smiled and said candidly: "You were not misled. You were told the truth. I lied, I swore and threw rocks at my cows when they strayed." **(23)**

His humility and candor were both undeniable. But the words of that little confession should, according to some, have made good Rousselot frown. "I lied, I swore." Well aware of Maximin's ignorance, people were more apt to overlook his swearing. Lying was more worrisome, especially in someone presenting himself as witness to an apparition. Fuller details would be hoped for here, at least to be sure that the faults were of the benign type.

The problem of insincerity does not seem to have bothered Maximin's observers very much. They imagined that a child's falsehoods cannot be judged according to the norms of an adult conscience. They knew how much this particular child's education had been neglected. They saw too much spontaneity in him to be astonished even if, on certain occasions, his reactions were instinctive rather than deliberate regarding the truth. They did not consider that his veracity in the La Salette affair should be questioned. Rousselot's willingness to believe him lies in the fact that he did not think the scatterbrained Maximin capable of sustaining a lie for any length of time or of fabricating one that would not have some kinship or connection with current events.

Father Arbaud, having interrogated the Superior of Corps on the "mores, the habits, the dispositions, the intellectual capacity of the two children," received the following answer on the question of sincerity:

> They never missed a chance to pull off some prank, some escapade. But since they knew that retribution always followed swiftly, they sometimes tried to excuse themselves with devious answers. They were not able to sustain their little lies for very long, however, and were soon brought to admit their guilt. **(24)**

These observations probably applied to Maximin more than to Mélanie. In any case, they provide us with a valuable point of reference. What happened with good Mother Thècle must have happened also with Giraud the wheelwright. When Maximin admitted to lying before the apparition, what could he possibly have had in mind except those alibis and the store of devices which all scatterbrains of his type use as soon as adults begin hounding them. The most pleasurable escapades, unfortunately, have to be disguised. Maximin again made use of craftiness and guile with Father Mélin who gave him Latin lessons, but no one would impute morality at this stage of Maximin's life. Before the apparition, though, if one considers the poor quality of the child's education and the tenderness of his eleven years, it would have been rash to burden his child's conscience.

We must realize in matters of sincerity a child's mentality does indeed make the same judgments and hold the same uncompromising standards as the adult conscience. In this regard, one of Mademoiselle des Brulais's anecdotes completes Maximin's psychological portrait:

> The superior told me that during the early days, Maximin tried to steal Mélanie's secret: "Tell me your secret and I will tell you mine." Mélanie was very scandalized and repulsed the tempter as he deserved. Maximin was accused of almost disobeying the Blessed Virgin. "Oh no!" he protested. "I would have taken her secret and I would have kept mine." (25)

Tell me your secret... I would have kept mine.... His moral judgment had not evolved enough for him to realize that trapping Mélanie was disloyal. Those who assume that the children were little stoics and those who believe that an apparition would make them so will be disillusioned. For those of us who simply want to see the credentials of witnesses of the supernatural, this last incident says much about Maximin's inner attitude toward truth. We do not hold that all of Maximin's lies were unconscious, since he himself admitted having lied. But the childlike mentality he reveals in this instance allows one to think that in other circumstances he did not judge any differently the little twists he gave to the truth.

How all of this relates to his credibility as a witness to an apparition cannot be decided absolutely until the event of La Salette has been analyzed. For the moment, we can say that Maximin's lies were occasional. They were motivated by a kind of necessity in the life of a child. They do not exceed the power of invention and the stubbornness that can be expected from the most ignorant and giddiest child that one can imagine. Nothing in him revealed a real tendency toward falsehood. Never did he lie freely, compulsively, or for the sheer pleasure of mystifying people. This is why, in spite of his peccadilloes, which he cannot help admitting, we can subscribe to the portrait the mule driver of Corps drew of him to Mademoiselle des Brulais: "Is this child honest?"—"Oh! You will see, Madame, he is completely natural. He does not know how to lie."

An innocent and childlike heart that even the worst possible education could not corrupt; a spontaneity and an open spirit totally free of duplicity or craftiness—these are, after all, titles splendid enough to attract the Blessed Virgin and strong enough guarantees to have him become her servant. If the Lady of La Salette is the same as that of the Magnificat, then Maximin is one of the humble people she must love. And if, in an apparition, proof of the divine begins where natural capacities leave off, then again Maximin is one of the instruments best suited to accomplish the purposes of God.

-6-
Maximin and Mélanie
—Face to Face—

I would like you to tell me if Marcellin and his sister will confide their secrets to me, wrote Cardinal de Bonald to Father Rousselot after the Ars incident. "I pray you, Bishop," he wrote again three months later to Bishop de Bruillard, "to ask them (their secret) and have it sent to me through the bishop's office."

More than four years after the event of La Salette, the Bishop of Grenoble's metropolitan superior was so ignorant of the facts that he assumed the children to be brother and sister. This casual attitude toward history is the stuff of nightmares. At best it blinds a person to essential aspects of the question.

It is crucial to the verdict to be brought on La Salette to know whether the children were brother and sister or whether they had met the day previous to the apparition, as history assures us. The credibility of their testimony rests on it.

In reality, Maximin and Mélanie, both born in Corps, had never noticed one another, had never exchanged a word in the streets of the town. Mélanie's rare mid-winter stays with her family, the difference in their ages, the fact that their homes were at opposite ends of the township, all contributed to keeping them apart. Chance or Providence brought them together at Les Ablandins. The man who was God's instrument in this case tells us more. "On Sunday, September 13, 1846," testified Pierre Selme, "I went to Corps to fetch a little boy who was to watch my herd of cows. The shepherd I had hired had fallen sick a few days before. Unable to find another, I went to Giraud, the wheelwright at Corps, and I begged him to let me have his son for some eight days. At first he refused, but after a while he agreed. Giraud had sent his son Maximin, normally called Germain or Mémin, to Saint Julien to run an errand with Mister Vieux. The latter, seeing the child at nightfall, did not let him go home but kept him overnight. I went to fetch him the next day, Monday, the fourteenth of the same month, at three in the morning, and brought him to Les Ablandins." **(1)**

Main road of Corps with the local Parish Church

Maximin, later questioned by Lagier, added a few strange details:

> *His little daughter was sick. He went to the neighbor. This man's price was a little too high. He was asking fifteen francs for the two month's stay. Then he said to my papa: "Here, give me your boy for two or three days." My papa told him that I had to watch my goat. He asked to let me go for two or three days to see if his little daughter would get better or to give him time to hire another shepherd. And then the man said: "Anyway, he can bring his goat up there while watching my cows." I stayed six days.—"What day did you go?"—"Monday."*

The error concerning the little girl he replaced is not important. What interests us in these conversations is that they candidly open up Maximin's world for us. In fact, he was replacing a young boy who said afterward: "I had bad luck. If I had not fallen sick I would have been the one to see the Blessed Virgin." But Maximin's error, assuming that it is his more than the copyist's, simply proves that the need to verify his thinking never occurred to him. His perception of people and things was likewise simple, delightfully childlike. He repeated the words of that conversation between adults like a lesson he had learned (probably from Selme): fifteen francs is a little too much.

Of the dickering between his father and Selme—which must have been an enjoyable diplomatic contest if we keep in mind the sensitivity of Giraud, a journeyman wheelwright of France—Maximin remembered only the pretext veiling a polite refusal: "My son has a goat to watch." The whole world revolved around that reality. Whether he went up to Les Ablandins or remained in Corps, there was only one thing necessary: that he watch his goat. He was a delight, this little man who felt indispensable, who was fond of his bosom companions, the goat and the dog he brought everywhere with him, even to Mr. Vieux's place on a Sunday evening. The next day, at sunrise, walking between the two of them, he made a triumphant entry into Les Ablandins.

All this self-confidence did not free Selme from worrying about his herd—the fortune he would place in the hands of an untried shepherd. Already, on the way up the mountain, Maximin's friskiness, his curiosity, had alerted Selme. He made a mental note not to let Maximin out of his sight. Fortunately, Selme's distrust of Maximin allows us now to reconstruct Maximin's entire week, day by day, almost hour by hour.

Selme's report goes on:

> This child went that very day and the following days to watch my
> four cows in my field on the southern slope of the mount named
> "aux Baisses," not too far distant from the cross recently planted
> on top of that mountain. There are private properties all over this
> entire slope. The La Salette commune owns the plateau on the
> north slope where the recent events Maximin Giraud and Mélanie
> Mathieu say have taken place. Since I feared that little Maximin

would not keep a close enough watch on my cows, which could easily fall into the numerous mountain ravines, I made it a point to work in that field on Monday, the 14th of the same month, as well as on Tuesday, Wednesday, and Friday of that same week. I testify that during all of these days Maximin was not out of my sight for an instant.

It was easy for me, in fact, to see him at whatever point of my field he could be, because there are no hillocks blocking the view. I only wish to add that on the first day, Monday, I brought him to the plateau I just mentioned to show him a fountain to which he could bring my cows. He brought them there every day at noon and he would immediately return to place himself again under my supervision.

On Friday, the 18th, I saw him play with little Mélanie Mathieu who was watching cows for my neighbor, Baptiste Pra, whose field is adjacent to mine. I don't know if the child knew her before working for me or if he had made her acquaintance at the village of Les Ablandins. I had never seen them together. They both went to their fields very early in the morning. They would return in the evening and would go to bed after eating their soup. Saturday the 19th, I returned to my field as usual with Maximin. At about eleven-thirty in the forenoon, I told him to bring my cows to the fountain on the plateau situated on the north slope of the mountain. The child told me then: "I will call little Mélanie Mathieu so we can go together."

That day, after having brought my cows to drink, he did not return to me in my field. I told him: "Well, Maximin, you didn't come back to join me in my field."—"Oh!" he said, "don't you know what happened?—What happened? I asked him. And he answered: "Next to the spring we found a beautiful Lady who stayed with us for a long time and who spoke to Mélanie and me. At first, I was afraid. I didn't dare fetch my bread, which was near her, but she told us, "Do not be afraid, my children, come near, I am here to tell you great news." The child then told me the story he has since repeated to all those who have questioned him. I add that on one of the days of the week the child was with me, he went to watch my cows in the field called "Babou." He was never alone that day but was supervised, as on the other days, by my wife or by me.

Pra Concurs:

> During the six days that Maximin Giraud, of Corps, kept the cows of Pierre Selme, my neighbor whose shepherd was ill, I was not aware that the children knew each other. They might have met, however, either in my field, next to Pierre Selme's, or when they brought their herds to drink on the north slope of the mount "aux Baisses." Saturday, September 19, 1846, they both came to tell me what they had seen and heard on this plateau. (2)

With these statements, we can readily believe the children's testimony denying any previous acquaintance. Their masters had seen no sign of it. Their answers to the interrogator's questions made it clear that they had met for the first time on Thursday at Les Ablandins. "There is a little girl who brings her cows on the mountain. You may go with her if you want to." This word from Selme urged Maximin to seek out Pra's unfriendly shepherdess. But in the bustle of that first evening they could only agree to meet on the mountain. The next day, shepherding in neighboring fields, they did not meet, according to them, until the afternoon. They went down together to the village and took leave of one another with the challenge: "Tomorrow, we will go back up the mountain. We'll see who is the first one up." (3)

Half a day's acquaintance on Friday and as much on Saturday! This would have to be the time frame upon which to build the supposition that the children schemed to invent a sacrilegious fairy tale. What we know of their character, their simplicity, their total indifference to money removes the element of motive in such a plan. How could we suspect them of such a perverse and gratuitous lie? We see such collusion as not only improbable but outrightly impossible when we consider the complexity of the La Salette event and the short span of time available to the accomplices in which to agree on every detail of the vision, the message, the costume, the actions of the beautiful Lady, the children's own reactions, and their own words.

The Two Witnesses were Believable and Reliable

The story of the apparition as we have told it according to the testimony of the children would be difficult enough to retain even by someone with a trained memory. An easy experiment will allay any lingering doubt: let two people of average intellect attempt to learn in the same amount of time what the children had to learn. Then let them recite this separately to a qualified panel to see if their agreement is absolute, if they omit any sentence from the discourse, or if they change the order of it, if their narrative is free of any detail that would point to contradiction. Mélanie's verbal memory was well below average and Maximin's was always handicapped by his inability to concentrate. Both lacked training. The discourse was absolutely beyond their comprehension. Having to recite it in French constituted one more obstacle. Nevertheless, the children underwent ordeals of cross-examination in circumstances that can only be called terrifying.

But this comparison outlines only a small part of the difficulty they would have to overcome. Let us note this well. They had not been presented with a paper to memorize but with an absolutely original drama they would have had to invent and plan down to the last detail. The most futile as well as the most insidious questions would surprise and harass them daily on such points as the Lady's words, her shawl, her stockings, her roses, their own actions and responses, Maximin's staff and his dog, and so on. Sherlock Holmes working with a playwright could not have managed it. And two children pulled it off? And these children? The hypothesis of collusion is decidedly absurd. Conclusive proof is to be found in the manner in which they sustained their testimony.

For a moment, let us simply observe the scene. Do these children look like conspirators on the slope of the Planeau as they watch their herds on Saturday morning a few hours before the apparition? They walked up together led by Selme, and each child went to his or her field. At approximately eleven-thirty, Maximin's employer called out to him and told him to bring his herd to the brook and Maximin answered calmly: "I will call Mélanie and we will go together." Where

The two children napped near the bed of the ravine

was the excitement of childish secret meetings as the plot's fateful
hour approached?

There are random strokes of chance, some may say. Agreed, the children had no concerted action or plan. They probably would not have
succeeded anyway. But what if by some incredible coincidence such
a thing did happen? And if, spurred on by the first success of the
evening of the 19th, they had decided to prolong the hoax, could they
not have elaborated the details as they went along?

All suppositions are allowed except those which facts forbid. The
entire population of Corps could see Maximin in the hamlet the very
next day, while Mélanie stayed with the Pra's. And nothing better
calms wild imaginings than Selme's juridical precision:

> The next day, my neighbors and I sent the two children to see the
> parish priest of La Salette who told his parishioners at Mass what
> the children had seen and heard. This is what my neighbors told me
> because I did not attend Mass at La Salette but brought Maximin
> to his father at Corps, as I had promised. The child never returned

to Les Ablandins, where Mélanie stayed until early December. He only went through the town as he accompanied the many pilgrims who walked up the mountain.

Thus, after their second retelling the children were separated. They were so, in fact, after the first. Henceforth, all hope of communication was gone. Each one alone would face questioners coming from every point of the compass. Their accounts and their answers were recorded by human and fallible memories, but also by the written word under their own dictation. The test was fearful. Every statement one child made was compared with the other's. If they were telling the truth, heaven might save them from substantial contradiction. If they were lying, it was impossible for the hoax not to surface.

The very notion of the risk involved in all this never entered their minds. They parted company at La Salette in front of the church. Maximin returned to Les Ablandins; Mélanie attended Mass. Their parting was totally unemotional. There was no regret. During the entire day of Sunday, each one, without worrying about the other, proclaimed the great news of the beautiful Lady as he or she knew it. Thus it was to be every day that autumn, until Mélanie's contract with the Pras expired. Then, at the convent of Corps, she joined Maximin who had already been there a fortnight learning the alphabet. If some variation between their stories was to surface at this time, we can say that the harm had already been done. In fact, thousands of people had heard the children. Investigators by the hundreds had turned them inside out and in all directions, especially the local priests, mandated or not by the bishop.

The reason for this new meeting was certainly not to consult with one another or to share sympathy. Bishop de Bruillard, yielding to many pressures, had wanted to provide for their education in a house he could supervise. The people of Gap claimed them insistently. Through the testimony of the Sisters and the children's visitors, we are amazed at how they remained indifferent toward one another throughout their entire four-year stay in the convent. "They don't seek each other out nor do they avoid each other," says Sister Thècle. "Called on and interrogated every day separately, they don't tell each other who called or what questions they were asked." Often, in the interrogation reports, one can find answers like this one: "But Maximin, told me this. Shall I have him come?"—Well if he told you that, he is a liar." Or, reversing the roles: "Mélanie told me just the opposite a while ago."—"If she told you that, she lied, that is all." They never tried to know what the other had said. "Do you talk to Maximin sometimes about what the Lady told you?" Mademoiselle des Brulais asked Mélanie in 1847. "Why should I talk to him about that? I don't need to, he knows it as I do," she answered.

In everyday life, they never missed a chance to needle one another. Marie des Brulais often witnessed their teasing and did not hesitate to present it as characteristic of their relationship.

In 1849 she wrote:

> *I often had the occasion this year to recall a note I made two years ago: Maximin and Mélanie have nothing in common except the apparition. Their temperaments could not be more opposite. This is evident immediately and they make no attempt to hide the scant affection they have for each other. "if you become a missionary," I once said to Maximin, "Mélanie can help you convert the savages, since she wants to be a religious in foreign lands."—"Oh!" he shot back, "Mélanie can go wherever she wants. I don't want a woman following me."*
>
> *Here is a little scene that will reveal them even more. A while ago, they had a disagreement, which is a frequent occurrence. "When I become a missionary," shouts Maximin, "if you come to my confessional, I'll give you such a long penance that you won't be tempted to return!"—"If I'm the only one to go to your confessional, you'll have a very lonely confessional!"* (4)

"They can hardly look less like conspirators. If they were, they would need unprecedented genius to be always faithful to themselves throughout the two years that this rigorous investigation has lasted." (5) Bishop Dupanloup wrote those words only after close observation of the children's characters and relationship. We can judge for ourselves as we follow them through their unfolding ordeal.

-7-
Faithful Witnesses

Maximin's fickleness and Mélanie's volatile memory made it absolutely astonishing that they could recall the beautiful Lady's long discourse, as well as every detail of the apparition, after hearing it only once. That their descriptions agreed on every point emerged from the thorough interrogations. The most trustworthy documents, those of the official investigations of 1847, testify to the historical truth of this phenomenon.

A man like Lagier, a bit of a skeptic and determined not to be put upon, also found this amazing.

"But you knew no French," he hinted to Mélanie, "I thought sure she had taught you how to remember all she said."

"No, she said it to me only once."

"Since you did not know French," Lagier insisted, "and you never learned it in school, it must have been difficult to remember all that."

"Well, no. She said it to me once and I remembered it well."

Lagier, like all the other interrogators, had to acknowledge the evidence. He could never find the flaw that would convict these illiterates of lying. Peytard, Mélin, Perrin, had tried that before him. They had interrogated the children separately and again on the mountain. Other people by the hundreds threw treacherous questions at them. The children's answers were always in harmony. The situation was more dangerous during the first months when Mélanie remained in Les Ablandins and Maximin, more vulnerable because of his airy temperament, was in Corps, within easy reach of the inquisitors and the curious.

In early December, when they were both reunited once again at the

Sister's convent, people seized opportunities to question them. One of the children would be called to the parlor, placed in the presence of a woman and asked, "Was the lady you saw shorter or taller than this one?" Then, the other would be summoned. Both would answer, "Taller." They would ask Maximin if his dog had barked during the apparition; he would answer no. Mélanie would then be asked and she would answer likewise. The children never spoke of the apparition to one another nor would they speak about their visitors and about all these questions.

Are we then witnessing an ongoing miracle by which all human element was canceled from their testimony? Father Bossan had collected almost every primitive document and sought all pertinent information from the authors. His observation on this topic is useful:

> The children have always repeated the Blessed Virgin's words as they had heard them. People noticed that sometimes they would shorten their account, especially after they had recited the same story many times. They would not summarize but rather omit certain details, or merely allude to them. Some people concluded from this that the children did not always say the same thing. They then formulated objections against La Salette with nothing better to offer as proof. The children always said exactly the same thing, but they sometimes did not fully narrate their story, which is quite a different matter.

The special Providence of God must not be expected to abrogate all the laws of his day-to-day Providence. A miracle happens, becomes visible in the texture of natural events, only as much as it is necessary to realize its purpose, not to entertain. One should not be surprised, then, if in telling what they saw and heard, Maximin and Mélanie remain subject to psychological fatigue and to their individual temperaments. (1) What is crucial is that their accounts do not show any trace of progressive development. Neither Father Bossan nor the witnesses he interrogated imply any such thing. Apart from human weaknesses from which no witness of the divine can escape, there are enough indications of superhuman strength in their behavior with regard to the apparition to allow anyone to recognize in all this God's special Providence.

First, the children's moral strength far surpassed the normal capacity to sustain a hoax. Both had been beaten by their fathers not once but many times, first because people did not believe them, then because of the troubles their story might ultimately cause their families. Civil authorities threatened them to the very limits of the tolerable. One gendarme, on the road to La Salette, held Maximin over the abyss and, letting fall on him a hail of curses, shouted: "I will drop you here and now if you don't admit that all you have told us is false." (2) There was always the prospect of prison and that constantly harassing manner of people towards them. "Maximin, I would not want to be in your place and I would prefer to have killed someone rather than have invented all you said." (3)

The Town of La Salette drawn circa 1850

We now move to the court scene where a judge alluded to the death penalty in the event of falsehood. Surely, no hoax could stand up to such pressure. (4) After all, these children were poor and simple little country adolescents. The giant of a man who had held Maximin over the edge of the precipice heard the boy say, "No, I will not admit it, because all I said was true." On September 19, Mélanie had been so frightened that she had dropped her staff. This same girl replied to the judge who had alluded to the death penalty, "Your honor, people die only once."

Flattery alternated with threats. The mayor's twenty francs represented a fortune for Mélanie and Maximin. Without consulting one another, without knowing what the other would do, both refused the money. Two years later, Father Dupanloup offered the same bait to obtain the children's secret, with no better result. With Maximin, Dupanloup pulled out all the psychological stops. He played on all the adolescent incentives such as curiosity, friendship, filial piety—to the point that he himself began to feel squeamish about his own tactics. He wrote a letter to du Boys that gives an exact notion of the power of seduction he had used, of the skill with which he had exploited situations and had calculated results. At every turn, he had to concede defeat:

> I had a traveling bag with a lock that opened and closed in a secret way without a key. Since the boy was very curious, touching everything, looking at everything and always in the rudest manner, he didn't miss my bag. He saw me opening it without a key and asked me how I did it. I told him it was a secret. He frantically insisted that I show him. The word secret made me think of his. I took advantage of the situation and said to him, "My child, this is my secret. You did not want to tell me yours so I won't tell you mine." I was half serious, half teasing.

> "It isn't the same thing," he shot back "And why not?" I asked. "Because I was forbidden to tell my secret. No one said you could not tell yours." It was a masterful reply. Appearing not to have understood, I answered, "Since you did not want to tell me yours, I will not tell you mine." He insisted again. I provoked him by mysteriously opening and closing the lock. He could not break my secret. For many hours I shamelessly held him this way in utter suspense. Ten times he insisted that I show him my secret. "All right," I said, "but you tell me yours."

> At this, the religious character of the child surfaced anew and his curiosity seemed to disappear. A moment later, he again pressed me.

I gave him the same answer and met the same resistance. Finally I told him, "But at least, child, since you want me to tell you my secret, tell me something of yours. I am not saying you should tell it all, but tell me what you can. Tell me at least if it is something happy or unhappy. This is not telling me your secret."

"I can't." This was his only answer. Since we were in a friendly mood, I noticed an expression of sadness in his refusal.

I gave in finally, and showed him the secret of my lock. He was fascinated and beside himself with joy. He opened and closed my traveling bag many times. I told him, "See, I told you my secret and you haven't told me yours." This new insistence and this sort of reproach distressed him. I thought it best not to repeat this tactic. I was convinced as anyone knowing how human nature can be, especially that of a child, that this little boy had just overcome one of the most violent moral assaults one can imagine.

But the tempter did not give up so easily. On the trip down the mountain, he secured Maximin's trust with small gifts and the genuine pity and sympathy he showed for his father's plight. Then, at the sentimental peak of this conversation, he threw in this tormenting word, "But, my child, if you were to say only what you can say of your secret, your father could receive much help." Finally, in his hotel room at Corps, he let Maximin play with a purse filled with gold coins. The boy counted them, stacked them in many different ways. Dupanloup himself was delighted with the scene. Then in a moment of warmth and friendship, he said, "Well, my child, if you were to tell me what you can of your secret, I would give you all that gold for you and your father, I would give it all to you, and right away. Don't worry, I have other money to continue my journey.

At that moment, confessed the tempter, surely, I witnessed a unique moral phenomenon and I am still gripped by it as I write. The child was totally absorbed by the gold. He enjoyed looking at it, touching it, counting it. When I spoke these words to him, he suddenly became very sad, quickly drew away from the table of temptation, and said to me, "Sir, I cannot." I pressed on, "But this gold means happiness for you and your father." Again he answered, "I cannot," but his voice and manner were so firm that I felt defeated. To avoid the appearance of defeat, I said in a scornful, sarcastic tone of voice, "Maybe you don't want to tell me your secret because you don't have one. It's all a joke." "Oh yes, I have one, but I can't tell you." "Who forbade you?" "The Blessed Virgin."

Then and there, I stopped the useless wrangling. I felt that the child's dignity was greater than mine. With affection and respect I placed my hand on his head.

Father Lagier likewise wove a web around Mélanie that seemed to be a sure trap for the child. To have her tell him her secret, he invoked his priesthood and the fact that they were both from the same village, the interest he had in her spiritual welfare, and his personal need of divine counsel. He touched feelings most capable of moving a young girl educated by the Sisters. Still, the investigator's persistence, more than his words, the art of repeating the same demands after a brief respite, must have cast after many hours a kind of spell and numbness that even the most resolute adult might not have resisted. The following conversation carefully recorded by Lagier will give an idea of the tension.

Father Lagier: "You never thought of getting on your knees?"
Mélanie: "Oh no!" (smiling).

Father Lagier: "And now, you will tell me what she told you?"
Mélanie: The child looks at me with a smile and says with assurance, "Oh no!"

Father Lagier: "You won't say it to a priest you know, who comes from your own town?"
Mélanie: "No."

Father Lagier: "And why not?"
Mélanie: "No, because..."

Father Lagier: "Now, tell me why not?"
Mélanie: "Oh! No."

Father Lagier: "You won't tell it to a priest, who can keep your secret?

If it's something that doesn't concern God, all right! But a priest who can receive all secrets, who is obliged in conscience to keep them, can surely keep yours. If this was the Blessed Virgin, it would seem that she would not have forbidden you to tell it to the priests. Other people, yes, but to priests? I don't see what could oblige you not to tell them. And then, you are still very young and you might need counsel. Those priests you can trust, or another good person you can confide in, your father, your mother, all these people can surely receive your secret and are able to keep it!"

Mélanie: "Oh! no. I am not telling it."

Father Lagier: "To no one?"
Mélanie: "I don't want to tell it."

Father Lagier: "Not even to a wise person?"
Mélanie: "Wise or otherwise, I don't want to tell it."

Father Lagier: "You can..."
Mélanie: "No, I really don't want to."

Father Lagier: "Why not?"
Mélanie: "I don't want to."

Father Lagier: "Are you afraid that if you told it, it would not be kept absolutely secret?"
Mélanie: "Even if it were to be kept well, I don't want to tell it."

Father Lagier: "But why?"
Mélanie: "Because I was forbidden to tell it, and I don't want to tell it, and I will never tell it. There!"

Father Lagier: "And does this secret concern heaven or hell?" I was still speaking when the child interrupted me, saying:
Mélanie: "It concerns what it concerns. If I tell it you will know it and I don't want to tell it."

Father Lagier: "But without telling me what it is, you could at least tell me whether it concerns religion or something else."
Mélanie: "Whatever it is about, I don't want to say it."

Father Lagier: "Well, since you don't want to tell it, I won't ask you

any more. It seems that it concerns you."
Mélanie: "Whatever it is about..."

Father Lagier: "Well, I will ask you something else (I pretend to sharpen my pencil, I raise my eyes and say to her), "I would like it if it concerned me, or the other priests. I would be happy to have come here, in this painful circumstance of my father's illness; (the child does not answer me, she lowers her head). Well, aren't you going to say anything to me?" (She raises her head again and answers me, smiling.)
Mélanie: "What do you want me to tell you?"

Father Lagier: "Mélanie, I'm going to tell you something. If the bishop, who is the successor to the apostles, and the Holy Father, who is the Vicar of Jesus Christ, were to ask it of you, I think well enough of you to believe that you would tell them?"
Mélanie: "Oh! No." (The child says this with astonishing assurance.)

Father Lagier: "Oh well!" I say.
Mélanie: "No, no. I will not tell it." (I am startled by the firmness of her words.)

Father Lagier: "Listen, my child. What you have just said worries me. I have the strangest feeling. I don't know what to think any more as I hear you saying that you will not reveal it even to my bishop who is a saint, a complete man of God, or to the Holy Father, the representative of Jesus Christ on earth. I would tell them all I have done, all I have thought, all I would have the most trouble breathing to any soul on earth. On the contrary, I would be very willing to tell them even my greatest faults" (The child stops me and says,)
Mélanie: "I would tell them that too, but not this. No." (I don't have the courage to go any further. My conscience is reproaching me for putting the child through such an ordeal.)

Father Lagier: "Well, my poor Mélanie, you must have seen the devil instead of the Blessed Virgin, because the Blessed Virgin forbade you to tell it to the ministers of religion, because she has no consideration for the ministers of her Son's religion." (The child does not raise her head, her face is calm but very serious. I wait till she looks at me. She

stays in the same position, maintaining the greatest reserve, modesty and sternness. I say to her), "Have I just hurt you?"
Mélanie: "No."

Father Lagier: "Are you sure?"
Mélanie: "No. How can that affect me?" (I stop. To go further would be tempting God. In any case, I can't....)

Lagier's confession is not a sham; we are reading words intended only for himself. (5) When he states that he cannot proceed further, he is referring to his own odious suggestion that the devil, instead of the Blessed Virgin, appeared to Mélanie. In reality, the struggle went on fiercely between the two adversaries. Lagier asked Mélanie if it was the pastor of La Salette who had taught her to say that she had a secret. He asked her if the secret was in French or in dialect, and if she knew Maximin's secret. Little by little the heat of the contest rose with the voices.

Father Lagier: "Germain told me he had told it to you. I did not ask him to whom he had told it, but he told me he had told it to you. Anyway, why would he have hidden it from you? Didn't you tell him yours?"
Mélanie: "No."

Father Lagier: "And why didn't you tell him?"
Mélanie: "Because..."

Father Lagier: "You did well. I will then say that you did not tell me in so many words," "Yes, Germain did tell me his secret," but that you implied it."
Mélanie: "No. Say what you want, but I did not tell you that he had or had not told me. I'm not telling you he told me.

Father Lagier: "Listen, I don't want to write lies! I want to write the truth."
Mélanie: "Well, why are you writing those lies?"

Meanwhile, a Sister had entered, probably to remind the visitor that it was late. In her presence, Lagier surrendered.

Father Lagier: "Yes, you must not repeat it, Mélanie. To anyone, since she forbade you and that it would be better to die rather than tell it." (No reply from Mélanie.) "Isn't it true that you would rather suffer and die than repeat it?"

Mélanie: "Yes, rather than say it."

Father Lagier: "Because she ordered you to die rather than tell it?" (She answered nothing and I decided to stop. Tormenting a child for three hours with the same question was enough.)

This long passage depicts a typical scenario for Maximin and Mélanie since they began making known the message of their beautiful Lady. Lagier's passage was only one example of the hassles they endured every day, a summary of the tortures, of the moral vivisection, of the incredible exhaustion to which they were subjected. Would the children have freely chosen to lead this kind of existence so foreign to them and so incompatible with their youth, with no hope of gain, purely for the thrill of mystifying people? Those who complain that the Blessed Virgin did not make saints of them should examine instead what superhuman strength she bestowed upon them for the sake of making her message known.

And what may be more wonderful still is the divine assistance clearly visible in their attitude and in their words when they proclaim the apparition.

Father Arbaud writes:

> "When people question them they become recollected. Mentally they place themselves at the spot and in the presence of the person who appeared to them. Their tone of voice changes. They lower their eyes, take on a serious air, and repress their normal behavior. In this way they bear witness to the spiritual power that was given them without their expecting it or wanting it." **(6)**

Every time he saw Maximin at La Salette during the school vacations, **(7)** Father Bossan was amazed by his inner transformation as he began the narrative. And Bishop Dupanloup, who can hardly be accused of preconceived enthusiasm, adds to all this the insights of his psychological acumen.

Upon arriving in Grenoble, I had been warned about the way the children would narrate what had happened to them on the mountain that day. I was told that they recited all this like a lesson. True, I was also told that they could be excused for that since they had been repeating this same account so many thousands of times during these eighteen months that routine was surely to be expected. I was actually well disposed in this regard as long as the recitation did not reach the point of the ridiculous. Before the narration, the children displeased me extremely and still did so thereafter. Still, I must confess that the narration was done, in both instances, with a simple, serious, and religious bearing which contrasted sharply with the generally crude and rude attitude of the boy, and with the glum, surly personality of the young girl.

During these two days, I was almost constantly amazed. Each time the rough hewn boy (Maximin) was brought, even unexpectedly, to speak of the great event, a startling change came over him. It was deep, sudden, instantaneous. The same thing happened in the little girl. They quickly became so grave, so serious. Almost in spite of themselves, they took on such simplicity, such ingenuousness, they became so respectful of themselves and of what they were saying, that they inspired their listeners with a religious awe for the things they related and with a respect for their own persons.

According to all the information I could gather on the spot, they never talked about the apparition uselessly with anyone, neither with their own friends, nor with the Sisters educating them, nor with strangers. When they were interrogated, they answered, neither adding nor subtracting to what was essential. You could multiply indiscreet questions all you wanted: their answer was never indiscreet. Discretion, that most difficult of virtues, was natural to them (in this matter only) to an unheard-of degree. People could pressure them, but there was something self-contained about them of which they were unaware themselves, which repelled all attacks and made light of the sharpest and strongest temptations.

Our experience with children in general, our knowledge of how fick-

le, impulsive, vain, talkative, indiscreet, and curious they can be, has led us to wonder if we have been beaten by these two youngsters or by a superior and divine power. **(8)**

There is an abundance of anecdotes showing these little illiterates facing antagonists and puncturing objections with a witty, lightning-quick answer, and amazing everyone. They alone were unmoved, as if strangers to their own words.

A parish priest (from Vallouise, in the diocese of Gap) to Mélanie: "The Lady disappeared in a cloud!"
Mélanie: "There was no cloud."

The parish priest insists: "But it is easy to wrap oneself in a cloud and disappear!"
Mélanie (vivaciously): "Sir, wrap yourself up in a cloud and disappear!"

A questioner to Maximin: "You must tell your secret to your confessor, from whom you must hide nothing."
Maximin: "My secret is not a sin. In confession we are obliged to tell only our sins."

Another: "If you had to tell your secret or die?"
Maximin: "I would die. I would not tell it."

Father Albertin, professor at the major seminary of Grenoble: "Aren't you tired, little one, of having to repeat the same thing every day?"
Maximin: "And you, Sir, do you get tired of saying Mass every day?"

There are numerous examples of such exchanges. **(9)** Could this talent have been natural

Maximin and Melanie
with parish priest

to the children, or did it come from daily practice? In ordinary life, Maximin and Mélanie showed no sharpness of mind. The Sisters we have interrogated, Mademoiselle des Brulais who lived many weeks in their company, and many other occasional observers all agreed in finding them poorly endowed. From the very beginning, the priests of the diocese of Grenoble agreed with what Bishop Dupanloup held as a proof of his conviction: the children's many spontaneous replies to interrogations and approaches of all kinds were definitely beyond their age and ability.

In late October 1846, Father Chambon and the professors accompanying him were already saying: "We have been truly struck by their ability to defend themselves when pressed hard, in spite of their candor and their simplicity. They have easily been able to escape all our little ruses and all our traps. It has been impossible to wear them down."

"Their ignorance is total," wrote Father Rabilloud to the Bishop of Grenoble in December." "They don't know the elementary truths of religion. But when they speak of their Lady they are little doctors. They reply with disconcerting and disarming ease to objections meant to intimidate and contradict them."

Yet these factors do not constitute the radical truth of the event of La Salette. Impressive as all these signs are, they become a factor in a prudential judgment only if it is rigorously shown that the testimony of the witnesses is totally free of contradiction. The inquiry of the bishop's commission assured this. So, we ask, how valid was this inquiry in the eyes of modern-day psychology?

The inquiry whose outcome was to be the doctrinal pronouncement of September 19, 1851 lasted five years. It included a number of very complex facts and documents. The report of commissioners Orcel and Rousselot was published very early. Today, as we come to know the testimony at the heart of this report, we can assert that the inquiry was conducted by prudent men who overlooked no means of investigation, even if they did not assign to each detail the meaning or the importance we would give it today.

We know in fact that Lagier's notes were scrutinized and that some were commented on by Rousselot. It can also be said that Lagier instinctively practiced the methods of clinical investigation advocated by present-day psychologists. **(10)** He described them for us almost unawares, apologetically, in a preface to Mélanie's narrative addressed to a few of his friends.

The account given here was written entirely during my interviews with the young shepherdess. I have not written it from memory nor with the help of other accounts, but from dictation, so to speak I myself am a native of the region and I understand its dialect perfectly. The entire interrogation was conducted in dialect. In all the conversations I had with her, the shepherdess expressed herself only in the local dialect. If at times I accidentally slipped into French, she conversed in French, but I noticed that she repeated her answer in dialect in order to express herself better.

There are many repetitions. The same ideas are often presented in different ways. This weakens the flow of my report, making it diffuse and without sequence. But you can imagine the handicaps I had to overcome. I sought primarily to record faithfully all our conversations. In good faith I wanted to get at the truth of such an extraordinary event. I did all I possibly could to pursue and understand the ideas that seemed related to the truth.

My sole concern was to know the truth and to make it known, and so my goal was to report my conversations with Mélanie exactly as they had taken place, with the same words and the same expressions, without fear of repetitions or of being prolix. I pursued truth alone; the rest was secondary. In any case, I wrote for my own benefit. I never thought of passing these notes on, even to a few friends.

I was skeptical of the apparition, and so all that interested me was the truth. I don't hesitate to admit that I began my conversations with the young shepherdess in the hope of uncovering a hoax. I had decided to use all of my God given abilities to embarrass, surprise, intimidate, and frighten this child. I wanted to obtain a certain result and I hoped it would match my first impressions. A reading of my various conversations will show whether I succeeded. All of

these reasons account for the confusion, the absence of sequence,
and the repetitions. The reason I returned to the same topic so often
is easily explained. I was looking for the truth and I knew I would
more easily discover it in the uniform responses of the young girl to
varying questions on the same subject...."

The use of dialect, his title of native son and compatriot, and a real gift for investigative reporting allowed Lagier to establish a friendly rapport with Mélanie. The narration would naively drone on when suddenly a question would flash, sometimes endearing, at other times cruelly intimidating, always insidious. To paraphrase Saint Augustine, the skepticism of this seeker without a mandate serves best to shore up our belief. Here again, a choice must be made among the many passages that could be presented.

Mélanie: "The cows were on one side and we climbed the other in order to see them. We saw them, all lying down, and I began to descend and Mémin was right behind me."

Lagier: "Where were you going."
Mélanie: "We were fetching our little bags and then we were to feed our cows. We were going down into the ravine where we had slept, near the fountain."

Lagier: "But you told me the fountain was not in the ravine."
Mélanie: "No, not at the very bottom, where the cows drank, not quite. I was ahead and I told him," "Let's go quickly get our bags." Mémin was behind me as I was going down. I looked ahead of me and I began to see a light."

Lagier: "Where did you see this light?"
Mélanie: "It was over there, on the stones piled one on top of the other, our bags were on them."

Lagier: "So the light fell also on your bags?"
Mélanie: "Yes. Then I said to Mémin, "Look, there's a light over there!" He was two or three steps behind me, then he came down. "Where is it? Where is it?" And I said, "O moun Diou!" And then I saw the brightness rise, it was roundish."

Lagier: "When you saw the light, there was no one in it?"
Mélanie: "No "

Lagier: "You could see nothing but the light?"
Mélanie: "Yes. When it began to move, we almost couldn't look at it. It dazzled us."

This scruple for detail can be intimidating for a child, especially when her interview has lasted fifteen hours and all of her statements are compiled and compared one with another. A little further, intimidation again comes into play.

Mélanie: "On Monday, I saw a fountain there, where the Blessed Virgin's feet had been."

Lagier: "But you told me you hadn't seen her feet."
Mélanie: "Yes I saw them, when she rose and went down lower."

Lagier: "Tell me, while she was speaking French to you, you told me you did not understand and that you had whispered to Mémin that you did not understand. Was it then that she spoke to you in dialect?"
Mélanie: "No. I didn't tell you that. I was about to tell him."

Lagier: "Well, I'll show you where you told me you had said to Mémin you did not understand. I wrote it here (I pretend to leaf through my notes. She answers,) "Oh no! I was about to ask him, but I didn't ask him" (she says this with extraordinary assurance.

Maximin's narrative is likewise riddled with interruptions whose very cleverness lay concealed in their casualness.

Maximin: "And so we had our snack close to the fountain on stone slabs placed there by shepherds to sit on."

Lagier: "Did you help place them?"

Maximin: "Oh no!"

Lagier: "What did you have to eat?"

Maximin: "We had bread and cheese."

Lagier: "Didn't you have wine?"
Maximin: "Oh no! We had water. After we had eaten, we fell asleep one next to the other."

Lagier: "Were you asleep a long time?"
Maximin: "I don't know. About an hour, an hour and a half."

Lagier: "When did you awaken?"
Maximin: "Mélanie was the first to wake up. Then she called me and told me to come right away, that we had lost our cows, that we didn't know where our cows were. We went to look for our cows and we saw them there on a rise. When we had found them we saw a great brightness."

Lagier: "Were you going at that time, or returning?"
Maximin: "We were returning."

Lagier: "Where were you going?"
Maximin: "We were going down where our snacks were, Mélanie's lunch bag and the jacket I had taken off and in which I had placed my lunch, "lous satsous" we had left near the fountain. We were going down."

Lagier: "Were you aware of the brightness?"
Maximin: "Yes, we looked at it."

Lagier: "Who saw it first?"
Maximin: "It was Mélanie. Then she said, "Look, there below, the beautiful light.""

Lagier: "While looking at the light, you saw nothing?"
Maximin: "No. Nothing. When we had seen this light, Mélanie did like this, "O moun Diou, qu'ai a quo?" We were both frightened."

Lagier: "While you were looking at this light, you saw no one?"
Maximin: "No, we saw no one (dungu) in this light. And then, all of a sudden, we saw a lady. The light was lowered and when it was lowered toward her feet, as if it were opening up, then we saw this lady."

The result of all this, we repeat, is that in fifteen hours of close questioning, Lagier was unable to find any contradiction in Mélanie's tes-

132

timony. Furthermore, Bossan carefully transcribed their testimonies in parallel columns which reveal compelling agreement on minute details.

Mélanie: "She had a beautiful white dress all covered with spangles. Her apron was yellowish red. Like the dress, it went down to the shoes. There was a square buckle in the same color as the yellow apron and there were roses all around."

Maximin: "Her shoes were white. On top of the foot there was a buckle like papa Prudhomme's, if you've known him. They were russet like that" (Napoleon's statue: he shows me the yellow epaulettes and the pommel of his sword).

Mélanie: "A cross hung in front of her by a little chain, also yellow, about the thickness of a finger."

("Was this cross very large?")

"Not very. It was on her breast. It was as long as this" (the child shows me a small stick about 10 inches long with the crosspiece in proportion to the upright).

Maximin: "She had a white dress, there were pearls all over it. She had a cross about so long (ten inches: the child points to the sword in the statue as a model). It was between her neck and her folded arms."

The similarity of these descriptions appears quite natural. To exclude all suspicion of collusion, we point to the "insignificant differences" between the two testimonies, referred to by Bishop Ginoulhiac **(11)** and which "in the mind of Saint Thomas, as in that of all theologians and of all jurists, make the testimony more indubitable. "Aliqua discordia in talibus facit testimonium credibilius."" Sometimes the difference is a point on which one of the children insisted more than did the other, or a detail one singled out and the other omitted. Here is a particularly significant example.

According to Mélanie's testimony, the children cast no shadow when they stood in the light of the Beautiful Lady. From the earliest stages of the narration, priests of the Chambon group had noted it. "The young girl noticed that her [the Lady's] body cast no shadow, in spite of the sun's brightness; neither did theirs, as long as they stood near her. But as she began to move away from them their shadow reappeared." Mélanie alone made this observation and it seemed to have struck her. She mentioned it to Lagier at each interrogation, and said it to others also. She explained it: "Our shadow should have appeared on the ground and at least on her apron." She stated having brought it to Maximin's attention right after the apparition. But Maximin did not mention it to Lagier, or to anyone. Why the omission?

Child psychology gives us a clue. According to Piaget's research, **(12)** children, on the average, succeed in correctly explaining shadows at about ten years of age. But Piaget's observations are based on city children attending school. If we remember that Maximin was just barely eleven years old and Mélanie almost fifteen, that both of them were like little primitives, and that their mental age was certainly much below their chronological age, then there is a valid reason for the difference in their perception and behavior. They were not at the same stage of mental development. Mélanie clearly understood the reason for shade. She insisted so much on it that it would not be rash to conclude it was a recent discovery in her life. The link between shade and the sun's light probably escaped Maximin, especially in this case, where the disappearance of shade caused by another source of light failed to attract his attention. For him, the problem did not exist. He did not understand or remember Mélanie's solution to it.

This example, along with many others, makes it clear to us that the testimonies of the two witnesses are independent of each other. Those who might study La Salette from a psychological perspective should appreciate its importance.

The diocesan inquiry had kept track of the more competently conducted interrogations. But it had also observed the children when left to themselves. It was clear to all that the spontaneous reactions of the children in the total absence of constraint and supervision could be at least as revealing as verbal responses obtained in the context of interviews, where many suspected them of being guarded. As an observer who could watch unseen, so to speak, none was better suited than Marie des Brulais.

"Small details," she says, "can reveal the secret thoughts of those you live with. A thousand nuances, almost invisible reactions that an eye accustomed to children can grasp have uncovered before me the inner core of the children in such a way that I find it impossible to harbor the least doubt as to the deep conviction of these young witnesses of the apparition. I would share two incidents that I found most enlightening and that I remember especially well."

On Thursday, September 16, 1847, I went up to La Salette for the second time. Mélanie, who is naturally neither joyful nor expansive, seemed to come alive when she heard that I was going to the Mountain. As I was leaving she ran towards me, placed both her hands affectionately on my shoulders (this is completely out of character for her) and said to me enthusiastically, "You are going to the Mountain. Say a prayer for me there, won't you?" Would she have asked me this had she not been convinced of the miracle? Isn't this a child's nature at its most candid and charming?

The huge crowds of the 18th and 19th brought great joy to both of them, especially to Mélanie. But when she heard that police had been assigned to the Mountain on the 19th for crowd control, she was displeased. "I don't like that," she said. "If all goes well, people will say it was because of the police." Isn't this one more proof of her deep and inner conviction? (13)

Many other anecdotes from the Echo are interesting in ways its author could not have imagined. The school teacher looked upon her students as they were then and did not anticipate what they would later become. Who can blame her? But we who know how unsettled Mélanie's life was to be must guard against reverse prophecy. We know the exuberance of her imagination at a later time of her life and we want to be certain that this excess played no part whatever in the account that she jointly proclaimed with Maximin. Mademoiselle des Brulais, without intending it, provided the psychological proof besides those proofs coming from other quarters that Mélanie did not influence the mind of her little companion.

In reading the Echo, we clearly understand that the children of La Salette were not friends. Maximin in particular missed no opportunity to express his independence from Mélanie. Neither did Mélanie hesitate to provoke Maximin, especially with regard to the apparition. Maximin's ruse, "Tell me your secret, I will tell you mine," was reported by her to the superior of the Sisters. She in turn must not have praised him for this but reported it to Lagier, to Marie des Brulais, to the diocesan commission, and probably to others. Would we not expect that if La Salette had been anchored to an agreement between children that a hurt, resentful Maximin would have denounced it?

The following example is revealing:

> Yesterday, the superior was telling me that the two children were taking their recreation with the Sisters and that she had to reprimand Maximin for his bad manners (he was sitting on the living room floor). Mélanie was in a better mood that day, and a little mischievous. She said, "Oh! How do you want him to behave, Sister, he couldn't even hold still before the Blessed Virgin?" "What did he do?" "Well, he had his hat on his head, then he took it off and placed it on his staff and twirled it around like this (she imitates Maximin). Then he put his hat back on. He took his stick and pushed stones back and forth with it, up to the feet of the Blessed Virgin." "Now listen," said the embattled Maximin, "don't believe that, Sister. Not one stone touched the Blessed Virgin!" "But you were actually playing with stones?" "Yes, but not one reached the Blessed Virgin. That is sure!" (All this took place without the least trace of self-consciousness.)

> I just received confirmation of this little incident. Maximin came in a while ago without greeting anyone, like a real scatterbrain, as often happens. "Well, Maximin," said the superior, "you will never change! You didn't even greet Mademoiselle des Brulais. When will you ever have manners?" Without a sign of temper, Maximin returned to the door, and playfully greeted us very politely. "My poor Maximin," I say as I return the greeting, "it is not surprising that you should forget to greet us, since you didn't even remem-

ber to greet the Blessed Virgin. Didn't you keep your hat on in her presence?" "Oh! Yes. At the beginning, but I still took it off." "Yes, to twirl it around your stick?" "Well, I didn't know who was speaking to me." "Didn't you roll some stones up to the feet of the Blessed Virgin?" "I'm not answering that any more. I'm ashamed of it" (he heads for the door, I stop him). "Now, dear Maximin, say it only to me" (he lowers his voice). "Oh yes! I rolled stones like this with my stick (he raises his voice) but nothing touched the Blessed Virgin. It's Mélanie who said that and it embarrassed me." "Did Mélanie tell the truth?" "Yes, but she had no business saying it. It embarrassed me." **(14)**

Whether we see them relaxed, as they are, or pressured by hard-nosed inquisitors, the children of La Salette give a clear message: they say only what they have seen and heard on the mountain. Whether the children were planners of or accessories to a hoax, their spontaneous reactions only attest to the grip this event has had on their deepest instincts. Where would their heroism come from in the presence of people who would pay them to recant? How could they organize such coherence in presentation and such harmony of detail, both definitively demonstrated by the most punctilious, the most subtle and exhausting investigation? It is most correct to proclaim that many verified incidents allow a believer to recognize special assistance from God, especially in the quality of their testimony during five years. And if no single one of these incidents is truly miraculous, we can certainly call phenomenal the concerted, unfailing strength and the constancy of these frailest instruments heaven could possibly have chosen.

-8-
The Seal of God

The La Salette event rests entirely on the testimony of two children. From the outset, serious people were initially wary of such sources. The venerable Chapter of Grenoble, consulted by Bishop de Bruillard at the close of 1846, not surprisingly advised him to delay all further action by reason of the mistrust automatically inspired by the testimony of children.

"We cannot see," said the canons' report, "what could be the basis for a decision approving this event. Until now we have only the testimony of the two children. We do not have undeniable proof that these children were not induced into error or did not intend to spread a hoax of which they would have been victims or accomplices. How could church authority legitimately approve such an event basing itself solely on the testimony of two children?" **(1)**

The professors of the major seminary had been better informed by their colleagues of the Rondeau seminary (Father Chambon and his professors) and were thus able to look beyond this negative stance and draw a research plan leading to a supernatural explanation of the event. "Observing the disarming naivete of the two children almost creates a bias toward the apparition in all who interrogate them." True, there were certain aspects concerning the truth of the beautiful Lady's words that inspired distrust and they did ask for clarification of these doubts. However, showing clear-sightedness, they added that the children's testimony could be "confirmed and made unassailable by an intrinsic examination of what they say and their manner of saying it, or, better still, by miracles, the authentic stamp of divine action." **(2)**

The canons had not categorically dismissed the apparition. The following year they were better informed about the children's exact statements. They heard them personally and looked into the wonders wrought by the apparition. Then, unanimously, they asked their bishop to proclaim the miraculous intervention of the Virgin of La Salette. However, what came through in their first response was a widespread tendency, when testimony was involved, to look for credibility in the external qualifications of the witnesses more than in the substance of their statements.

Examining the La Salette Cures

Memorial of healing through intercession of Our Lady of La Salette

For them it was mostly a question of tone. Once the prejudice against the children of La Salette had disappeared, they examined the message critically and decided whether or not the words and actions of the Lady justified a Christian's trust in them. For other opponents, the prejudice was insurmountable. Following his thorny interviews with Maximin and Mélanie at the time the secrets were en route to Rome, Cardinal de Bonald wrote to Cartellier: "I hope Rome will go easy on this and not rush into a judgment. This would be really unfortunate. It should become clear that the children's statements are not enough." In the logic of these serious men, the value of a testimony is gauged by the quality of the witness. If his conduct, his past honesty, his social standing are commendable, then a witness's statements are worth believing and should be given credence without hesitation. Should these recommendations be lacking, he merits nothing but contempt. From the very beginning this had been Cartellier's position. The Cardinal had always held, fortunately, that heaven must supplement this deficiency, but he still demanded many signs in order to believe.

In our own day these severe judges have successors: they are all those who would believe in La Salette only if Maximin and Mélanie were to be canonized saints. But holiness has nothing to do with the matter. In this particular instance holiness would not have prevented two young children from being victims of an illusion. The guarantee of a testimony from the normal behavior of a witness can, in reality, only be of surface value. The testimony itself in its inner truth must be grasped with complete confidence. The seminary professors felt this way when they suggested certain conditions to Bishop de Bruillard which, if fulfilled, would render the children's testimony unassailable. Let us follow the path they have marked out for us. If it reaches its destination, none of the prejudices against these witnesses will matter much. We will believe because they are children and more precisely these particular children.

"The specific analysis of their message and their manner of communicating it," according to the professors, provided sufficient grounds for belief. For five years, the most discerning observers saw in the very manner of the children's testimony a convincing reason to recognize the presence of the miraculous. Lagier and Dupanloup were convinced that they were neither authors of nor accessories to a hoax, at least not consciously. In fact, they seemed to be led by a power beyond them. Did they really see the Blessed Virgin and did she speak through them to all her people?

Our Christian instinct must now grasp the content of their testimony if we are to attain complete trust. A celestial person's appearance and discourse must contain a degree of perfection inherent to it. Pascal says that a wealthy man praises wealth, a king speaks casually of a great gift he has just granted, and God speaks well of God. Does the Virgin's hallmark appear on the message as well as in every detail of the apparition? This basic criterion will determine our opinion of

La Salette.

The specific analysis is of prime importance. If, in fact, the words of the Lady were found to be incompatible with what we know of her through faith, they then would have to be ignored. But the difficulty of such an analysis gives us pause. We would be engaged in weighing otherworldly realities. What are the available measuring instruments? We do have faith, theology, spiritual experience perhaps. But what of the ability to perceive the supernatural in an event not of faith? Does this perception belong to the realm of logic? Of intuition? Can it convince anyone who does not hear its voice in his or her own spirit immediately? And what if the Virgin had placed within the event a sign to perplex the blasé and the superficial and summon them on a journey to a deeper faith? If we are attracted we will want to understand. But what are we to say to the person who does not find that open door and walks away?

Research methodology in this area can be theoretically conclusive, but experts quickly add that trust and conviction are still better assured "by miracles, the authentic hallmark of divine action." The perspective we adopt in examining the event will be altered if we are granted the sign of miracles, allowing us to see the presence of God in La Salette. Instead of summarily rejecting obscurities—which are present in any manifestation of the supernatural—we will want to know if they help express the mystery of Mary in our human language. Without indulging in illusion we may see these obscurities turn into light. Care and respect are essential to this specific analysis. It is only fair to approach it with this disposition when God himself reveals that La Salette is something in which he is well pleased.

This testimony of God, hoped for by theologians as well as by the prayerful laity, has not been lacking. Twenty-one verified cures attributed to prayer to Our Lady of La Salette were already being mentioned in Rousselot's report, published in August 1848. All of them do not qualify in an equal manner as miraculous, but their combined strength nevertheless bears witness to God's favor for the title that prompted the prayers of the needy. The Episcopal commissions of that time were as well aware as those of the present day of the strict canonical stipulations governing declarations of miraculous healings. The Commission examining La Salette in 1847 chaired by Bishop de Bruillard accepted the cure of Sister Saint-Charles of Avignon, as well as that of Mélanie Gamon of Saint-Félicien (Ardèche), as meeting the requirements formulated by Pope Benedict XIV and were declared miraculous in the strict sense. On November 21, while the Commission was in session, Antoinette Bollenat rose suddenly from her deathbed at the close of a novena to Our Lady of La Salette. "Let her die in peace," the doctor had said as he left her room on the 19th. On November 22 he said: "If I had to, I would sign my name in blood to testify to this miracle." The judicial investigation begun by Archbishop Mellon Jolly of Sens came to the same conclusion. "We declare that Antoinette's cure, brought about following a novena to the Blessed Virgin Mary, the Mother of God, invoked under the title of Our Lady of La Salette, possesses all the conditions and all the characteristics of a miraculous healing and constitutes a miracle of the third order."

A balanced and thorough research study on the miracles of La Salette was written by Bishop Giray, former rector of the Shrine and the future bishop of Cahors. (3) It relates and appraises 185 occurrences judged miraculous, whether in the physical or the moral order, which took place between 1846 and 1879, from the time of the apparition until the solemn crowning of the statue. The monumental work, by its reliable information and its exacting critical method, justifies the author's conclusion: "God has his own language and it is that of the miracle."

There is no need to pursue once again such a comprehensive study. But one must insist that God's language has indeed made itself heard and that it has a meaning. It is simply not enough to praise the works that publish it and then point to them as destroyers of all the opposition La Salette has ever encountered. For many people this is all irrelevant "After all," they say, "the Blessed Virgin is the same everywhere. Whether you invoke her under one title or another, what she answers are prayers that call upon her in faith." What this opinion overlooks is that among the miracles in the physical order claiming the patronage of Our Lady of La Salette, some have been petitioned precisely to confirm the truth of the apparition. Such is the cure of Sister Saint-Charles as well as the three signs given to the Curé of Ars. Also overlooked is that in their great number and expressed purpose they engage the very truthfulness of God. We readily admit that God's language has to be interpreted and understood. If a confirmed miracle were to abet accidentally something we know to be patently false, we would have to see in it nothing but the reward of sincere faith. But is it conceivable that God would be so consistent and coherent in reinforcing error as to suspend the laws of nature in favor of so many people placing their final hopes in a few drops of water and a few invocations to the beautiful Lady of La Salette?

It is possible, of course, to deny all miraculous intervention, and to appeal to the unseen powers of nature or of the unconscious. But can the Christian who wants to reopen this old debate pride himself in knowing more than bishops of the day in the official exercise of their mission? La Salette is also compared to Lourdes. We regret that the light of the former is less brilliant. We yearn to see waves of healings sweeping away every doubt and objection. But does God's grace ever show itself in the same way twice? It accomplishes at Lourdes what it does nowhere else. At La Salette it performs deeds that have become its hallmark: sudden, unexpected, lasting conversions.

In any case, miracles are essential to a prudential judgment on La Salette. Their relevance has been clearly defined in Bishop de Bruillard's doctrinal instruction: "Considering that the wonderful consequences of the La Salette event are the testimony of God manifesting himself through miracles, and that this testimony is superior to that of men and to their objections. ..."

The Religious Purpose of Mary's Message

Moreover, it seems that the opinion of the canonical judge reflected that of the professors which guided his entire instruction. First, he examined the event in itself, as he had to, and considered it impossible to explain "other than by divine intervention, in whatever manner one would wish to consider it, either in itself, in its circumstances, or in its basically religious purpose." Obscurities that a minority opposition sought to magnify to the detriment of this clearest evidence were eventually resolved. The canonical judge needed only simplicity of heart, born of piety, and the desire not to frustrate what could be God's grace. He was also watching shortsighted exegetes obsessed with trivia and offered them the argument of miracles, not as a way of magically substituting truth for error but more as an added light restoring perspective and equilibrium. "God's testimony is superior to that of men and to their objections." To clarify this sentence one need only compare it to what Cardinal de Bonald wrote to Bishop de Bruillard in answer to his Instruction:

> And what about the prophecies that never materialized? Or the Blessed Virgin's language not understood by the children, for which she had to substitute the local dialect? And what about Mary's seeming unawareness of the children's ignorance of French? Had she continued to speak French, would she have accomplished God's will with regard to the children? These are serious, unresolved difficulties. This is why, according to the Council of Trent, the provincial council had to examine the allegedly miraculous event of La Salette.

This well-known example shows how the specific analysis of the apparition can be influenced by subjective perceptions. If his mind had been open, the Cardinal would not have sided openly with Cartellier by giving credence to such stumbling blocks. There was also the objection made by some theologians regarding the anthropomorphic conflict between the Mother and the Son in the discourse. Other critics claimed that the discourse was nothing but a copy of the "Letter from Heaven." This sort of exegesis suffers at the outset from a very subjective negative bias.

There is probably only one way to keep such an insidious prejudice from slipping into so-called objective research. This would be to accept the favorable and justified presumption found in the manner of the children's testimony as well as in the miracles. We want to be sure that the words and actions that the children assign to their beautiful Lady are worthy of the Virgin reigning in heaven. It is better to seek expecting to find, yet all the while remaining diffident towards ourselves and not towards God.

The apparition of La Salette is both a unified and a complex reality. In the history of apparitions, few have as long a message and are so varied visually. Yet, from all of this, a guiding thought emerges with the greatest of ease: *"For how long a time have I been suffering for you!"* she says. What is the weeping and beseeching woman suggesting by her words and the language of her body? Is it not the power of her eternal compassion and its wondrous activation in the presence of sin? Prior to analysis this oneness must emerge. Many people have failed to understand the meaning of the apparition because they have separated and isolated its elements rather than distinguishing its parts in an integral whole. La Salette cannot be reduced to a discourse, nor can the discourse be limited to a single item, isolated, then found shocking. La Salette is a whole with three principal elements: the discourse, the action, and the particulars of time and place. Moreover, these elements are interrelated. Each one in its own way, every detail in its place, contributes to the meaning of the whole. The discourse also constitutes a whole in relation to its components. Each one of these elements receives a new meaning and a new inflection from its relationship with the whole. Whoever will not consider them in this way will never discern the person identified with them. The parts are contained in the whole and the whole in the parts: a seemingly trite principle but one whose value soon becomes evident.

Let us now study the discourse and attempt to sort out and identify its statements in the light of Christian teaching.

The beautiful Lady's first sentence to the children is a preamble inspired by their own feelings, an invitation to come near and to listen without fear to the great news she has come to tell them. (We know that Mélanie and Maximin had experienced great fear upon seeing the globe of light in the center of which the weeping Lady was sitting.) With solemn clarity and power she immediately states the basic theme of her message: *"If my people will not submit, I am forced to release the arm of my Son."* Everything is contained herein. Already she has expressed the meaning of her dramatic visit and has presented

"A famine is coming...potatoes and wheat... walnuts and grapes..."

all its actions with their respective parts: her rebellious people, her angry Son, and herself, the Mediatrix, whose role had now become impossible to fulfill. What follows will develop this general proposition.

She now goes into detail. The situation is such that she can no longer restrain the arm of her Son. This is indeed the role long assigned to her in the economy of salvation. But people pay no heed. They should realize that nothing they can do will ever compensate for all the sorrowful Mother has suffered for them, from that distant day on Calvary.

She utters in her own vivid words the cry of her Son: *"I gave you six days to work. I have reserved the seventh for myself. And no one will give it to me."* She explains: *"This is what causes the weight of my Son's arm to be so crushing."* She attaches the same gravity to blasphemy.

And so, she goes on, do not be surprised if the harvest is spoiled: *"It is your own fault."* It will punish as well as instruct you. I had warned you last year by the rotting potatoes. Since you paid no heed they will go on rotting. This coming Christmas there will be none left.

You will also see diseased wheat, famine, the death of small children. All this is your penance. Understand this when you see it, when you see the walnuts turn bad and when the grapes rot.

Then come the secrets which we naturally imagine to be an extension of the preceding passages. But historical critics must admit knowing strictly nothing of them except the general sense revealed by Pius IX to Bishop de Bruillard's representatives and later repeated to Father Giraud in a still more general way: "If you do not deny yourselves you will all perish."

The messenger then turns from threats to promises. *"If the people are converted, the stones will become mounds of wheat."*

But the stipulation is that they be converted. What is now happening? First, what is the personal disposition of these innocent children? (*"Do you say your prayers well, my children?"*) They themselves do not give to religion the place it deserves in their lives. Their countrymen even less. On the whole, they live only for their bodies. (*"They work every Sunday all summer long. In winter, they go to Mass only to scoff at religion. During Lent they go to the butcher shop like dogs."*) This is what must change; otherwise, people greedy for worldly pleasures will be punished in their own sin. Must they be scolded through signs such as the prophets of old gave to the princes of the day? Do they need to see, in order to be convinced, that nothing escapes the eye of God? The Lady recalls for Maximin, who had forgotten it all, in detail and with the precision of an eyewitness, the rotten wheat he had seen on the farm of Coin. That is enough. She knows Maximin's story more intimately than he knows it himself. The story then becomes intelligible, within everyone's reach. The Messenger concludes by twice saying: *"My children, you will make this known to all my people."*

No one can deny the unity and the coherence of these lines of thought. One idea follows the other logically. There are levels of thought, the universal governing the more concrete and particular, shedding light upon them. Thus, an organic oneness emerges among them that the human spirit can readily grasp. The transitions of the discourse demonstrate its sequential strength, its real order.

"During Lent they go to meat market like dogs..."

The hierarchy of ideas must be stressed because many capable minds get distracted by a particular image and fail to see the forest for the trees. A country priest is scandalized at the mention of potatoes and thinks it unworthy of the person of the Blessed Virgin. Some goldsmiths such as a Mr. Josse, can see only one sentence in the discourse, a detail concerning their own craft. Violations against the holiness of God's day are condemned by the Virgin, but one cannot argue from this, as a well-known writer once did, that blasphemy was given only token attention, or that Lent can be ignored.

Addressing the people of God as a whole, the Lady of La Salette condemns the more concrete forms of its godlessness, the main beachheads opening the way to materialism. Moreover, it is quite clear that these reproaches are not isolated one from another, nor from the whole of the discourse, which has nothing in common with the dry shopping list type of conscience examination. Everything is set in a living framework. The precepts and reproaches, the threats and the promises all draw their unity and their absolute originality from the relationship first established between Messenger and people: *"How long have I suffered for you!"* We need only obey the rule of objectivity and every detail of the discourse becomes clear in the light of the

148

moving and concentrated prologue wherein the Virgin describes her mediating role. *"If my people will not submit, I am forced to release my Son's arm."*

This is the essential, basic theme of the La Salette discourse. This is the prevailing idea, which explains everything else. The rest of the prologue develops it in moving terms. The reproaches, the threats, the promises are a concrete expression of it. When this is agreed upon, it is difficult to deny the originality of the message. And to deny this originality is to turn our backs on the facts. So much for the goldsmiths of the time. But we cannot give equal weight to a "letter from heaven" calling for Sunday observance as we do to this La Salette discourse whose theme is nothing less than the mediation of Mary.

Indeed, many pseudo-problems are quickly dispelled and the real questions are properly answered when one maintains a clear view of the basic ideas of the a La Salette discourse.

We can be surprised by this use of the present tense: *"How long it is that I am suffering for you!"* For us this might be incompatible with heavenly existence. We could picture a conflict between Mother and Son when we read, *"It is so heavy, so pressing that I can no longer restrain it."* It is disconcerting to hear only of punishments and rewards of a temporal nature. But stopping at details, at imagery, impedes our ascent to the essential meaning of the discourse.

To theologize the elements of the La Salette message makes visible a facet of Catholic dogma in a new and uniquely moving light. It is not a new dogma or a new revelation. Revelation ended with the last of the apostles. But there exists in the revealed teaching of the Church a specific place where all that comes to us from the apparition of La Salette can be inserted with perfect assurance. "I believe in the Communion of Saints," the Creed says.

This is where we can enshrine what the beautiful Lady has told us of her suffering, of her concern, and of her power. Mary's mediation finds resonances in the Church's deep-seated intuition, although it is not defined teaching. But the Communion of Saints is an article of

"If they are converted... rocks will be changed into mounts of wheat..."

faith that none can set aside without ceasing to belong to the Church. Are we able to discern how La Salette exemplifies this teaching and what new and pressing reasons we now have to let it shape our behavior?

Christians know that by their solidarity with Christ each one of their acts can strengthen or weaken the Mystical Body whose members they are. The best of them, like Saint Paul, fill up in their flesh "what is lacking in the sufferings of Christ for the sake of his body, the Church." Now the Virgin reminds us that she, the sinless one, has obeyed this law of universal solidarity. At La Salette, her tears are only a sign of this participation. What is real is that on Calvary she experienced the most unspeakable sorrow any mother has ever tasted. These real tears have a permanent value and allow her to repeat this real complaint: *"How long have I been suffering for you."* We do say, and rightfully, that sin renews the Passion of Christ.

What she tells us about withheld punishments, about blessings and rewards of conversion, is a result and an image of her spiritual mediation. Essentially, she is mediating in the supernatural sphere. But, for us human beings, the supernatural is in every way involved with the natural. A bad harvest can bring a farmer to blaspheme or to turn to God. It is important for him to see a spiritual meaning within this natural event. This is why the beautiful Lady warns: *"If the harvest is spoiled, it is your own fault."* The threat of hunger is a most insuperable obstacle to the spiritual life of the poor. Thoughts of heaven have very little prominence in the mind of a man like Maximin's father, obsessed by this ever-present threat: "Well, my son, eat some bread this year anyhow. I don't know who'll be eating any next year if the wheat continues to spoil like that." The Mediatrix of all graces can therefore not be unconcerned for the "minimum well-being required for the practice of virtue."

"If people are converted, the stones will become piles of wheat." We should not be misled. Promises of material prosperity following upon inner conversion are clearly meant to draw us closer to the realm of the spiritual. They recall the words of the medieval poet: "Heavenly Lady, empress of earth." Mary's concern means to drive us into the loving embrace of Jesus. "Live with my Son," she tells us, "live by my Son and in him. Hold faithfully to the place he has assigned you in his Mystical Body. Generously fulfill the role of service and self-giving he asks of you in favor of the Body you are united to as I am who serve as go-between with him who is Head of all the members."

Essentially, this is the message of grace that Our Lady of La Salette brings to those who want to hear it. Objections to details of wording can be easily resolved as soon as we examine them in their context within the whole. In fact, what remains of the theological hurdles opposing the apparition? Will we again have to face the oft-stated objection that it was not the Virgin who gave humankind six days to work and reserved the seventh? Maximin and Mélanie always answered candidly: "I don't know. I just say it as she said it." And why should we object to her way of expressing it?

The early commentators suggested that after the statement, *"I have given you six days to work,"* the words *"said my Son"* were understood by the context. The problem would then be solved. The style of the discourse, passing immediately from the first to the third person, stresses that the offense is directed against God—*"This it is which*

"Six days I have given you... The seventh I have kept for myself..."

causes the weight of my Son's arm to be so crushing"—and allows one to accept this solution. We believe that present-day theologians would not be shocked to see attributed to the Virgin in person the command she voices here. Mother of God and Mother of grace, Mary is so closely associated with the work of redemption that in a unique manner, she has become one mystical person with Christ, and can assume as her own all of her Son's intentions.

It might very well be that this apparition's singular purpose, more than any other, is to introduce us into the mystery of Mary's mediation and to allow Christian intuition to anticipate the thinking of theologians.

We observed how, in the beautiful Lady's discourse, the events of this world appear to be obedient to her. We noted how she attributed to herself the warning given to her people by the spoiled potatoes: *"I warned you last year."* It is in her role as Mediatrix of all graces that she rules over temporalities in a world where all is grace. All blessings created by God for the temporal needs of people are also made holy by her Son's redemption and ordered to eternal salvation. Mary exercises complete sovereignty over them. But if we proclaim her

Queen of this world, "Empress of earth," can we refuse her the right to speak to us as Queen and to give us, in her own name, commands coinciding with her Son's will? She makes them her own in the hope of reaching us more completely, since, in a sense, she is closer to us because as the Mother she is the Mediatrix between her Son and ourselves.

To accept literally the expression she used and to give it the same obvious sense it has in the rest of the discourse would be to understand with wholehearted enthusiasm the title of Queen of the world given her by tradition. It would be to see her in the fullness of her role. Logically, this would also mean to attribute to her in the order of execution the same power of mediation that none refuses her in the realm of intercession. If we are happy to see her between her Son and ourselves to bridge the chasm caused by our evildoing, we can also grant her the right to prevent us from doing it—and the right to speak to us as Queen even when the commands she gives us are expressions of her Son's will. She who said "Do whatever he tells you" in the Gospel also said, *"This it is which causes the weight of my Son's arm to be so crushing."* She will not usurp her Son's place. The contrast between this last statement and the preceding one is enlightening. Even though she speaks as Queen, and makes her Son's orders her own, she does not pretend to be the offended party when these orders are violated. It is the arm of her Son that we are making heavier. As if she were telling us: my Son has the supreme authority, to Him alone belong vengeance and justice.

Nothing here suggests conflict between Mother and Son. The beautiful Lady of La Salette embraces the cause of justice as much as the most exacting theologian would hope. In the end, she is only claiming the rights of her Son. She is only asking the children to make this plea known to all her people. Would we want her to abstain from making us understand in the only way we can that her mercy also pleads for us?

We can understand divine realities only in human terms. We even distinguish between mercy and justice in God. We acknowledge a host of saintly intercessors between God and ourselves, leading to the person of Christ. We would have to hold guilty of anthropomorphism every Christian invoking Mary as advocate. Fortunately, we realize that all of these apparent conflicts are resolved in the unity of God. A careful reading of the discourse clearly shows that Mary's maternal intercession is subordinated to her Son's justice. *"If my Son is not to abandon you, I am obliged to entreat him without ceasing."* We could not find more appropriate or more admirable terms in any course of theological study.

The fulfillment of the prophetic threats of the discourse is part of the historical data of the La Salette event. Contemporaries of the event attached great importance to the realization of these prophecies, to the point where believers were sometimes prevented from seeing the religious meaning of the message while opponents claimed easy victories.

In 1847, in his correspondence with the bishop, Father Mélin scrupulously recorded the signs of famine and the rise in infant mortality in the Corps region. Among the parish's 1300 people, 13 children under 14 died in 1845; 24 under 10 died in 1846. On April 10, 1847, 33 children under 10 had already died. By the end of that year, the total number of deaths rose to 99 among whom were 63 children. **(4)**

The author of the *"Mémoire au Pape"* (*Report to the Pope*) countered the Lady's prophecies. He reassuringly declared the wheat to be promising, while just about everywhere vineyards and walnut trees were diseased, which, he said, the Lady had not foreseen, but which the diocesan authorities had shamelessly included in the prophecies.

Cardinal de Bonald himself sided with this infamous report and asked: "What about these unfulfilled prophecies?" On July 19, 1856, the *Illustration* replied: "Pictin, a disease affecting standing grain, has caused great losses in 1851 and 1852. Since then it has wreaked destruction on wheat. Diseased plants are stunted and very quickly take on a yellowish color characteristic of mature plants...." Even the *Constitutionnel* replied in the March 1856 issue that the estimated number of deaths in France due to the high cost of food had risen to 71,000 in 1854 and to a minimum of 80,000 in 1855.

It would be unfair to simply dismiss both parties in this affair. Mélin's figures are based on facts. Cartellier's ramblings reflect his prejudices. Going through the newspaper morgues of this period we could draw up a list of calamities strikingly similar to the contents of the discourse. (5) It would not be difficult, even today, to research the year 1847, a frightful year for the poor, a banner year for profiteers. "The year of the great famine," still so called by the Irish who have heard former generations tell of it. But we know that we can easily rationalize the harshness out of these events and deny that the calamities ever reached the level of divine chastisements. It seems more useful to note that the prophecies are conditional: *"If people are converted the stones will become mounds of wheat and it will be found that the potatoes have sown themselves."* At what time has this condition been fulfilled? If we cannot answer this question, neither can we complain that the threats did not materialize.

Bishop Villecourt felt the need, as all did in 1847, to discuss this subject with his readers. "Many people will be almost scandalized to learn that France, or a certain part of France, was threatened with calamities which never occurred. Still, the famine that devastated our provinces this year was quite something. And who could dare say that conversions did nothing to halt still worse disasters? "But," they say, "children did not die trembling in their mother's arms as the Blessed Virgin had foretold!" "Those who speak this way know nothing of the dreadful mortality that swept so many little ones away in many parts of France, and especially in Corps, in the course of two months last winter." (6)

During this same period, life became more simple for the children of La Salette. "The Lady deceived you," Maximin was often told. "She told you a famine would come and the crops are good all over." "So what?" he would answer. "She told me that, and it's her business." At other times, like Mélanie, he gave a standard answer: "But what if people are doing penance?"

There exists a more humble yet irrefutable proof of the prophetic light inspiring the Lady of La Salette. This proof does not depend on statistics and is immediately recognized as valid by the person involved. "It's very true, Madame. Now I remember it. Until now, I didn't," admits Maximin when the beautiful Lady reminded him of details of his visit to the farm of Coin. Prophetic vision is not only exercised in the prediction of things to come but is relative to any event, past or future, whose knowledge exceeds the natural powers of the human mind. Here we have a sure example of it. Only a heavenly visitor could possibly bring back from the past a scene that had no witness. *"Well my son, eat some bread this year anyhow. I don't know who'll be eating any next year if the wheat continues to spoil like that."* We could retain this episode which converted Maximin's father in preference to the ambiguous proofs of history. It proclaims the presence of the Virgin at La Salette and in each of our lives.

Given the orthodoxy and the spiritual wealth of the discourse, we can rightfully state that it is worthy of the Blessed Virgin. It would be rash to imagine another author. An impostor or a deceiver could not attain this purity of craftsmanship. Such a ruse would have produced an encumbered theology and muddled logic and would have been clearly overcautious.

This ring of truth is further enhanced if we attend to the tone of the discourse.

There is in this message something direct and concrete, simple and vibrant, bringing it wondrously in tune with the "people" it speaks to and with the heart that speaks it. One senses that it is spoken by a real person to other persons no less real in such a way as to settle between them a personal and specific matter.

We rarely hear the vocabulary of the supernatural used by people who really belong to it. The entire abstract nomenclature of the catechism—sin, blasphemy, hell, justice, punishment—we use admittedly with some distancing. The Lady of La Salette does not use it at all. But she speaks of these things as someone who deeply feels their reality and is very involved with them. Everything she says about them reveals an experience. From the depths of her being come the telling words: *"How long have I suffered for you!"* "The words of the Virgin in the Gospel" noted Father Philpin, "rarely assume dogmatic overtones and appear remarkable more by the seeds of divine life they contain than by their own importance." (7) Likewise at La Salette, when she speaks to us of her role in heaven there is between us and her a direct contact of souls more than of minds.

But she is speaking to human beings and she must show them she also belongs to the earth. To be Mediatrix is to belong to two worlds. To bring her hearers to realities that no longer touch them, she adopts their language, relies on words and images familiar to them. She uses concrete words, carnal words, as Péguy might have said. Like Maximin and his father on the road to Corps, she reminded them, in a vocabulary they can relate to, of what they were doing as they drove carts or harvested potatoes: *"You swore, you abused my Son's name."* In a language stripped of medical jargon she jarred them in their own flesh when she said: *"Children under seven years of age will be seized with trembling and die in the arms of parents holding them."* But they feel her very close to them and to their human race as they realize, by the words she uses, how deeply the Lady shares their misfortune: *"You took two or three ears of wheat in your hands. You rubbed them and they crumbled to dust."* Then she expressed peasant resignation: *"Well, my son, eat some bread this year anyhow."* Then comes an image of incredible prosperity, the secret yearning of every peasant, of all of these mountain people who scratch out a meager existence from the rocky soil of the Corps countryside: *"The stones will become piles of wheat and it will be found that the potatoes have sown themselves."* It is the biblical expression of heavenly abundance adapted to the dreams of our western land-clearer's as the "streams of milk and honey" were to the shepherds of Canaan.

The thrust of the discourse also focuses on experience. Abstract theorists would probably wish for a more pronounced distinction between what is said to the children and what concerns the people. Laurent the haberdasher, boasting literary skills, separates material concerning the people from words concerning the children. This distinction, however, is everywhere in the tone.

When the beautiful Lady addressed the children she spoke to them directly, with an affection that filled them with happiness: *"Come near, my children... You don't understand, my children?"* She recognized

their negligence in religious matters and this added a little gravity to her tenderness: "Ah, my children, it is very important to do so." When the beautiful Lady looks beyond the children and speaks to the people, this people is present there and is also challenged in a collective "you" that leaves no doubt as to whom she is addressing. And when she said vous autres, there is an added nuance of reproach and of disappointed tenderness.

In reality, the discourse is not a monologue. She is conversing with the children and challenging her people to a response. She passes from the first to the second without ever losing contact with either. This is the manner she prefers because it is so close to life and reality. At one point, as she speaks to the people, Mélanie's inability to understand allows the Lady to manifest concern: *"You do not understand French, my children. Well then, listen. I will put it differently."* One question she asks them allows her to return to the topic of the observance of Sunday. *"Do you say your prayers well, my children?... Only a few elderly women go to Mass in the summer."*

Perrin and Cat, who might have consulted one another before writing their accounts, place this warning after the first reproaches

concerning Sunday and blasphemy. These men are an example of abstract theorists. The flow of ideas and textual criticism overrule their objections. There is no longer question that the day of the Lord be seen as a debt to be repaid in justice; the prayer consecrating this day and the respectful inner disposition that must enliven it are what matter. After this, we are quite naturally called to a spirit of penance (*"During Lent, they go to the butcher shop like dogs."*) This living unity of the discourse provides a much more cogent proof of its authenticity than do labored and artificial divisions.

And it is such a simple style, with few obvious transitions and no sentence requiring long concentration. The syntax uses few subordinate clauses conditional, temporal or relative commonly known to her people. The rest of the sentences are independent statements, complete and straightforward in themselves. The Messenger adapts herself to the thought patterns of her listeners and thus maintains contact with them to the very end. All who have spoken this message before a Christian audience have seen with what attention it was absorbed. They have seen its power to reach hearts. With words such as these, the heart of the Virgin speaks to our own.

Some say that the Lady did not communicate with the two children. How could the Queen of heaven not know that the little mountain children had no knowledge of French? Indeed, what an objection there was in this avowed misunderstanding: *"You do not understand, my children? Well, then, I shall put it differently."*

As we recall, she communicated so well with her two witnesses that they seemed to "eat her words." But she communicated with them differently than with her people. Neither Maximin nor Mélanie were the true addressees of her message. They were heralds, go-betweens. The beautiful Lady prepared them for the role they would play, and she made of this very preparation a sign for her people. Under the guise of a familiar conversation she disposed them to an awareness of the supernatural character of what they saw and heard. From the outset she showed them that she could see their hidden anxieties. *"Come near, my children, do not be afraid."* Again, with concern she answered Mélanie's unspoken question about potatoes: *"You do not understand. I shall put it to you differently."* Father Giraud, in his Pratique de la Devotion, compares this behavior with that of Our Lord in the Gospel before the multiplication of loaves, when Jesus asks: "How many loaves of bread do you have?" Our Lord and the Virgin speak as ordinary people do. For the people to whom the message was addressed, there is this advantage: they will see the wonder of two poor shepherds, whose ignorance is well-known, able to repeat these admirable words in a language totally unfamiliar to them.

It should be further noted that the beautiful Lady expressed in French that part of her message containing matters of principle and in dialect that which held a more restricted meaning. The latter illustrated the former. The shift in idiom highlighted the order of ideas. Had people noted this difference sooner, attention might have more quickly been focused on essentials, on the broad views of Mary's mediation, rather than on threats and promises whose realization was awaited with anxiety or mockery.

It would be ill advised, however, to regret the children's incomprehension of the French part of the discourse. True, Mélanie did admit to repeating all this "like a parrot" **(8)** or "a bit like when she read Latin at Vespers, for example." **(9)** But she provided an answer to potential scruples: "Even when I did not understand well," she told Lagier, "when I repeated what she said, those who understood French learned about it. That was enough for me, even if I didn't understand." **(10)** Far from showing a lack of adaptation, the beautiful Lady's strategy served a twofold purpose: the communication of her message by her two little heralds as well as the conversion of her people.

We could pursue this analysis further. What is important, though, is not so much to dissect but to understand the inner unity of the text as well as the intangible, quickening element called tone. What we have said will hopefully convince a reader to listen to Maximin and Mélanie's beautiful Lady with a simple heart, without prejudice, seeking to recognize her by the sound of her voice. The learned can be put off here. There is a type of criticism which consists of cutting up a text into little pieces, eagerly seeking to find in some far distant reference the source of a line or of a section of verse. Four matching, identical words make one a plagiarist. Pascal was also called a shell picker. He compared himself to a handball player using the same ball his opponents used but placing it better. "I would prefer," he said, "to be told I am a user of ancient words. As if the same ideas did not form a different whole by a different disposition of parts. In the same way, the same words form different ideas by being disposed differently." Other ideas result in a different whole, and another ring, would he have said, had he known what more than anything else attracts us to him.

In any case, the people were not misled. For them, the discourse was signed. Under the harshness of the reproaches and threats as well as under the lavish promises and the concerned watchfulness that followed Maximin, the people heard the same heartbeat. In each word of the discourse was the same persistent cry: "Forever have I been suffering for you."

The conclusion is clear. The La Salette discourse, by the nature of its concepts and their coherence in a single whole, by its vivid, concrete form marvelously adapted to its audience and to its purpose, and finally by its tone and ring, can, from the viewpoint of internal criticism, claim the character of authenticity attributed to it by Bishop de Bruillard when he declared that "the apparition of La Salette bears within itself all the characteristics of truth."

We have dealt at some length on the discourse because in the complex fact of La Salette, it represents, for the cerebral types we are, the outstanding element. But one might also give as much scrutiny to the scenario in which the message was expressed. From a critical point of view, it is most important to know whether the scenario and the discourse complement or contradict one another. One cannot accept the viewpoint of those who speak the final word on La Salette by calling the discourse apocryphal and yet have overlooked this challenge. Indeed, it has been historically proven that from their earliest accounts, the little shepherds gave at least a summary description of their Lady and of her conduct and actions. (11) From the mystical point of view, for the person searching out the Blessed Virgin's intentions, the scenario itself might illustrate more clearly what is not grasped in the discourse.

Only with great difficulty could a Christian artist describe the inner dispositions of a heavenly being, who is attempting in her glory to tell us that her predominant characteristic is to have been the most distressed creature who ever was. Whoever would illustrate the discourse would have to enflesh this twofold reality in visual symbols, blend both in a living harmony and a perfectly balanced whole. Our eyes of flesh must be allowed to see Mary's power of intercession, the title that justifies it and gives her the right to speak to us as well as the hope of reaching us. That title is her unfathomable compassion. For an artist with the background of a theologian, the task would be difficult. Here is how the beautiful Lady of Maximin and Mélanie fulfilled it.

She appears in the midst of glory. "It was as if the sun had fallen there," was Mélanie's first impression. A double halo of light envelops her as her outline slowly appears, the closest light seeming to radiate from her. She is weeping, but her tears disappear in light. Literally, she is decked in glory. Her dress and her shoes are speckled with light. The crucifix and the golden braid on the shawl are dazzling. Everything is bathed in light. The poverty of their vocabulary forces the shepherds to speak of a yellow apron, yellow stockings, reddish buckles. But Maximin had been so filled with the scene that twenty years later he preferred to say that all of this was light, all light. The Virgin could not show us more clearly that in the unchanging glory she inhabits, mourning is gone and suffering is transformed. "Her voice was not broken by her sobs and as she wept her face did not grimace," Mélanie candidly tells Lagier. Her movements dispense with the laws of gravity. She glides above the blades of grass without bending them. We are clearly being told that this person is happily free of the vicissitudes of earthly life.

Still, she had to show us her suffering, had to move us, and to reveal it to us in such a way that we feel a part of it and that even now we are able to affect it. Time does not exist between her and us. On Calvary, on the day in which her motherhood was fulfilled, she bore each one of us in her maternal bosom, according to the expression of Grignion de Montfort, in order to create us anew in the image of her Son. The nineteen centuries separating us from this meeting with her are only the thin veil of time. This encounter remains an unchanging and ever-present reality in that she still suffers for us regardless of our docile obedience or our proud obstinacy. "How long have I suffered for you." She can direct this cry to any person born on this earth. Yet it is a cry she utters only at La Salette, and it has to appear on a face gripped with sorrow.

She appears on this deserted mountain sitting on the shepherd's stone bench, her elbows on her knees and her face in her hands. Generations of pilgrims, seeing this statue of her at a turn in the path, believed that they were hearing the prophet: "Come, all you who pass this way, look and see whether there is any suffering like unto mine."

In the central scene of the conversation, as she tells of her mediation and the limits imposed upon it by our sin, the young shepherds see her tears flow. They are amazed by the modesty of her dress and of her demeanor, but both agree that the Christ resting on her breast seems to be the focal point of all her glory. She has identifying hallmarks: three garlands of roses recall her title of Queen of the Holy Rosary; and an apron, a headdress, a shawl are signs of her choosing to remain with the people, especially the little people whose misfortune touches her. We can sense that this shimmering Crucified Christ pervades all her thoughts, her tears, and her entire penitential demeanor. And the tongs to the right and the hammer to the left of the crossbar poignantly recall our choice of atonement or of sin in our ongoing role in the Lord's Passion. Facing this scene we can better understand the challenge the Lady of Compassion places before us: *"No matter how well you pray in the future, no matter how well you act, you will never be able to make up to me what I have endured on your behalf."*

Between the scene of the conversation and her disappearance into glory, there occurs a unique trek up the side of the ravine. It harks back to the way of the cross. We too easily scoff at mystical interpretations. This one has a foundation. The Lady must have had a reason for tracing an open "S" pathway to the top of the ravine. She might have walked straight up or followed one of the two paths leading to the summit. It is not surprising that, before rising to heaven, Mary should follow the general configuration of the painful way her Son trudged in Jerusalem from the Pretorium to Calvary. This very action teaches us a lesson embedded in the heart of the apparition.

This entire scenario as described by the shepherds is very coherent. What is most remarkable is that it develops in tandem with the discourse. The dominant themes of Mediation and Compassion are not only made more moving by the power of the image, but are also enlightened by a deeper insight. Each element has a place of its own and its own importance. In this way, the most uneducated of Christians, starting with the two shepherd children, can grasp the whole meaning of the apparition. Any critical examination of the La Salette event must recognize the organic unity of word and action and acknowledge therein its supernatural origin.

In the end, the fact of La Salette, as the historian can grasp it, comes forth this way: one afternoon, Maximin and Mélanie came down from the mountain with a story that they could never have thought up. There is no choice but to see that their minds have been filled with something out of the ordinary, immeasurably stretched beyond whatever might be expected of them. We know them. With the help of the most diverse observers we have been able to gauge their natural abilities. We will not go over this ground once more.

How could these ungifted children have suddenly become theologians juggling abstract dogma, or preachers speaking with charisma and authority, or artists able to see intellectually conceived realities?

Such is the question internal criticism asks the psychologist. There is no natural explanation for such sudden giftedness. Moreover, the question here is one of enrichment, not growth or development, since the progress has been clearly circumscribed to one area. Beyond the area of the event they relate, they have not changed. If we carefully take into account the two givens of the phenomenon, namely the children's original level of growth and knowledge and the nature of the narrative, we readily concede that the apparition has an outside, objective cause, foreign to the children. It would be morally impossible to have such an account come from their own minds. Groping for causes in the infinite possibilities of abnormal psychology and psychopathology means taking refuge in mythology. Whether they were normal or abnormal, the principle of causality demands that these children previously possess at least the seed elements of their story.

Yet, could there have been other causes? Might the daily life of this remote countryside have somehow affected the subconscious mind of these children? Could the famous "letter from heaven" have stricken Mélanie's fanciful imagination?

The literary characteristics of this mediocre piece of writing, in reality a fabricated sales pitch used to rekindle Sunday observance, are such that whoever might hope to fashion a discourse remotely resembling that of La Salette would do best by dismissing the idea outright. Even a gifted impostor would find it excess baggage. An ignorant child would be hopelessly lost. In religious content, in style, in structure and tone, the letter from heaven is as different from the La Salette message as night is from day. The two texts might have expressions in common but the similarities are so random and so merely verbal and accidental that they can be discounted.

In summary, the letter is a lifeless piece. It could not be the seed from which would come the clear, admirable discourse we have examined. The harmony between the external scenario and the discourse could only be the work of a veritable religious genius. Who could have successfully taught these children, barely able to recite the *Our Father* and the *Hail Mary*, to retell in sight and sound the orthodox concepts of the Mediation and Compassion of Our Lady? Lagier's interviews with Mélanie prove that the children still had not understood the meaning of the discourse two months after the apparition. They could have described a smiling Virgin. They could have filled their story with childish and grotesque imaginings. The investigation proved also that no chapel in the region could have provided an image or model of the Virgin so characteristic of Our Lady of La Salette wearing on her breast the crucifix with hammer and tongs.

Then there is the whole world of hallucination, "an unstable, uncertain, mysterious universe, where, it is said, a light, strange but identical to the light of day, shines on wonders never seen." (12) The impression given is that of an intellectual hyperactivity able to draw fantastic combinations from the stores of memory.

We shall not undertake to decide whether in terms of descriptive psychology Maximin and Mélanie's vision is related or not to hallucination, that is, to perception without object. Whatever awareness of reality the two witnesses may have had, their eyes could possibly have seen images and their ears heard sounds caused by no external stimulus. Theologians say that the value of prophetic revelation is not measured by the sensible images that express it but by the truths it reveals. The value of a revelation is measured by the power it has to draw us to God. Whether the vision follows an objective or subjective manner of perception changes nothing of its supernatural nature, as long as what finally emerges is a truth exceeding the knowledge and natural capabilities of the subject. (13) The matter of knowing to which of the two modes La Salette belongs is therefore secondary. Moreover, there probably is no answer to the question because we do not know God's secrets. The only sure and important thing is that we could speak of hallucination here only in a very special sense, inasmuch as God's supernatural intervention would be as necessary as if the vision were objective.

Natural hallucinations, if we may so speak of pathological symptoms, require a relaxed state of consciousness as a precondition. This was certainly not the case for the two children between their awakening from sleep and the time they first saw the brightness. Their entire consciousness was directed to one purpose: finding their flocks.

Maximin's warning, "Keep your stick, Mélanie," shows no openness to invading outside images. In the course of the apparition, they have normal and expected reactions to the words of the Lady, to her departure, to her disappearance. In this extraordinary world they have just entered, they react in their normal, day-to-day behavior, very attentively and not in a tense, artificial manner. In any case, multisensory hallucinations are rare and there is no record of one simultaneously affecting two persons with such precise and varied images. Natural hallucinations especially do not have results such as those manifested in the children. In every case, incoherence is the price paid for this kind of intellectual exaltation experienced by victims of illness or drug abuse. Labels are not important. Some insist on the term hallucination to describe what might have been the children's manner of perception at La Salette (do not all apparitions present the same problem?). But the coherence, the lofty meaning, the religious impact of their story give evidence that if hallucination there was, it cannot be explained by natural causes.

The Lamerlière Trial

We can conjecture endlessly. Maximin and Mélanie's account requires an external cause, hence the supposition arose that a secret person might have planned everything while they served as accessories or victims. What immediately comes to mind when one decides not to be duped is to imagine that the children were tricked by some conspirator who would have played the role of the beautiful Lady. The civil authority of the day had first followed that lead without success. After the interrogation by Long, Giraud the registrar, meeting Father Mélin one day, confided to him his suspicion of his neighbor d'Ambel. It was later discovered, however, that the neighbor did not believe in La Salette. **(14)** Later, after having maintained that

Maximin and Mélanie had seen nothing on the mountain, Déléon presented the Lamerlière fable, propping it up with outrageous lies that quickly collapsed in a hearing conducted by Jules Favre. Poor Miss Lamerlière really had no need to turn to the courts for compensation in a defamation of character suit. The children's account relieved her of all suspicion. It is difficult to imagine Miss Lamerlière, "more than ordinarily obese," **(15)** and having long passed her fiftieth year, attempting to play the ethereal Lady of the apparition, brushing the blades of grass as she walked, surrounding herself with light and disappearing into the heavens. In fact, we cannot imagine her or anyone else inventing the scenario and the discourse of the apparition and implanting it in the children's sieve-like memories. Surely Déléon jests. His entire argument is extraneous to the fact he seeks to explain. Those who believed him in good faith showed that they had not understood the real issue.

Mademoiselle de Lamerlière, falsely accused of dressing as Mary during the actual Apparition

One might still imagine the children learning their role from a hidden third party. We can actually weigh the chances of success this scheme might have had. Where could one have found this mysterious stranger? Would he have been an ordinary person? An intellectual? A clergyman? An anti-clerical? One should have some suspect in mind. Is it not strange that not a trace of this mystery-person has ever been found? He had to have been a highly skilled pedagogue besides. His successful gambit was great enough to have lured him out of the shadows. One might as well conclude that, historically, this hypothesis is purely gratuitous. Compare this with the positive data we possess: two children, known to everyone, who at a given time claim responsibility for their story. "We say only what

168

we have seen and heard." They repeated this during the five years of the investigation and for the rest of their lives. Early in any interrogation one is made aware that they are not reciting a lesson but a lived event. Their simple reactions mark every gesture and almost every word of their beautiful Lady: keep your stick, we were no longer afraid, I thought it was a lady from Valjouffrey, I was about to ask Maximin what potatoes were, etc. They answer the Lady's questions, describe the path they had walked with her, their position, their actions, their feelings, and their words. Can one seriously think that all of this was suggested to them, or that they invented it all to tighten their instructor's plan? There are simply too many spontaneous reactions and they are all too true-to-life.

One could imagine many mysterious strangers instead of only one. In his fertile falsehood Déléon points to that possibility without ever exploiting it himself. He suggests that the legend gained strength by the concerted action of the people of Corps and of La Salette. Lagier himself, the discerning Lagier, allows himself to be swept up by the desire to gift his compatriots with a lucrative, miniature California. Déléon forgets to explain how the purported sacrilegious scheming of an entire population was not given away by a single honest person or by a malcontent. However, if someone wanted to assign Maximin and Mélanie's story to a collection of editors, then he or she would have to explain how, from such massive, collective ignorance and indifference, such a flawless masterpiece of religious experience could have emerged.

Yes, an endless series of hypotheses can be proposed to explain naturally the event of La Salette. Besides the fact that they all lack historical basis, they also practically all need miracles to maintain an intrinsic likelihood, so difficult is it to counterfeit the perfection of the discourse and the scenario as well as their intimate harmony. Think of the theology, the imagination, the simplicity of soul, the precision and intricacy of detail needed to blend all the elements of this complex symphony. More exactly perhaps, what such a story would need is an individual endowed with all of the religious experience of the person appearing, namely of the Virgin Mary herself. It is easier for the Christian to believe in an intelligible miracle than in an absurd one.

There are signs in the life of the believer that are valid for him or her alone. Even if a particular event occurring as the result of a certain prayer cannot be presented to an unbeliever as an argument, the believer can still logically see it as a response from Providence confirming his faith. Such is the case for the set of circumstances surrounding the apparition relative to the fact itself. Every fact and detail, and each on its own strength, becomes a sign for one who has discerned the presence of the Virgin within the event and the message of La Salette.

The children following the mountain paths to the Planeau on the morning of September 19, 1846 had no idea that this day was the last of the fall Ember Days and that on this afternoon the universal Church would sing the first Vespers of the feast of Our Lady of Seven Dolors. The affinity between the mystery of the apparition and the liturgical circumstances is obvious. The children's ignorance in this matter need not be shown. Neither can it be considered very likely that an impersonating accomplice would have chosen precisely this day and this hour to put his plan in motion as well.

The harmony between the apparition and its scenic framework is felt by every pilgrim. At this altitude, surrounded by a mountain fortress blocking out the city, the spirit is naturally recollected. Already prepared by silence and solitude to listen to God, one has no trouble understanding that it is fitting to weep over sin.

But many other mountains could have inspired the same awe and prepared pilgrims for the cleansing act of grace. Why was this one chosen?

Probably because the Virgin of La Salette, following the example of her Son, came to save what was lost. As much as anyone, we believe in the universal relevance of the message. However, what we do know of the religious climate of the Corps region at the time of the apparition leads us to think that the choice of this site by the Mother of divine grace is due to the special love of the Good Shepherd for the lost sheep. When the beautiful Lady complains of the neglect of God, of people's contempt for Him, she certainly condemns all forms of blasphemy, the subtle and the crude, that of the written word as well as that of the cart drivers. But her reproaches are directed primarily to compatriots of Maximin and Mélanie, among whom *"only a few rather old women go to Mass, and who cannot swear without bringing in my Son's name."* She was literally speaking to them. In 1846, the Corps region was already the mission country that half of all our French rural districts have now become. Father Champon writes:

> *The spirit of insubordination, the blasphemous language, the desecration of Sunday, the avoidance of penance, the neglect of Lenten fast and abstinence, an unbridled love of public pleasure and drinking places such was the moral state of our people. Corps, the county seat, was especially notorious for all of these disorders and led all the surrounding communities down the primrose path to perdition. Two examples illustrate this.*

> *A clergyman could not walk through the town without being insulted. The sacraments were abandoned to the point where only two men performed their Easter duty, and that very early on a weekday to escape being ridiculed by others.*

> *Dance parties and balls were publicly organized and even presided over by the town's magistrates. The patronal feasts of Corps and of its neighboring parish, Saint Jean-des-Vertus, had become a particularly scandalous time of the year. During fifteen days there was nothing but dancing. Not even the frightful fire that consumed Corps in 1822 and motivated a general diocesan aid collection managed to interrupt similar goings-on. The sound of the violin accompanied the felling of trees used to rebuild the area.* (16)

Could not this deep spiritual misery justify a special intervention by God if one considers such an action in the light of the Gospel? "I have not come to call the just but sinners." We cannot overlook the fact that the conversion of the Corps region was one of the most remarkable results of the apparition.

"We have just had a clear proof of the good influence of the apparition in the entire area," wrote Father Mélin to his bishop early in the summer of 1847. "Saint-Jean-des-Vertus, a shrine of faith and of miracles, as its name seems to indicate, saw similar disorders and scandalous behavior every year on its patronal feast of June 24. This year, the feast was celebrated very religiously and there were far more people on the mountain than at Saint-Jean's. They went to the mountain to get away from carousing and to pray."

"There was still the feast of Saint Peter, everywhere remembered for drunkenness, dancing, the deafening din of musical instruments, day and night, from the eve until the following morning. This year, everything took place in church. No music was heard elsewhere. No one danced. What touched me most was the joy everyone felt afterward. It proved to me that their conduct was born of deep conviction and that it would endure. May God grant it and Mary come to our aid!" (17)

During the meetings which took place at the bishop's house in 1847, Canon Rousselot approved Father Mélin's and his colleague's collected testimonies bearing on the past as well as on the present. He highlighted the "prompt and sustained conversion" of the whole township and its environs in favor of the apparition. On Ascension day the previous year, not one man had been present in church; now many came prayerfully. (18) Explaining how conversion might have warded off famine, he stated that in the Corps township, with a population of five to six thousand people, hardly one hundred had not returned to church. (19)

That such a mountain-place of reconciliation should renew this ungrateful earth does not constitute proof for the unbeliever but it is a sign for the believing person. If, then, the hoped-for intervention occurred, it cannot be attributed to a hoax perpetrated by Maximin and Mélanie. Could such innocent, ignorant, and religiously indifferent children have known how much this little township needed healing?

La Salette is Truly Unique

The apparition of La Salette has its own individuality. Historically, it is dependent on no other private revelation. Since no human influence was brought to bear on its witnesses, it would be pointless to conjure up arguments against it from a parallel incident about which some readers might still wonder. We believe it to be all the more impressive that the authenticity of La Salette comes from its own inner characteristics and its very uniqueness.

In the time during which Mélanie and Maximin lived their carefree lives in the Corps township, a nun called Sister Marie de Saint-Pierre was favored with extraordinary graces and was revered at the Carmel of Tours. On November 24, 1843, Our Lord had told her after Holy Communion: "The holy name of God is blasphemed and the holy day of Sunday is desecrated. This is the height of evil. These sins have risen to the throne of God and have provoked His anger which is ready to lash out if His justice is not appeased. Never have these crimes been so flagrant. I strongly desire that an approved and organized association be founded to honor the name of my Father." **(20)**

Many times, Christ spoke insistently to his servant, the Bishop Morlot of Tours, convinced of the truth of these revelations after a long investigation, was still putting off establishing the desired association. At Christ's persistent urging, and wondering what her role regarding sinners might be, this good Sister was told one day that she was in charge of the entire country of France.

"I saw then," wrote the sister, "that the only hope and effectiveness I had lay in prayer through Mary's powerful intercession. I recited the Rosary each day to obtain the salvation of France and to begin atonement in all the cities of the country. All my prayers, all my communions, my desires, all my thoughts were directed toward this work so dear to me. I would have wanted, had this been possible, to proclaim throughout all of France the misfortunes that threatened my countrymen. I suffered so much from being the sole confidante of such an important task, one that I am obliged to hold within the silence of the cloister! Holy Virgin, please appear to someone in the world and share with him or her what was said to me about France." **(21)**

Our Lord continued speaking with her and revealed to her his Holy Face as a perfect means of atonement. "The face of France has become hideous to my Father. Offer him the Face of his Son in whom he is well pleased."

Thereupon followed a long silence. Sister Saint-Pierre received no word in prayer from March 23 to October 4, 1846. Early in September, a friend of the Carmel, Father Dupont, journeyed to his home in Brittany and stopped by the Convent to take some errands from the Prioress.

"I was obliged," he related, "to write down quite a long list of errands she was giving me. Then we spoke of Sister Marie de Saint-Pierre. "Here is what she has just told me" adds the Reverend Mother. As I already had pencil in hand, I wrote down what follows: "Our Lord, speaking to the Sister, said: "My Mother has spoken to people of my anger. She wants to calm it. She has shown me her breast and said to me: "Here is the breast that nourished you; let it lavish blessings on my other children." Then, filled with mercy, she went to speak to earth. Have confidence in her." **(22)**

"This is mysterious language," thought Dupont, "where the past blends with the present and the future. Yet, it became clear to me when I received the first letter from the parish priest of Corps, on October 22 of that same year, relative to the apparition of the Blessed Virgin at La Salette on September 19. It was the fulfillment of the prophecy of the first days of September. I made a copy of it and hurriedly sent it to the parish priest of Corps who in turn replied: I believed from the very first day. Today, if I can so speak, I believe twice as much.'"

Naturally, the Carmelite of Tours looked upon this as a striking confirmation of the mission confided to Sister Saint-Pierre.

In the course of the following months Our Lord repeated His requests but intimated that success was at hand. Finally, on May 5,

1847, He told her that He had placed all things in the hands of the Most Blessed Virgin and that the Sister was to have recourse to her powerful intercession.

> *Very confidently, I turned to this Mother of mercy, begging her to be my advocate in God's cause, fervently commending this great work to her during the beautiful month of May. I had not prayed to her Son in vain. She considered the tears of her servant. Soon she inspired the Bishop of Langres, who had heard of the project, to take a lively interest in it.* **(23)**

When he heard of the wishes of Sister Saint-Pierre, Bishop Parisis admitted that he had also been "preoccupied with this kind of idea, and had wanted to found a similar confraternity in his diocese." He had previously heard one of his priests, Father Marche, parish priest of Saint-Martin-de-la-Noue at Saint Dizier, tell him of the conviction he had brought back with him from La Salette and of his desire to react against the two great crimes denounced by the beautiful Lady: the desecration of Sunday and blasphemy.

Father Marche was thus referred to the Carmel of Tours and then sent to Rome to ask that the new work be given the title of archconfraternity. Pius IX granted the request enthusiastically and requested that his name be the first in the register of members. He also granted a plenary indulgence for the recitation of the divine praises with which benediction of the Blessed Sacrament still terminates to this day.

Writing to Bishop de Bruillard on September 11, 1847, Bishop Parisis declared unequivocally that La Salette had been the determining factor in his decision. "While awaiting a canonical decision, it seemed to me that we could not atone soon enough for the two great crimes indicated in the children's declaration at Corps. To this end, I have established in my diocese a confraternity which Pius IX, by a brief issued on July 30, has erected as an archconfraternity with many indulgences."

Two paths from heaven thus crossed and led to the same goal. They quickened Christian piety with the same spirit of atonement. Between them no human dependence was ever established. A true joy for any believer.

We cannot offer any judgment on the revelations of the Carmelite from Tours. The least one can say is that around 1846 a saintly nun in her cloister felt the need to atone for the capital sins of France—the desecration of Sunday and blasphemy, the neglect of God or contempt for Him. The ecclesiastical hierarchy recognized that in this she was led by the Spirit of God. This spiritual diagnosis is confirmed for us in the general history of that era. (24) The intervening event of La Salette, the complaints of the beautiful Lady, lightly held by some, are rather a sign of credibility for anyone gauging as an historian and as a Christian the depth and the breath of the evil it condemned.

-9-
The Incident at Ars

Various forms of inquiry have each brought us to the same conclusion: La Salette can only be explained supernaturally. The children's testimony, the Virgin's discourse, and the miracles all point to the single conclusion that moral certainty must result from the fabric of these tightly woven elements, barring any valid opposition. We have followed the path marked out for us by the canonical judge and we have seen the inherent weaknesses of more than one objection. Might the Ars incident present a more serious problem? It was tenaciously used against Bishop de Bruillard and there is no doubt that to this day its shadow still clouds the perception that many Christians have of La Salette. We will attempt to clarify Maximin's conduct in order to assess honestly the impact of the incident.

Adolescence is universally characterized by instability, rebelliousness, and contradiction. But in Maximin's case these traits were exacerbated by a whole combination of unfortunate circumstances. This must be taken into consideration if we are to understand his attitude toward the saintly priest of Ars. A mature person in touch with the

Rectory of Curé of Ars in Ars-sur-Formans, France; photo: Benoît Prieur

vicissitudes of a 15 year-old boy will not be shocked by the sudden mood changes and the urge for self-expression which underlie this unfortunate misunderstanding. Such a person knows the unpredictable behavior of this age. He can see brittle self-confidence give way to bruised feelings at a single word and move beyond the point of no return to the savoring of the shock value of rejecting proffered friendship. Maximin gave in to this kind of impulse but with mitigating circumstances. Hence the necessity of providing this story with more background.

In the spring of 1850 Maximin was no longer the lightheaded boy, the endearingly repentant dynamo described by early writers. He was in his fifteenth year. The three years of sheltered life with the Sisters weighed heavily on him. His adventures had consisted in shuttling between convent and rectory where he muddled through Father Mélin's tutoring. He strove hard to take on the schoolboy's discipline but also found ingenious ways to escape it. The mountains and the woods beckoned to him from beyond the narrow alleys of Corps. He fidgeted with the need to run, to climb, to be free, to escape the convent walls and the cloying tenderness within.

One day, the inevitable happened. He took to the open fields. It was a first violation and the panic-stricken Sisters lectured him severely then covered up the whole escapade. The second offense was reported to the pastor who reported it to the guardian, and the heavy hand of Uncle Templier impressed upon the delinquent boy the advantages of the sedentary life. (1) The third flight was longer in coming but of longer duration. To escape his uncle's clutches, Maximin walked as far as Les Ablandins and hired out as a domestic with Baptiste Pra, who after three days brought the prodigal son back. Father Mélin then served notice that this was to be the last prank he would tolerate. But Maximin's natural craving for freedom erupted a fourth time. After this he had to abandon Latin and the Sisters and was exiled to Uncle Templier's drab tenement. It was like going from prison to solitary confinement. The guardian kept his charge on a very short leash in order to prevent future escapes.

Toward the end of August, an enterprising Marist brother named

Bonnefous visited La Salette. He was a friend of Baron de Richemont who dreamed of doing great things with Maximin. He offered the distraught boy a place with the Marist Fathers in Lyons. The guardian and the child readily agreed, the one more than happy to find a place for his charge, the other yearning to discover new horizons. Bonnefous went back to Lyons, promising to return when the arrangements were complete.

Meanwhile, Templier took Maximin and his sister Angélique on a trip during which the shrewd mind of the guardian discovered an unsuspected source of revenue. He had traveled to Crémieu to ask a maternal grand uncle to be the young girl's guardian. The plan never materialized, but enroute, Maximin was recognized by the Count of Certeau who offered them the hospitality of his castle at Passins. Templier was impressed by this gesture and upon his return home spoke to Mélanie's father. Both agreed on the advantages of showing these well-known children far and wide. Nothing could have pleased Maximin more.

Bonnefous returned to Corps on the fourth anniversary of the apparition. He announced the consent of the Marists to lodge Maximin with the reservation that they could not defray the entire cost. Then and there, a colleague named Houzelot offered to make up the difference. Two other pilgrims, Verrier and Brayer, who were interested in the children of La Salette also volunteered to share in this charitable work.

Unfortunately, Bonnefous sought still further assurances, this time mystical ones. To be more certain of Maximin's vocation he had brought with him from Lyons the strangest seer one could imagine. He was Antoine Gay, a former Trappist brother, who had had to leave Aiguebelle because of some "nervous illness" and who now was reputed to be a devil worshiper. Cardinal de Bonald had confided him to the care of Father Chiron, a holy man forever in quest of self-giving and self-abasement. In 1850, this pair traveled every road in southern France and eventually came to La Salette. On the site of the apparition, in the presence of a few pilgrims, of Bonnefous's group, of Maximin and Mélanie, a scene at once grotesque and sublime took place. In a fiery sermon, Father Chiron sang of his confidence in Mary. He was interrupted by the "devil" who, in spite of himself, confessed the purity of the Immaculate Virgin in the voice and words of Antoine Gay. Maximin was afterwards brought before the poor man whose vaunted power could not read the boy's conscience nor discern his secret. It was quite an experience for an adolescent lacking the support of a normal home.

Bonnefous's friends were at best wary of his judgment and suggested consulting another adviser. Would not the Curé of Ars shed more light on Maximin's vocation? The boy agreed immediately. "I had asked to be brought to Ars to get away from my uncle," he declared at a later date.

(2)

Acceding to the pressure coming from all sides, Templier authorized an eight-day leave for Maximin. Father Mélin's was the only dissenting voice. With growing concern he had witnessed the scene with the possessed man and observed the overbearing solicitude of these people. He knew Maximin more than anyone, and he had the uneasy feeling that his time for stupidity had come. Yet there was nothing he could do to control Maximin's wanderlust.

On Sunday, September 22, Maximin boarded the coach in the company of Brayer and Verrier. They expected it to be a non-stop trip to Lyons, but at Grenoble the connecting coach had already left. They had to wait until the next day.

Monday morning, Maximin asked to visit Father Rousselot and Father Gerin, parish priest of the cathedral. Only Father Gerin was available. He saw Maximin at approximately five in the afternoon. Meanwhile, the bishop, aware of Maximin's whereabouts, had told Father Auvergne, his secretary, to attend the meeting. The bishop forbade the shepherd of La Salette to leave the diocese and ordered him to go to Saint Joseph, a school directed by the Brothers of the Christian Schools, while waiting for the opening of classes at the Rondeau minor seminary.

The frustrated group headed toward Saint Joseph. They were received by the Brother Superior. Maximin was restless. Verrier reasoned with him: "You must obey your bishop. You must give up the idea of going to Ars."

St. Joseph School near Corps, the first La Salette Seminary for poor boys

"Your youngster wouldn't by any chance be thinking of running away, would he?" asked the brother.

"I am not responsible," answered Verrier. The boy put up such a fuss that he was allowed to have dinner in the city with his protectors, after which he categorically refused to go back to Saint Joseph. Anger, tears, and all of the pent-up explosive force accumulated in him by the abnormal constraints of Corps finally overthrew all opposition. That same evening the party, Angélique included, set out for Lyons.

The travelers arrived in Ars around six-thirty in the evening of September 24. They went directly to the church where the saintly priest was praying his breviary. His curate, Father Raymond, after reading their letter of introduction, (3) told the visitors to wait for the pastor at Providence house. He would let them know when they could see the pastor.

Father Raymond had already visited La Salette and had come away with almost militantly negative biases. He had seen meat served at the Corps hotel on a Friday. He had witnessed dancing in the public square. He had concluded that Corps's much-publicized conversion was a fable. With but a little open-mindedness he could have seen these happenings as part of the celebration of the patronal feast. He had entered Father Mélin's rectory and had surprised him slipping correspondence under his napkin, had assumed that he was hiding meat, and had quickly concluded that the pastor was no better than his flock. The coup de grâce had fallen when Father Perrin, parish priest of La Salette, had not allowed Father Raymond to celebrate Mass for want of a *celebret*.

"I must say, Maximin," Father Raymond goaded, "you are more courteous than I am. I went to La Salette and I made no effort to see you. You come to Ars and you visit me. Come, my friend." (4) With this mocking tone, he led Maximin and his companions to his own room. Turning to Verrier whom he assumed to be the leader, he said, "Why are you bringing Maximin here? Would you perhaps think the Curé has some special revelation for him?" The child is not looking for any special revelation, Verrier answered, only some word of counsel from the Curé concerning his own future. (5)

"How can he be undecided on this matter?" responded Raymond, "if he has seen the Blessed Virgin, if she has spoken to him at length and given him a secret?" With that, he launched into a diatribe against La Salette, railing against the parish priest of Corps, against false miracles and false witnesses. The children of La Salette, he asserted, were liars, just like the three little girls, of whom the last one had just retracted herself at Ars eight days before. And he proceeded to tell them a bizarre story which, according to him, impressed Maximin. It is clear even from his own testimony (6) that he was excitable to the point of monologuing out loud and of not being able to distinguish between his own feelings and the reactions of his listeners. Even conceding the accuracy of his own version, the fact remains that he was unable to obtain a retraction from Maximin and that he had gone to the limits of provocation.

Two years later, Maximin, pressed by the Jesuits of La Louvesc to narrate the Ars incident, painted a scene which agreed with the testimony of those who spoke with Father Raymond that evening and the following days.

I've never seen anything quite as ludicrous and unseemly as that evening," wrote Father Rabilloud, who had been present, to Father

Rousselot.

Let me tell you about it, as Maximin himself described it so many times in my presence at Louvesc and elsewhere and before many other people. Maximin sat calmly in a corner of the room. Father Raymond paced the floor in every direction. He bluntly denied La Salette, ridiculed it, ran it down with a stream of disparaging descriptions.

"Wait," yells Maximin. "Let me tell you..."

"I know more than you do about La Salette. I know all about it's false miracles."

"But wait. Give me a chance. Then you can talk"

"What could you tell me that I don't already know? You didn't see a thing. You're nothing but a liar..."

After a half-hour of futile efforts to speak, Maximin sarcastically threw out the remark "Ah! You won't give me a chance to speak, so I grant you: I didn't see anything. Don't believe it." **(7)**

A parishioner of Ars named Azum de Bernétas attributed the following words to Raymond: "You see, Maximin, if you have the gall to maintain having seen the Blessed Virgin, you are a liar and there aren't enough thunderbolts in heaven to strike you." Maximin is said to have answered: "I never said I saw the Blessed Virgin. I said I had seen a beautiful Lady. But suppose I did lie. Why should I care?"

"Oh, well, now we agree. You only saw a beautiful Lady. That's all there is to it, and you came to Ars to retract."

"And so," added de Bernétas, "everyone agreed on what had been said that night, the next day, and on the following days. All repeated the very same story. Some people added that the curate ended with the following words about which there was some joking: "You only saw one beautiful Lady? I've seen more beautiful ones than you have!" Ending the interview, he dismissed the visitors and left to see his Curé, repeating as he went: "We must destroy La Salette. The child has contradicted himself," words that we would hear many times." **(8)**

That evening and the following morning, Father Raymond tormented the holy pastor with these so-called retractions. Harassing Maximin who was already in a contentious mood, turning Father Vianney against him, Father Raymond was setting the stage for the misunderstanding that was to come. Father Raymond is the person principally responsible for the Ars incident, and he cannot be excused for having been an excitable and easily provoked adolescent himself.

St. John Vianney (1786–1859), a friend of La Salette who lived nearby in Ars

Maximin did not appear more emotional than usual as he left for church on Wednesday, September 25. "Nothing," Brayer later wrote, "in his attitude or his actions, in his manner or his speech, betrayed the least worry or anxiety. At the very most, his features expressed desire and curiosity, but not tinged with anxiety." (9)

It was nine o'clock. The curé was in the sacristy blessing holy cards and rosaries. The crowd slowly left and Verrier entered alone with Maximin and locked the door behind him. Father Vianney sat down. Maximin knelt before him and spoke with the priest for some ten minutes. Verrier retreated to a corner of the room and knelt, blocking his ears and preparing his confession. Maximin rose and left. Verrier fell on his knees before the pastor and said to him: "Maximin will not have traveled here for nothing!"

"Are you happy?" Angélique asked her brother as he left the sacristy.

"So happy," answered Maximin, "that I would not exchange this trip for two hundred thousand francs." Indeed, he looked happy. (10)

Mrs. des Garets, the mayor's wife, saw him leaving the church. "Well, would you tell your secret to a bishop, to Bishop Dupanloup, for instance?" she asked.

"No "

"To our pastor?"

"I have already told him." **(11)**

After his confession, Verrier returned to the hotel. Maximin embraced him and repeated what he had told Angélique: "I couldn't be more satisfied if I had been given two hundred thousand francs." But the Curé of Ars had advised him, he said, to return to Grenoble and to do the bishop's bidding. Disappointed at this, the guardians brought him again to the church for further consultation. They thought the flighty boy had misunderstood the pastor.

Shortly before eleven o'clock, Maximin again met with the Curé of Ars behind the altar where the latter heard men's confessions before teaching catechism. He came out after a few minutes, repeating that he must return to his diocese. The group then prepared for the return trip on the two-o'clock coach to Lyons.

But rumors were flying in the village. The public ear had heard Father Raymond's comments. Brother Athanasius saw the Curé who told him, "If what Maximin told me is true, he has seen nothing." The Curé added that he had even demanded a written retraction. Maximin answered that he had maintained all this up to the present for the good of the people. He refused to recant. In the sacristy the brother found a sheet of paper on which the following words, not in the hand of the pastor, had been written: "I declare that..." and nothing more. The brother assumed this to be the beginning of the retraction. Maximin had not wanted to finish it. **(12)**

The directress of Providence house, Catherine Lassagne, had also come to the sacristy and had seen a much-preoccupied Curé. Maximin had told the Curé that he had seen nothing but that the belief should not be disturbed for the good of the people. **(13)**

Father Raymond bestirred himself and the news spread. A half hour after Maximin had left the pastor, the Count des Garets, on his way to church, met the assistant priest who was precisely on his way to the Count's home to inform him of the retraction. The mayor advised prudence, but in vain. The curate had spoken about it to everyone and was already writing to many people on the subject.

In the evening of the fateful day, Father Raymond walked the pastor back to the rectory. "Let this La Salette thing rest," said the saintly pastor very simply to his curate. But the next day Father Raymond found an occasion to settle the matter. Seeing in the sacristy a letter addressed to the Bishop of Grenoble, he asked the pastor what it meant.

"I had wanted," the pastor replied, "to give a letter of retraction to Maximin for the Bishop of Grenoble, but he refused to take it to him. He was unhappy with me. I was unhappy with him." Twice, Father Vianney told Father Raymond: 'If Maximin told me the truth, then he has not seen the Blessed Virgin." **(14)**

We already know how the curate used this disclosure and how much suffering it brought to the saint.

In Lyons, however, Maximin's friends felt somewhat embarrassed. In spite of Father Vianney's advice, their protégé refused to return to Grenoble. Did he dread his uncle Templier's grand plans for him? Did he have some idea of the storm he had unleashed? Waiting out the eight days allowed by the guardian, his companions paraded him through the legitimist salons of the Count de Richemont's following.

The opposition led by Cartellier and Déléon made much of this whole display. They maintained that Maximin, through his secret, identified the Baron de Richemont as the future Louis XVII, and that from the very beginning this had been the purpose of the entire La Salette story. In defense, Rousselot stressed the coincidental presence of so many supporters of de Richemont in the company of Maximin and right away concluded that a careful plan had been developed to kidnap the two children of La Salette. But the involved parties pointed to the fact that Mélanie had stayed behind in Corps. They vehemently denied the alleged intrigue, all the while remorsefully acknowledging the imprudence of disregarding the bishop's orders back in Grenoble. It must in turn be recognized that their responsibility in the Ars affair was purely incidental and that it basically changed nothing. They simply provided the opposition with a ready-made pretext which greatly complicated the whole question.

On Friday, September 27, Verrier and Brayer had decided to return Maximin to his guardian. By a happy coincidence, Father Bez learned from the pastor of Saint-Pierre that the child who had once so fascinated him was now in Lyons, staying at the hotel du Parc. He hurried there. Maximin ran to him and begged: "I want to stay with you. Take me wherever you want." In a few days, through the priest's efforts, Maximin was brought to the boarding school of Ecully directed by Father Collard. There, under the assumed name of Joseph Bez, nephew of Father Bez, he enjoyed three happy weeks, sheltered from all curiosity and indiscretion. His guardian was advised in order to obtain his consent, and Bishop de Bruillard was duly notified.

Mr. Dausse, the Bishop of Grenoble's emissary, arrived on Sunday, October 20. He brought with him an order summoning Maximin to the Rondeau minor seminary. The prodigal son finally returned home. He balked a little, perhaps anticipating what awaited him.

The rumors from Ars were now racing through Grenoble. At the end of October, Father Gerin, traveling through the "Roches de Condrieu," could not resist pushing on to Ars. The saintly pastor greeted him warmly (they were already acquainted) and related Maximin's conversations, suggesting that he report them to his bishop but to no one else. Father Raymond added his own inevitable comments. As a result, Bishop de Bruillard ordered Maximin to appear before a board of inquiry composed of clergy and laypeople, over which he himself would preside.

To questions from all sides, Maximin replied that he never recanted at Ars, that he will say what he has never stopped saying, what he would say on his deathbed, that he saw something at La Salette. Asked what he meant by "something," he answered, "A beautiful Lady who spoke to us and disappeared." He admitted not having heard the Curé of Ars clearly and of having answered "yes" and "no" indiscriminately.

In order to be more certain, Father Rousselot chose to question Maximin at his own apartment on November 1, and at the Rondeau seminary on the following day. Maximin repeated what he had said before the board. On November 2, he signed a statement in which the vicar general had summarized the conclusions of his interrogations.

> To render homage to the truth and for the greater glory of God, in honor of the Blessed Virgin, I, the undersigned, Maximin Giraud, testify to the following facts:
>
> 1. That I did not confess to the Curé of Ars.
> 2. That neither in the sacristy, nor behind the church altar of Ars, did the pastor question me on the apparition or on my secret; that he told me only two things: that I must return to my diocese, and that after such a grace I should be obedient.
> 3. That in none of the answers I gave to the pastor or to Father Raymond did I say anything contrary to what I have told thousands of others since September 19, 1846.
> 4. That I have never said that my secret concerned Louis XVII.
> 5. That I persist always in everything I said at the office of the Bishop of Grenoble, to the Bishop of La Rochelle, to Father Bez, to Father Mélin, pastor of Corps, and to many others on the fact of La Salette. In witness whereof, I sign this document, ready to testify to it under oath."

Minor Seminary of Grenoble, November 2, 1850.

(signed) Maximin Giraud.

Canon Henry of Grenoble also had the opportunity to test Maximin. Having met him at his niece's home, he drew him aside and said to him:

Canon Henry: "My little one, I have always liked you, but now I like you even more."
Maximin: "And why, Sir?"

Canon Henry: "Because today you are a good boy. Before this you were a little liar, but today you have just admitted having lied at Ars. Today, you have become a very sincere, a very honest boy."

Maximin: "But Sir, I never retracted."

Canon Henry: "We know better. You have retracted everything. This is why I now hold you in high esteem."
Maximin: "Sir, you are mocking me."

Canon Henry: "No, my friend, I am not mocking you."
Maximin: "Today, Sir, people laugh at La Salette, but it is like a flower we cover with dung and mud in the winter, but which in the spring or summer rises beautiful from the earth." (15)

But La Salette had another witness. The day after Maximin's testimony, Father Gerin, a member of the bishop's commission, went to Corenc to question Mélanie.

Father Gerin: "Well, Mélanie," said the priest abruptly, "you have been deceiving us for four years now! Maximin has just admitted to the parish priest of Ars that you both had seen nothing on the mountain.
Mélanie: "Oh! the wretch!" exclaimed the girl. "I myself will always say I have seen something."

Father Gerin: "And what do you mean by 'something'"?
Mélanie: "I mean a beautiful Lady who spoke to us and disappeared."

Father Gerin: "And she told you what you have been telling us now for four years?"
Mélanie: "Yes, sir."

She signed an affidavit which the emissary would later show to Bishop de Bruillard.

The Bishop of Grenoble did not confine himself to this. He sent Fathers Rousselot and Mélin as a delegation to the Curé of Ars. They were bearers of Maximin's statement at the end of which they had him write this postscript:

> *In addition, if I have revealed anything to the pastor of Ars, made any disclosure preventing him from believing in La Salette, or said anything which was related to this event, I willingly authorize him to make it known to Fathers Rousselot and Mélin.*

The Minor Seminary of Grenoble, November 6, 1850.

(signed) Maximin Giraud

The bishop's secretary, Father Auvergne, received this new document with its signature. Giving it to Father Rousselot, he reported the conversation he had had with Maximin. The boy wished to add a few words for the parish priest of Ars. "What do you want to write?" asked Father Auvergne. "Let me be," he said. "I will write: 'Reflect well on what you will say, in order to say all you have heard and not what you have not heard.'"

The Curé of Ars must have admitted to the official emissaries from Grenoble what he had already confided to a few of his acquaintances, because Maximin wrote again in response to his grievances.

Dear Father,

You have just told Canon Rousselot and the pastor of Corps that I have admitted having seen nothing and having lied as I narrated my story and that I have persisted in this untruth during three years because I saw the good it was doing.

You asked me for permission to share this avowal with the Bishop of Belley as well as for my address in order to write to me if necessary, and you added that after having given you the authorization and the address I withdrew both a moment later.

The report dictated to me by Father Rousselot proves that I was unable to make myself clear to you, Father. Allow me to say in sincerity that you misunderstood me completely.

I never meant to say, Father, and I have never told anyone seriously that I had not seen anything and that I had lied and persisted three years in this lie because I saw favorable effects.

As I left the sacristy, all I told you, Father, was that I had seen something and that I did not know whether it was the Blessed Virgin or another Lady. At that moment you met the crowd and our conversation stopped. Shortly after, I was sent to you again behind the altar, where you were hearing a man's confession, to ask you one more time if I should return to my diocese or remain in Lyons. You repeated that I should return to my diocese and you added a few words I could not understand. But I never heard you speak of the Bishop of Belley or ask me for my address. I am certain I did not give you my address or ask you to write to the Bishop of Belley.

I make this statement with a clear conscience and I am resigned to being expelled from the minor seminary, where I am very happy, and even to suffer anything, if this statement is in any way contrary to the truth.

Grenoble, November 21, 1850.

Maximin Giraud

With this letter, Bishop de Bruillard included a personal note. He invited the Curé to consider the question anew in the light of Maximin's statements. He suggested that there might have been some misunderstanding between him and the boy. The Curé of Ars replied:

Dear Bishop,

I had great confidence in our Lady of La Salette. I blessed and distributed numerous medals and holy cards illustrating the apparition. I distributed pieces of the stone on which the Blessed Virgin had sat. I kept some on my person and even had some of it placed in a reliquary. I often spoke about the event in church. I believe that few priests in your own diocese, Bishop, have done more than I for La Salette.

Bishop Philbert de Bruillard, Bishop of Grenoble during the Apparition

I need not repeat here what I told these men. I was put out for a few days after the boy told me he had not seen the Blessed Virgin.

After all Bishop, there is no very great harm done. If this event is the work of God, it can never be destroyed.

I am happy, Bishop, to have been able to present my humble re-spects, to recommend myself to your prayers, and to ask for your holy blessing.

Jean-Marie Vianney, Curé of Ars

In spite of his regrets, the saintly pastor was holding to his position. At the office of the Bishop of Grenoble, however, the idea of a misunderstanding was becoming more and more evident. Proof of that is found in another letter, written this time by Mr. Dausse at the request of Bishop de Bruillard.

Father, you cannot have been for four years the great apostle of La Salette, as you yourself wrote to the Bishop of Grenoble, and then abruptly change sides because of some misunderstanding. Nor should you even be held back by a doubt resulting in such grave consequences after your previous professions of faith.

This unofficial intermediary even offered to bring Maximin immediately to Ars to clear up the misunderstanding.

Mr. Dausse's letter was never answered, but it very likely influenced Father Vianney. Toward the end of 1850, we witness a reawakening of his former belief. Father Bruno, a Capuchin, asked the Curé about this well-known retraction. At first he was only told: "I wouldn't have had this child come here for six francs, not even for twenty francs." The next day, in a long conversation, the holy pastor himself brought up the subject and was surprised to hear himself say: "I always believed in La Salette. I still do. I blessed medals and holy cards depicting Our Lady of La Salette and distributed a great number of them. I wrote all of this to the bishop of Grenoble. You see how much I believe." He then went to his bed, pulled the draw-curtains, and showed Father Bruno a large painting of Our Lady of La Salette, framed and hung on the wall above his bed. **(16)** We know that doubt would again assail him. His sense of fairness as he heard Maximin's repeated denials and his religious sense of docility in the face of ecclesiastical approval of the event prevented him from defiantly clinging to his opinion.

Whenever he confided in Count des Garets, his favorite parishioner, he told him the facts as he had told them to Catherine Lassagne and to Brother Athanasius on the first day; but he always took care to add what is surely one of the most beautiful examples of prudence that can be quoted: "After all, this doesn't mean much. The boy could very well have been ridiculing me as he had already ridiculed the curate. (17)

As for the confrontation planned by the Bishop of Grenoble and hoped for by the pastor of Ars as much as by Maximin himself, Bishop Devie saw fit never to let it happen. For whatever reasons, the Curé's bishop never attached any moral or juridical weight to the incident.

Canon des Garets wrote,

> Six months before his death, I happened to be at Ars with the bishop and I asked him if he had spoken to the pastor about Maximin's visit. When I expressed surprise at his negative answer, he said to me: "The good pastor is not competent in this matter. Father Raymond had hassled the child and no one knows what could have gone through his head. The pastor is not competent." In fact, he considered him so unable to deal with the matter that he hadn't even spoken to him about it. (18)

Not to grant the pastor of Ars even the competence of an ordinary witness can appear rather arbitrary. Before making that kind of judgment, however, we must remember that the bishop, with three of his assistants, had heard Father Raymond himself at length. There is more discernment in his sentence than in the whole controversy that followed: "Father Raymond had hassled the child, and no one knows what could have gone through his head."

La Salette now returned before the canonical judge "as it was previously" and we know how it all ended. After the Bishop of Grenoble's doctrinal pronouncement, the Ars question could have appeared resolved in the eyes of the faithful. In the preliminary considerations, the bishop in fact declared himself "thoroughly acquainted with the suppositions contrary to the supernatural interpretation of the event of La Salette." Some obscurity still hovered over the incident which the ensuing controversy did nothing to dissipate.

There is no doubt about Déléon's bad faith when he got hold of the Ars affair. The same can be said of Cartellier's stubborn pride. The provocative role played by Father Raymond was perceived and condemned by all of the saintly pastor's proven friends.

"I am afraid," stated Brother Athanasius, "that Father Raymond's manner of dealing with Maximin during the preceding evening had exasperated him and had been a factor in the answers he gave to the servant of God." At the time of the incident, the brother did not believe in La Salette. But Father Raymond's thoughtlessness, his eagerness to spring into writing, to scandalize, and to confuse, awakened the brother's sense of justice and his educator's instincts in the face of such a firebrand.

In his defense, Rousselot made the mistake of minimizing some of the Curé of Ars's statements which opponents had enhanced to bolster their positions. Thus, in the view of an impartial bystander, friends and adversaries of La Salette sometimes seem not to meet on any common ground.

The Ars incident was nothing more than a simple misunderstanding: this is the view of which Rousselot made himself the official champion. The good pastor, he held, misunderstood Maximin's words when he declared having seen a beautiful Lady who might or might not have been the Blessed Virgin. The whole incident can be reduced to this. One must add, though, to the defender's credit, that he was able to face the worst scenario. Let us suppose, he wrote, that Maximin had retracted or contradicted himself. This retraction or this contradiction in no way infirms and much less destroys the fact of La Salette. He concluded his arguments by saying that if indeed Maximin did contradict himself at Ars, it was then that he lied. **(19)**

There is no doubt that the canonical judge confronted and weighed this worst possible scenario in his investigation. He took great care to inform himself of the Curé's statements as reported to him by Fathers Gerin, Rousselot, and Mélin. He weighed Father Raymond's remarks as well and he still concluded that the retraction theory was "bereft of any kind of value." At Ars, Maximin might have expressed himself in a way interpreted by the pastor to be a retraction. But given the boy's firmness in maintaining the veracity of his previous testimony, it was quite clear that the contradiction attributed to him did in no way correspond to his true conviction. Contrary to what Father Raymond would have people believe, the trip to Ars was nothing but a kind of adventure. Maximin never undertook it to clear his conscience of some great sin but only because he wanted to travel. Finally, there still remained the other witness, as well as the impossibility of explaining La Salette in a manner that would be naturally satisfactory. There was also the event's religious impact as well as the miracles, "a great number of which it is impossible to reject without violating all the rules of human testimony." All these considerations allow one to understand why the diocesan authority did not lend the retraction the importance attributed to it by the adversaries. The authority is correct in calling the retraction a misunderstanding if this word is taken in its broadest sense. It is correct in rejecting the idea of retraction if this word is understood in its formal sense.

Thus, we must not be surprised that the bishop's pronouncement said no more than it did about the facts of the case, since only an act of prudential judgment was required.

Rousselot presented a true evaluation of the incident within its proper context, but the adversaries correctly faulted him for evading some of the basic facts. Adversaries also went to Ars. Their version of the facts was too slanted by Father Raymond and their own acrimony to be acceptable. Cartellier met Father Vianney personally at least once and Cartellier's writings contain remarks akin to those we have heard from Catherine Lassagne and Brother Athanasius. When we read from Cartellier's pen that the Curé allegedly said "that La Salette is nothing but a fable and that he had done well not to believe in it," we may justifiably decide that his writings deserve to be dismissed, for the aloof attitude underlying such works simply does not resonate with what we know of the saint's sufferings caused by La Salette. Yet this slanted report does contain some truth. From the point of view of the Curé of Ars and some of his friends, this whole incident could not be reduced to a simple misunderstanding. Vianney said very little about it to others, but he did speak at some length with Canon des Garets who comes through to us as a faithful witness.

Two of us were present. Here is what our pastor told us: "If what the child told me is true, then we cannot believe it. He came to see me and he told me: "Father, I have not seen the Blessed Virgin, but this has not hurt the people. I would like to make a general confession and enter a monastery." "My child," answered the pastor, "if you have lied you must retract." "Oh! That won't be necessary," said Maximin, "it didn't hurt the people: some have even converted. Then, after I have entered the monastery I will declare that I have told all and have nothing else to say." "My friend," answered the pastor, "I don't want to assume that responsibility and I must consult my bishop." "Well, Father, go ahead and consult!"

Then, Father Vianney wrote down Maximin's address and a moment later the boy added that it was not necessary to consult.

Here we have a reliable account of the pastor's interview with Maximin. The priest added: "This is not worth worrying about. If it isn't true it will fall of itself. All we have to do is send the boy back and then we'll see. They say I was deaf but I heard very well." **(20)**

Window of the Curé of Ars in Church of Saint-Marien, France

In view of the formal and repeated statements of the Curé of Ars, Father des Garets could see only one explanation: Maximin had lied to him to test his discernment. Father Raymond had challenged him: "You will be dealing with a saint. You can't fool saints." **(21)** We'll see, the flighty Maximin may well have thought to himself.

"In my opinion," concluded Father des Garets, "after having studied all the facts of the Ars question, after having knocked on every door in search of reliable information, realizing that even after having returned to his former faith, the pastor still said: "I believe, but only in spite of what the boy has told me," I am convinced that this is the key to the enigma, and I know for certain that Maximin has admitted this to a small number of intimate acquaintances." **(22)**

The misunderstanding went beyond the limits Rousselot wanted to impose on it. Maximin made remarks that the pastor could only construe as a formal retraction. Maximin's assertion that this did not harm the people, the flippant invitation to "go ahead and consult," the strange first line of a retraction statement, "I declare that..." — these are compromising details in a matter too serious to be accepted by any serious person as mere banter. The shepherd's silence on these matters proved nothing. His statements were contradictory and Rousselot seemed embarrassed to use them as arguments. Insisting on having the misunderstanding bear only on the point mentioned, the hapless Maximin groped like a drowning man. He did not dare acknowledge publicly the predicament into which he had blundered. Some of his semi-confessions, however, spoke volumes: "I didn't mean to tell you, Father," he said after Rousselot and Mélin's return from Ars, "and I have told no one seriously that I had seen nothing and had lied when I was making my story known." On another occasion he said to Mr. Dausse: "The pastor had the devil in his ear when I spoke to him." "And you had him on your tongue," replied Dausse. A knowing smile appeared on Maximin's expressive face. **(23)**

Father des Garets said that, in private, Maximin might have made more explicit admissions. At the rectory of Seyssins under the tutorship of Father Champon he is said to have let out this word of triumph: "I had heard that the priest of Ars read consciences. I wanted to make sure. I confessed to him. I told him that all I had reported about the apparition of the Blessed Virgin was false, that I had seen nothing. The pastor believed me, so he can't read consciences. So there! Your Curé of Ars is like all the others." It must be noted that this remark may have been distorted in transmission. It was heard by Miss Champon and reported much later to Canon Achard who passed it on to Bishop Giray in 1917. We would want to retain it only in its general sense: Maximin admitted that he had challenged the spiritual penetration of the pastor of Ars. **(24)**

What happened exactly between Maximin and the holy pastor? Are we to believe Father des Garets who explained that the boy deliberately lied to test the gift of prophecy he was told he could not outwit? The hypothesis is defensible. Ever since his confrontation with Antoine Gay and all those who had attempted to invade his conscience—the legitimists and the Raymonds—the boy probably tried hard to appear stronger than his attackers in defending his privacy. Still, another explanation may conciliate the Curé's remarks with Maximin's later statements.

It is at least possible that the conversation began with a misunderstanding. According to the Father Monnin, the pastor of Ars opened with: "So you're the one who saw the Blessed Virgin?" Could some distrust have filtered into the Cure's tone of voice as a result of his conversations with Father Raymond? After the taunts of the previous evening, could Maximin have heard in the pastor's tone of voice what actually was not there? We can easily see him on the defensive and rebutting: "I didn't say I had seen the Blessed Virgin, but a beautiful Lady." **(25)** Moved by the similarity of this response with the one Raymond had reported as a retraction, Father Vianney spoke firmly: "You must make a retraction."

"Oh! That won't be necessary," retorted Maximin tersely. "It didn't hurt the people. In fact, some even converted."

In order to interrupt this line of conversation, he asked to make a general confession. "After I enter a monastery, I can say I have told everything and there is nothing else to say."

Maximin is referring to his sins. The pastor hears it in reference to La Salette. "My friend," he decides, "I cannot take that upon myself. I must consult my bishop."

"Go ahead and consult, Father!"

Every word and action as seen from the perspective of Ars comes naturally in such a lively exchange. Each one of Maximin's statements finds its logical place. His contradictions can be explained by the need to bear witness to La Salette and by the impossibility of admitting publicly that he enjoyed making fun of the man of God. The reply he had once given to Canon Henry, "Sir, we make fun of La Salette today..." shows that he took insults to his beautiful Lady personally and allows us to imagine how deeply the curate Raymond's ridicule must have hurt. One might say he wreaked vengeance on the wrong person. But how can an adolescent in such circumstances be expected to show tact and poise? This is why it can be said that the person truly responsible for the Ars incident is Father Raymond himself.

How far did Maximin push this mindless game? Could he have admitted lying about La Salette? That question will never be settled. But, still, nothing is less sure. It could have been only a mistaken meaning progressively aggravated to the point where Maximin abruptly broke with the good Curé, unable to go further than this incipient retraction: "I declare that..." We can find a serious basis for such an interpretation in the words Maximin added to Rousselot's postscript and directed to the pastor of Ars: "Reflect well on what you will say, that you may say all you have heard and not what you have not heard." When the Curé quotes Maximin in an admission of falsehood this could be the result of his own interpretation. The words "after I enter the monastery, I will tell all," according to all the texts we have read, could be related to the general confession Maximin had asked to make. Maximin's admission to Champon has little value considering the manner it has come down to us. The fidelity of its transmission is very much in question. If the remark is true, there is still the possibility that after the passage of time Maximin is interpreting his memories.

Finally, psychological likelihood favors the initial misunderstanding. Part of Maximin's game might have been to deceive a prophet. Much later, the memory of that moment could have surfaced in his consciousness. All this is probable. For us to think that he would have come to the Curé of Ars with the deliberate intention of lying to him for the sake of an experiment would be to assume a perverseness out of character with him.

From the beginning of the conversation, there had to be a word, a tone of voice, arousing in him the suspicion of collaboration between the previous evening's insulter and the holy priest now listening to him. The bitterness born that evening was now revived. He bristled and threw out the senseless remark that poisoned everything: "This has done the people no harm!" He was happy and gave expression to his happiness when he left the sacristy that day: "I am happier than if I were given two hundred thousand francs!" But could that happiness make sense if it stemmed only from having stumped a man of God? It becomes comprehensible if we see in Maximin's smug triumph a vengeance on the Curé for the insults of his associate.

But how, one wonders, did the pastor lay himself open to the initial misunderstanding? And then, how could he have been fooled by this sudden about-face: "This is not necessary! It has done the people no harm!" The remark itself was so outrageous that it is hard for anyone to believe it could have been made in earnest. It would seem that in such circumstances the most mediocre confessor would have given it some thought before deciding whether or not he was dealing with a prankster or a cynic. There is here, on the part of the Curé of Ars, a truly astonishing kind of blindness. Said Father des Garets: "Not only did God not enlighten his servant with the supernatural insight He so often granted him to see into hearts and minds, but He did not allow him to understand what was so improbable in the retraction he thought he heard. Nor did He allow him to see the need to clarify this mystery."

Psychologically, in the realm of secondary causes, the explanation is simple. The curate's prejudices weighed on the mind of the pastor. The latter's readiness to believe the retraction is one point on which Maximin never wavered. "He believed the very first word I said about the retraction." This is how the mischief-maker expressed it in a conversation reported to Rousselot by Auvergne.

But the incident was to have such consequences that it is not foolhardy to see within it, in the interplay of secondary causes, a providential will guiding everything. The manner of the incident's denouement allows us to think that, granted the priest's lack of insight, it was to be better thus both for him and for La Salette.

"God writes straight with crooked lines," says a Portuguese proverb that Claudel illustrated with a masterpiece. These "crooked lines" become wonderfully clear in all this as with the passage of time they bestow meaning on the agitation of people. The boy's stupidity was believed to be the death-knell of the apparition. Scheming opponents pounced on it like a golden trump card. And still, at the end of this road, where wise men, from the Cardinal of Lyons to the Bishop of Grenoble, tread fearfully, lay victory for La Salette. Maximin one day candidly made the disarming assessment.

Miss des Brulais, the great friend of his childhood days, reproached him for the Ars escapade. She asked him why he had confided in total strangers.

"Why, to see the world!"

"You were heading for deep trouble. What were you thinking of?"

"Yes, it's true. I did a dumb thing. Anyway, it did help the secret get to Rome."

"How is that?"

"Well, the Cardinal saw all the publicity in the papers about the pastor of Ars and he wanted to have the secret. The Pope asked to see it and the Bishop of Grenoble sent it to him. There!" (26)

The boy's insensitivity to the saintly old man's moral agony is sad to behold. Would not the divine meaning of this trial be revealed to him, especially to him?

The saintly Curé's bewilderment and suffering in this matter are well known. He would try to convince himself that he had misunderstood the boy, but the words he had heard would return and would again plunge him into darkness. In simple imagery and profound feeling he would describe these fluctuations: "When I stop doubting I find peace again. I feel light as a bird. I fly. I simply fly! When the devil plunges me back into doubt, it's as if I were dragged over brambles." Without a doubt, the impossibility of settling his belief as well as the fear of doing anything against the Blessed Virgin became one of the greatest trials of his life. It was "the bloodiest thorn in his crown," testified Mrs. des Garets and her daughter.

His incredulity manifested itself in words and acts that opponents quickly seized and travestied, but it had nothing of their cocky assurance. He searched in painful anxiety. "I have qualms of conscience," he said to Catherine Lassagne. "I would want God to let me know if this is true or not. If it is true, I will speak well of it. If it is not, I will not speak of it again."

As the passage of years blurred the incident, he leaned more and more toward belief. On September 19, 1857, Father Chambon wrote to Father Auvergne from Vienne:

> I am speaking tomorrow at Saint Maurice. On this matter, the Curé of Ars told Father Ponton recently: "We not only may believe in La Salette but we must. I was made to look like an unbeliever. You can tell your colleagues and all who will listen that I am a fervent believer. The child confused me, telling me I know not what. We didn't understand each other." Without any prompting from me, the Curé had said this same thing to Father Nicoud on the previous evening. "Yes, yes. There is much good being accomplished there."

But the wound inflicted by Maximin kept opening. Human remedies were powerless in the face of such persistent pain.

One day in June, 1858, Amédée Nicolas, a defender of the apparition, said to him: "Father, I am coming to convert you to La Salette. Since 1850, your incredulity has made many opponents. If you were to revert to your first view, the opposition would be left without its main support." "It will be hard for me to return to my first opinion," he is supposed to have said. "The boy positively told me and in clear terms: "Mélanie and I invented this miracle." **(27)**

He still accepted to read a booklet his guest gave him — La Salette devant la raison et le devoir d'un catholique (La Salette before the reason and the duty of a Catholic)— and allowed himself three months to read it. Correspondence followed in July and August. But in his situation, rational investigation was nothing but a striving to believe against evidence. He had to clear this impasse. The Lord's good friend boldly chose another way: he asked for signs and he received them.

The only proof he asked for was that his mind be no longer troubled once he had said "I believe." It was a simple request and it did not tempt God. The good priest therefore restated the act of faith to which he had so often and vainly tried to cling. This time, however, a newfound and total peace was given to him. He admitted as much to Father Toccanier:

"I was troubled. I felt as if my soul was being dragged on gravel. I prayed to God and I said to myself: Why shouldn't I believe when so many bishops believe? At that very moment, I found peace." He said to Canon Seignemartin: "For many days I was plunged in deep sorrow. As a proof of the truth of the apparition, I prayed to the Blessed Virgin to free me, and I promised to believe. I was freed immediately." Canon Guillemin, Vicar General of Belley, whom Cardinal de Bonald had sent "to ask Father Vianney what led him to change his views on La Salette," wrote in his report: "He felt as if his shoulders had been relieved of a bagful of lead." **(28)**

But what if he were to lose this delightful peace once again? Couldn't the Almighty make it such that never again would it become a mirage? He boldly asked that heaven's response not be limited to the powers of his own soul. Good-naturedly and very soberly he told Father Descôtes about his struggle with the angel and its outcome:

"My friend, you'll never imagine what happened to me."

"What happened, Father?"

"I had long been troubled by the question of La Salette. One night, after having struggled with it for a long time, I finally said: 'My God, I believe. However, I still would want you to give me some sign or some proof.' My peace was immediately restored. But here is what happened. I was hearing confessions one morning when a priest suddenly entered. He was as tall as you are and he asked me bluntly: 'Father, what do you think of La Salette?' I answered: 'I think we can and should believe in it.'

"Without further ado, he turned around and left. I know neither who he is nor where he comes from. And that's not all. Before going to bed that night, I found my table covered with gold pieces. I picked them all up, as you can well imagine. I just happened to need money. Next morning, I again found my table covered with gold pieces. Now after this, do you think I should believe in La Salette?"

"If I were you I would believe," said the other priest.

After many years, Father Descôtes's remembrances have a certain vagueness about them. **(29)** We have more immediate and formal testimony about the priest's visit in the sacristy as well as its sign value. Canon Guillemin's report can be held as the conclusion of a true inquiry and it comes a few weeks after the event. With the help of Cardinal de Bonald's messenger we can place the detail in its proper perspective.

To confirm what had just happened, (deliverance from sorrow and doubt), Father Vianney asked God to send him a prominent priest from the diocese of Grenoble. The very next morning, while the pastor was in the sacristy, an ecclesiastic who said he was a professor at the Grenoble Seminary entered the sacristy and without preamble asked Father Vianney this question: "Father, what do you think of La Salette?" Father Vianney answered: "I think that we not only can but that we should believe in it." The priest from Grenoble immediately left the sacristy without saying another word. **(30)**

Further on, we will see this same sign attested to by Father Gerin in almost identical terms.

Father Toccanier also knew that a sum of money had been left on the table, but he knew it in a veiled way, it would seem. An understandable modesty, fear of vainglory perhaps, prevented the Curé of Ars from revealing complete details as well as their interconnectedness to his confidants. But testimonies corroborate one another and it appears that all the signs occurred barely within the span of twenty-four hours. Had the saint asked to have his prayers answered this promptly? Miss de Belvey states "that he had prayed God to free him from this indecision within three days." **(31)** Father Monnin went further and said "that the venerable servant of God had returned to his first opinion because Our Lord had granted him three signs he had asked to see in a single day." **(32)**

What we know for certain is that from this moment on the faith of the Curé of Ars in the apparition of La Salette was unshakable. To the end of his life he spoke of it with tears of joy. Father Gerin visited his friend at the request of his ordinary. On October 13, 1858 the priest wrote to Bishop Ginoulhiac from Lyons:

> *I am just returning from Ars, where I have been at your Excellen-cy's bidding. I am very happy to have gone. I have offered a Mass in thanksgiving for the comfort brought to me by the conversation I had with the holy priest.*

> *"I am grateful to you for having come to visit me," he said. "I have much to say to you about Our Lady of La Salette. I cannot tell you how much worry and anguish I have endured in all this. I have suffered beyond what words can express. I have felt like a man in a desert sandstorm, not knowing where to turn. In the midst of this kind of turbulence and suffering, I finally cried out in a loud voice: Credo! At that very moment I recovered the peace and tranquility I thought I had lost forever. I asked God to send a priest to me from Grenoble, one who would be learned and able, that I might share my dispositions and feelings with him on this subject. He came the very next day."*

> *"What is his name?"*

> *"I can't recall his name. He is a professor at the Seminary. Now it would be impossible for me not to believe in La Salette. I asked for signs and I received them. We may and we must believe in La Salette."*

> *He spoke to me about Maximin. I didn't understand him. I told him that Maximin was a little scatterbrain.* **(33)** *He nodded approval. Many times he spoke to me of the signs that had completely changed him. Embracing him, I took the liberty of asking him what those signs were. He sharply refused to tell me more. He forbade me to*

speak of our conversation to anyone in the vicinity of Ars. **(34)** *"But couldn't I speak about it to my bishop who sent me to you?" "Yes, yes, to your bishop and to everyone in your area. I sent everyone to La Salette and I have witnessed many miracles brought about by Our Lady of La Salette."*

I am relieved, Bishop, to have shared this with you. I couldn't keep it until I returned. It would have killed me. I consider these words of the holy pastor a formal retraction of the error in which he had been for eight years.

At this time the miracle-worker of Ars was the center of attention in all of France and the news of such a startling change could never go unnoticed. People came from everywhere or wrote to Father Toccanier, Father Raymond's replacement, to ascertain the truth. Whenever he was asked about the apparition the holy Curé invariably replied: "We not only may but we must believe in La Salette." **(35)** He was more willing to confide in those who were aware of his anguish: Father des Garets, Canon Guillemin, or Amédée Nicolas. This last, who had urged the happy transformation, learned of its happening in a letter from Father Toccanier. "There is a new incident at Ars," he wrote, "that will bring as much joy as the other brought sorrow." **(36)** Inasmuch as he can he makes the saint's joy his very own. "I saw his tears flow," he writes. "He was happy about his return to his first belief, but he keenly regretted having doubted for eight years as well as having created this impression all around." **(37)**

Was this a need to make amends or to share his joy? Would it not more likely be the fraternal gesture of one who had tasted clear spring water and could not rest until he had shown it to all who thirsted? "One day," wrote Father des Garets, "he left the place where he was hearing confessions, walked over to a priest about to begin Mass, and told him all that had happened to him. Then he returned to his penitent" **(38)**

Even in death, the renewed apostle of La Salette persisted in bearing witness. The new bishop of Belley, Bishop de Langalerie, learned on August 3, 1859 that the Curé of Ars was dying. From Meximieux, where he was awarding prizes, the bishop hastened to the priest's

The wax-encased body of the Curé of Ars, above main altar in Ars Church

bedside and arrived at seven in the evening. At two o'clock in the morning Father Vianney was called from this life. One of the last words, perhaps the last abiding thought of the dying priest, was of Our Lady of La Salette. Two years later, speaking in the La Salette Basilica on Christ's weeping over Jerusalem, Bishop de Langalerie told his congregation:

> Dear pilgrims, I have come on this holy mountain to bring, in favor of the apparition, the testimony of the one we love to call, while still awaiting the Church's decision, the saintly Curé of Ars. I was his bishop and his friend. He died in my arms. He told me he believed in the apparition of La Salette. From heaven he hears what I say and he will not deny my words. **(39)**

Such an endorsement of the La Salette event by the Curé of Ars challenges our own partiality or resistance regarding the apparition. Two notable personalities in the history of La Salette reacted to the Ars Incident most tellingly: Cardinal de Bonald and Father Cartellier.

At the beginning of October, 1858, Cardinal de Bonald had been visited by Father des Garets. The saint's confidant had told him what he had heard: "My friend, I have suffered incredibly. For a few days I was miserable. I suffered like a soul in hell. I didn't know whether I should believe or not. Finally, I decided to say very simply: I believe. I was immediately freed from my burden. I found peace again. I then asked the good Lord for signs."

The Cardinal was moved and stunned by this account that differed so much from the one he had heard himself from the saintly priest. He asked Canon Guillemin to establish the inquiry mentioned above. Did the Cardinal's belief stem from the report of that inquiry or did it evolve through progressive stages? We do not know. We do know that on October 23, 1862, "he spoke of the event and the devotion in the manner of a believer" to Bishop Ginoulhiac. (40) Furthermore, Father Giraud, Superior of the Missionaries of La Salette, invoked the Cardinal's allegiance to La Salette. The former was animating a Third Order of women at Lyons (41) when he wrote to Mother Marie-Thérèse, the foundress, on the very day the Cardinal died, February 25, 1870:

As I learned of the death of the Cardinal, my first thought was of you and your work. You must accept this loss in a spirit of adoration of and submission to the will of God. If you enter into these supernatural dispositions, I am convinced that there will be nothing but graces and blessings for you in this transition. Your work already has Cardinal de Bonald's blessing and this approval will be honored by the new archbishop. (42)

Cartellier, on the other hand, hearing of the Ars incident, wrote for clarification to Father Toccanier. The reply was clear and precise: the parish priest of Ars once again believed in La Salette after having obtained three signs from God. The author of the "Report to the Pope" no longer wrote for publication, but he committed the following to his diary:

We now hear loud and clear what had been previously only whispered, that Father Vianney believes in La Salette, that the venerable Curé petitioned God for a sign, one he refused to reveal but that he received. In any case, he now believes. A divine inspiration established his faith. It is therefore true that he did not previously believe. But does he deny what he has always said about Maximin?

Not in the least. What are we to think of what has been reported? Compare: Father Vianney believes when a vision is granted to him. All this is very personal and cannot be posited as proof. It is all invisible. Isn't it possible to deceive oneself even in the loftiest things? Father Vianney believed he would be damned for not fulfilling his duties as a pastor. This was the first point made by those in favor of La Salette. Yet who fulfilled such duties better than he? His timid conscience plunged him into what was, in our opinion, an ill-founded fear.

He was inclined by nature to the supernatural. Couldn't he have deceived himself in this case as he had on the state of his soul? This type of error is possible and it would prove that the excellent priest lived in an altogether spiritual realm. The fact is that Maximin retracted himself before the Curé of Ars. This is an ascertainable fact about which Father Vianney could not have been mistaken. This is real, this is positive, and we hold to it because the thing is sure and corroborated. This is a fact we can evaluate. Can the same be said for what the saintly priest might or might not have seen in his spirit during his last days? **(43)**

This is a vivid example of what Amédée Nicolas called the spirit of the opposition. It is all here: the creased forehead annoyed when contradicted, the brushing away of facts whose meaning he wanted to dilute, an anti-mysticism not far removed from outright positivism. Behind all this, perhaps, was a stubborn pride unable to concede error. There is, in any case, an absence of the humility necessary for true understanding, confirming Hamlet's observation: there are more things in heaven and earth than are dreamt of in our philosophy.

We have examined the Ars incident in detail. What should our conclusion be? Looking solely at the incident that took place in 1850, and considering the circumstances that explain it, we can state that, by right, its repercussion on the event of La Salette is nil. The opposition should never have used it as a weapon because Maximin clearly never had the intention of retracting. The diocesan authority was essentially correct in judging it a misunderstanding and one can only subscribe to the prudence of Bishop de Bruillard's doctrinal pronouncement.

As we objectively examine the testimonies, taking care to link together irrefutable facts according to their psychological plausibility, we find that the parish priest has a claim on our veneration for the way he suffered and Maximin on our understanding for the way he was inveigled. "The sad business of Ars," wrote the saintly Father Eymard in a note to Rousselot. "Maximin is a little scoundrel." (44) The remark is attributed to Bishop Ginoulhiac around 1870. These are verdicts of serious and well-informed men, but they rest on the assumption that an adolescent can in all circumstances behave rationally. Bishop Devie was more discerning. He invoked extenuating circumstances for the hassled child. Father Gerin, too, shrugging his shoulders and labeling Maximin a little scatterbrain, showed more judgment.

But when we consider the aftermath, when we link what occurred in 1850 with its upshot in 1858, we can no longer suppose the first part to have a meaning of its own. Rousselot's insinuation that the parish priest of Ars, believing in Maximin's denial, sinned through carelessness is itself short on wisdom. There is something supernatural both in the child's stupidity and in the saint's momentary blindness that eludes the mind's natural light. Bishop Devie again with his admirably keen intuition was aware of this when he assured the superior of the Marist Fathers early in 1851: "What happened in Ars was a trial and a storm provoked by the devil. La Salette will emerge dazzling from all this." (45) Had he lived longer, he would have rejoiced to see the calming of the storm. For those of us who can judge it after the event, his word does indeed seem prophetic. Considered in all its complexity, the incident at Ars is one of those contests where heaven and earth come face to face. The devil was able to weave his intrigue only because God had decided to untangle it.

In spite of what Cartellier says, the reasons compelling the parish priest of Ars to return to his first adherence do not all belong to the realm of the invisible. In answer to a hidden hope, a man comes before you. Your kitchen table is laden with gold pieces, on two separate occasions. Such signs are not produced by some fantastic obsession. Now that the credentials of the miracle-worker have been ascertained by the Church and that his realistic common sense has been made evident by historical research, his about-face invites the thinking Christian to say: "I believe." Saint Augustine's remark relative to the apostle Thomas applies well here, all due allowances being made: it was to strengthen our belief that this unbelief was allowed to take place. (46)

-10-
Senseless Hostility

*W*e must once again turn to the opposition that had sprung up in the meetings presided over by Bishop de Bruillard. It grew in noise and intensity especially after the Ars debacle. In 1854, the adversaries of La Salette appealed to the Pope against the bishop. The opposition leaders have long since left the scene and the general public hardly remembers their names. But because of them this same general public has the impression that all is not clear in the La Salette story. Some authors, having skimmed through the children's writings and compared the assumptions they drew from them with the way they think they know of the children's subsequent lives, conclude to the impossibility of coming to any decision regarding La Salette, until psychology will have made such progress that to the present generation, these assumptions will no longer matter.

Whether by ignorance or by superficiality, it is still deplorable to see a Cartellier and a Déléon referred to as authorities on a question demanding at least a minimum of depth. Wearisome as it is, we shall once again rehearse their machinations and take stock of their arguments.

We recall that the clergy retreat of 1851 in Grenoble had been the scene of unfortunate episodes. This is why Bishop de Bruillard had taken care before publishing his pronouncement to give the adversaries every assurance and proof that their objections had been weighed. He had reason to hope that, even if his clergy could not give intellectual assent—the document in fact did not demand it—it could at least manifest external compliance. There was no point in rehearsing "pretensions and suppositions" that the competent authority declared being completely aware of. But Cartellier, pastor of Saint Joseph's, believed he had as much right as his bishop to be heard by all of Christianity. He admitted having disclosed his "entire thinking" to his ordinary in the bishop's meetings. **(1)** But his opinion had not prevailed, and to the end of his life he sought vindication from the whole world.

Having recourse to Cardinal de Bonald was Cartellier's master stroke. From the beginning, following the pronouncement, we can readily see his stamp on the commonplace objections that the cardinal directed to his suffragan under the guise of "respectful representations." But under the cover of the storm created by the Ars incident, Cartellier managed to have him brandish his famous manuscript, which pitted the cardinal both privately and publicly against Bishop de Bruillard's decree. "If the voluminous report I have in hand were to be released, **(2)** I believe it would reduce to almost nothing the value of Rousselot's

Cardinal Bonald, archbishop of Lyon, circa 1860.

work." Thus did the cardinal thank the bishop for sending him his pronouncement.

The situation grew worse when this reservation crept into an official document. On August 6, 1852, the cardinal addressed a circular letter to his clergy on the need for prudence with regard to recent miracles. Admittedly, there was reason for caution. The letter refers to unfortunate incidents in the diocese of Lyons, and more than one bishop at that time anxiously witnessed the progress of the Vintrasian sect. The bishop of Grenoble could hardly miss the allusion to his pronouncement in the cardinal's admonition to the priests of his diocese.

> We forbid giving from the pulpit the recital of a miraculous event without our permission, even if its authenticity were attested to by the bishop of another diocese. We would grant such a permission only after having consulted with the Pope and received from him a rescript which would be for us a guarantee of the truth of the miracle. In two or three of our parishes, the pastors have read a decree from the bishop of another diocese without having consulted

us. *This is an irregular act.*

In response, Bishop de Bruillard had recourse to the authority that had encouraged him to go ahead the preceding year. His letter to Cardinal Lambruschini summed up the situation and appealed to the Pope against possible abuses of power by the cardinal-archbishop.

> *In a circular letter given to the newspapers, although addressed only to his clergy, the Archbishop of Lyons seems to attack La Salette without naming it, to confuse it purposely with reprehensible events occurring in his diocese, and to question my right to proclaim it. Your Eminence did not doubt that I had this right. Many bishops, Bishop Devie among them, who has just been taken from among us and whose learning equaled his piety, have recognized that right and have praised me for exercising it. The Council of Trent clearly grants it to bishops and stipulates the intervention of the provincial council only in doubtful and difficult cases. I now appeal to your Eminence, and through your Eminence to His Holiness, against all that the Cardinal Archbishop of Lyons might attempt against La Salette, an event so filled with consolation and hope, and enjoying such undeniable authenticity that it belongs less to my own diocese than to the whole Catholic world. (3)*

In point of fact, no personal initiative against La Salette came from Cardinal de Bonald himself. But he kept displaying a reticent attitude, giving everyone to understand that the whole thing had not been adequately looked into and that he would believe in it only if the Pope gave a formal pronouncement. He did not appear to have driven his inquiries beyond the summary notions he had formed from the Cartellier report. He placed complete trust in this informant, and all were aware of it. Nothing contributed so much to the strength of the opposition as well as to the contagion of doubt than did the cardinal's patronage.

However, support from on high was not enough for the pastor of Saint Joseph's, nor were the devious tactics by which he turned the archbishop against his suffragan. Ever since 1848, he had as collaborator a priest-journalist who had to retire from his parish in Villeurbanne. Father Rousselot, always partial to good journalism, had placed this priest-journalist in charge of the *Union Dauphinoise*. He was Father Claude Déléon. For years Cartellier hounded him with his own compulsion: La Salette is a fiction to be destroyed. "He serves me this mess of pottage on a platter every day," said Déléon to Father Rigat, pastor of Vienne. "This is what he wants me to write about in elegant French." At that time, Déléon believed in La Salette. He would send his parishioners of Villeurbanne on pilgrimage there. Until February 1851, the *Union Dauphinoise* published the articles of Father Chambon on his reasons for believing. Unfortunately, it happened that in 1851 Déléon's conduct forced the chancery to address him more severe reprimands. The alienated priest, opting for revenge, chose to challenge authority on another battleground, the one designated by Cartellier: La Salette.

What could Déléon hope to achieve by this tactic? At the outset, he had wanted to forestall the suspension of his ecclesiastical faculties, and later, having been placed under interdict, he would become a threat formidable enough to bring his bishop to a compromise. Such were the motives behind the short essay by J. Robert, already referred to above, as well as the sensational pamphlet previewed by Robert and signed Donnadieu. It came, in 1852, to spread turmoil anew in the diocese on the eve of the clergy retreat. It was entitled *La Salette-Fallavaux: Fallax Vallis, or, The Valley of Falsehood*.

In fact, Bishop de Bruillard had already been alerted and was informed of the direction the adversaries were about to take. Early in June, appalling verses had been covertly circulated. The old bishop had some reason to believe that some of his priests had had a hand in their composition and dissemination. He struck the authors and the disseminators with suspension of their ecclesiastical faculties, lest they be among the priests of his diocese.

But the new pamphlet far surpassed the "infamous songs" in insolence and sophistry. In manner and essence it was accurately previewed in the posters heralding it which covered the walls of Lyons even to the windows of the archbishop's house. "A religious critique according to the unchanging rules of the Church for the approval of new miracles, recalled on August 6, 1852, in a circular letter of His Eminence

Cardinal de Bonald, Archbishop of Lyons, Metropolitan of the diocese of Grenoble, delegate of the Sovereign Pontiff for the question of La Salette." Shading the truth in this way, it was impossible to lie more shamelessly.

Naturally, Bishop de Bruillard protested before his clergy gathered for the annual retreat. "Beloved collaborators, I know you already share my pain; only in my own diocese can we find such brazen opponents. I hope to God they are not among my clergy." Two hundred and twelve retreatants declared themselves "spontaneously and energetically against everything in this tract that is injurious to the first Shepherd of the diocese and to the colleagues in whom he has placed such warranted confidence, as well as against any similar writing that may appear in the future." But the scandal was universal. Bishop Depéry of Gap, who was partial to the opposition, called Donnadieu's writing a "work of darkness." Even Cardinal de Bonald himself was prompted to write: "Moreover, dear vicar general, the act of using my circular letter as a lead for an unworthy pamphlet certainly induced no one to believe that the Metropolitan could have been involved in such a despicable maneuver against his suffragan." **(4)**

View of Apparition site in 1861 showing
pilgrims climbing mountain with mules

It was Rousselot's *Nouveau Sanctuaire* (*A New Shrine*) that persuaded the cardinal to explain his position. He clearly disapproved any exploitation of his office that others like Donnadieu might attempt in the future. But Donnadieu Déléon, stung by Rousselot's epithets, declared: "I am now publishing the second volume of *La Salette-Fallavaux*." In March 1853, his second book of lucubrations appeared, and suddenly the people were given the key to the riddle that had mystified them for seven years: the La Salette event was simply a stroll in the mountains by an eccentric and mystical former nun. She was Miss de Lamerlière, and before the astonished children she had played the role of the white Lady. Was it worth writing a book attempting to prove that there was no one at La Salette only to arrive at this conclusion?

Meanwhile, Bishop de Bruillard had resigned. His successor having been installed on May 7, 1853, he retired to the convent of the Dames of the Sacred Heart in Montfleury, near Grenoble. What would be Bishop Ginoulhiac's attitude toward La Salette? The question was asked with anxiety and curiosity, especially in the presence of such turbulent and clandestine opposition. There was no longer any doubt that some priests were involved.

Déléon approached his new bishop. His mother was dying. The prodigal son wanted to spare her the supreme humiliation. At first, he denied having been the author of Donnadieu's pamphlets. Diocesan authority showed itself conciliatory. Bishop de Bruillard had been satisfied with a letter of apology, Bishop Ginoulhiac with simple promises. The priest-journalist would once again wear ecclesiastical garb, would avoid all controversial behavior, and would surrender all the unsold copies of the La Salette-Fallavaux work. At the end of July 1853 he was once again a priest in good standing.

Bishop Ginoulhiac soon noticed that the promises were not being kept, and early in 1854 he learned that Déléon was writing another tract.

In his own mind, the new bishop felt that after Bishop de Bruillard had published his pronouncement the issue was settled. As he left his diocese of Aix for that of Grenoble, his intention was to consolidate the work of his predecessor, to bring around through gentleness and persuasion the few entrenched obstinates who persisted in a pointless resistance. He had not studied the La Salette dossier with any thoroughness, but the opponent's agitation convinced him that he must. He read attentively all the documents assembled by his predecessor and had the diocesan secretary, Father Auvergne, bring in all the accounts still in the hands of the priests who had heard the children in October of 1846. He was then in a position to respond with a penetrating and definitive source-criticism to all those who questioned Bishop de Bruillard's decision. (5)

Believing more in prevention than in cure, he summoned Déléon. In remarks made later on the Deleon case, (6) Bishop Ginoulhiac explained: "His violation of one of the conditions imposed for lifting the interdict of January 30, 1852, provided us with an occasion to summon him. After having reprimanded him for this and for allowing the publication of his irreligious pamphlet, we told him we were aware that he was about to publish another book against La Salette. Father Déléon stated that this information was unfounded. We insisted. He persisted in his denial. We were not convinced, but it was useless to pursue the matter. We simply warned him that if the book did appear, we would be forced to intervene and perhaps even censure him."

This interview took place in July 1854. The *Mémoire au Pape* appeared on August 28. Such deceit was all the more frustrating because Déléon assumed the role of defender of conscience and reason.

This time, Déléon did not come alone. The somber Cartellier preceded him, his cold authority backing the exuberant zest of the journalist, confidently proposing to the Head of the Church the outrageous de Lamerlière farce. Bishop Ginoulhiac had expected a sniper; he faced a conspiracy.

Déléon had no sooner finished insisting on the purity of his intentions than the intrigue came to light. Cartellier and a handful of priests overawed by his argumentative posturing sidestepped the Bishop's authority, appealing to the Pope himself for a review of the La Salette question. On July 29, Cardinal de Bonald informed Bishop

Ginoulhiac:

> *Some ecclesiastics in your diocese have given me a report on La Salette to be sent to the Supreme Pontiff. I assumed you would not be opposed to forwarding this report. I gave it to Monsignor Vecchiotti, assistant to the Nuncio, who was returning to Rome. He told me that the Pope had not pronounced himself on the so-called apparition of the Blessed Virgin, although he did grant it certain privileges.*

Only a blind confidence in Cartellier, if it must be said, could explain the cardinal's conduct. But the scales quickly fell from his eyes. He soon received the same report he had sent to Rome printed now by Redon of Grenoble, who had published Déléon's earlier writings. The Holy Father also received it and was thus informed that the request now before him had become public. Personalities of the diocese and of Rome, bishops, newspapers, all persons of consequence in the mind of Cartellier were being solicited by personal copies of his book to embrace his cause.

Bishop Ginoulhiac asked for explanations. Cardinal de Bonald gave them, realizing a bit late that he had been taken in by a conspiracy.

> *Saint-Hippolyte, August 6, 1854.*

> *Bishop, I could not answer the letter you graciously sent me as soon as I would have wanted to because I am presently absent from Lyons.*

> *Many pastors of your diocese, headed by Father Cartellier, came to ask if I would send the Pope a report on La Salette. I told them that recourse to the Pope is always permitted, but that they would have to consult you beforehand. They told me they would consult you and send me a report. The report arrived well sealed. I did not want to read it. These people had promised me they would consult you before all else. Someone was leaving for Rome and I sent the package without opening it. Some time later, to my great surprise, I received a printed report. I did not open it. This, Bishop, is what has taken place.*

I am displeased to have relied on Cartellier whom I thought more deserving of trust. What these priests have done is most reprehensible. Your Excellency would do well to point this out to them. Had I read the report, I never would have sent it. But I now believe Father Déléon had a hand in all this, and I have no confidence whatsoever in him.

Cartellier himself received a note that must have sounded like a death knell. "I had confidence in you, Father. You have placed me in the position of having to make my disapproval of you known to Rome." But the poor cardinal had not yet exhausted his portion of disappointments.

With great publicity the Redon press launched, on August 28, a thick volume with a long and eloquent double title: *La Salette devant le Pape, ou rationalisme et hérésie découlant du Fait de La Salette, suivie du Mémoire au Pape par plusieurs membres du clergé diocésain de Grenoble.* In this way, Cartellier appeared with Déléon on the title page. His haughty aloofness tolerated the huckster's glibness: "one of them (among the most intelligent and the most conscientious priests of the diocese) has breathed life into this report" read one blurb. Moreover, he tried to lend plausibility to his colleague's most absurd fabrications by transforming the "highly placed civil servant" to "a highly placed official of the University of Grenoble," following Déléon's leads and searching Miss de Lamerlière's harmless behavior to arrive at apparently plausible conclusions. All of which goes to show that, in his frenzy to win out, the choice of means was of no importance to Cartellier. Still, this is the same man who had no illusions about Déléon as he wrote: "We can reproach Father Déléon especially for lack of precision in the details he reports. Even if what he says is true, he leaves himself open to proof of falsehood. He embroiders, so to speak. In his conclusions, Father Déléon seems to be a bit peculiar...."

Déléon's case posed no juridical problem for Bishop Ginoulhiac. Cartellier's, given his appeal to the Holy See, demanded more circumspection.

Having received his own copy of the Report, the Bishop of Grenoble had immediately asked Rome how he should deal with it. In a brief dated August 30, Pius IX sent the matter back to him in keeping "with the rule of the Holy See in this type of question, which is to refer to the judgment of the Ordinary, to whom legitimate testimonies and proofs must be duly remitted." This right of the bishop which was being ignored underlies every line of this document.

Referring first to the manuscript forwarded by Cardinal de Bonald, the Holy Father noted that he "returned it to the Eminent Cardinal who had sent it, asking him to examine it and to give him an account of its contents." Coming

Pope Pius IX
(1792-1878)

to the printed copy he had been given soon after, he described the report in terms Cartellier should have expected but which, instead, stunned and embittered him.

> As soon as we realized that this pamphlet was nothing but the manuscript, we could not help being astounded at this conduct on the part of unknown men who disregard the most common courtesy, to say nothing else, and who certainly intend to embarrass us by the anonymous publication of this work.

He then evaluated the situation, using Bishop Ginoulhiac's words.

> In this letter you express the regret that so very few men cause so much anxiety among the people and, worse, that the faithful, some of whom come to the mountain of La Salette from distant regions, find displeasure and reason for scandal....

Then came the means to be adopted to implement these directives, taking into account circumstances and the law.

> The fact itself has been made known in so many ways and has been recognized by your predecessor on the strength of proofs and documents you certainly still have in your possession. Nothing prohibits you, as soon as you find it expedient, from investigating it anew and publicly demonstrating the truth of it. Make every effort, Venerable Brother, to see to it that the piety and filial devotion toward the Queen of heaven and Sovereign of this world, so widespread in this

place, be faithfully maintained in your people and grow stronger day by day.

Father Déléon was summoned to appear before diocesan officials. During four sessions he defended himself, conceding only that his mistaken theology was due more to hasty writing than to malice. He admitted that the superior of the Missionaries had not, in fact, "sequestered" Mélanie. "His explanations, his excuses were attentively heard and received with fatherly concern," guarantees Bishop Ginoulhiac in his instruction of September 30. Unfortunately, Déléon persisted in maintaining that priests and even the faithful have a right, by way of the press, to protest against the ordinances of their bishop against what they believe contrary to the teaching and the discipline of the Church, provided these publications are restricted to a certain number of people.

Consequently, his ecclesiastical faculties were once more suspended and his book was banned as containing "on the one hand, propositions which are erroneous, reckless, scandalous, subversive, smacking of Presbyterianism or favoring it, and on the other hand, as containing allegations and implications against Bishop de Bruillard and respected priests of the diocese that constitute in the canonical sense a veritable defamation of character."

The *Mémoire au Pape* (*Report to the Pope*), if only because of its author's personality, was even more likely to create a serious bias against La Salette. Hence, Bishop Ginoulhiac took the time to check its assertions one by one before publishing, on November 4, 1854, an instruction which toppled this proud castle of cards and which cast at last on the question of La Salette a definitive light.

Bishop Ginoulhiac stated that he was not pronouncing a new judgment. Keeping in step with the Church, he was satisfied with bringing needed cures to present-day ills. Following the *Mémoire's* reasoning, he showed that the opponents had uncovered no new facts and presented no explanation invalidating the verdict handed down by his predecessor. In passing, he highlighted all the passion and bias that slanted a critique calling itself objective and inspired by the love of religion. He pointed out "grave and premeditated reservations, rash and even false assertions, baseless allegations injurious to our venerable predecessor and to respectable priests of our diocese, and, finally, insidious and even openly malevolent insinuations."

While refuting objections, and precisely in order to refute them, he recalled facts, put forth theological and critical principles, the whole of which could be considered a small apologetical summa, the most substantial ever written on La Salette. This is where we will always find the solid foundations establishing the truth of the event as well as the guidelines guaranteeing the Christian value of the devotion. There is no doubt, for example, that an axiom such as "La Salette is not a new doctrine but a new grace" will save us from many deviations. It is also very likely that all the attacks and the doubts later provoked by the two children's conduct would have lost much of their corrosiveness had the question of fact always been situated on the grounds on which the pronouncement itself had placed it.

> One would be oddly mistaken to believe that the proof of the apparition is derived from the moral character of the children at the time of its occurrence. Those who have written on the subject find their proof especially in that it was impossible for the children to have planned a hoax, to have been accomplices in it, or to have been tricked into it.

That this superb document reflected the authentic teaching of the Church can be seen in the rapid approval given it by Pope Pius IX. After its publication, Bishop Ginoulhiac had left for Rome. The Pope received him several times with extreme kindness. When he returned, he communicated to Cardinal de Bonald the epilogue to the question of the report.

> In my last audience with him, the Holy Father spoke to me about it on his own initiative. He told me he stood by the contents of his last letter to me. I then asked him if I had rendered the correct meaning of it in my own pronouncement, which I knew he had read. He answered yes, that I had rendered his thought accurately. (7)

After this communique Cartellier was faced with a dramatic choice. He had to submit or follow Déléon in open revolt. His book had been sternly condemned in severe terms and banned to all those in holy orders. His personal standing would be determined by his own reaction. "Hoping that the author of this book will give an example of praiseworthy submission," wrote the Bishop, "we reserve to ourselves the right to decree accordingly."

At first, he thought of evading Bishop Ginoulhiac's conditions by attempting a new recourse to Rome. Avoiding an official summons, he began calling to arms some of his well-placed connections, among whom it is not surprising to find a certain Father de Geslin, serving the opposition's cause in Rome. He was a very suspect character whose bits of gossip delighted Déléon. But Cartellier finally understood the futility of such recourses. Instead of going to Rome, he deferred to his bishop. Cardinal de Bonald's mediation seemed desirable to both parties. Thanks to him, a submission formula was worked out to the satisfaction of Bishop Ginoulhiac and which Cartellier agreed to sign. It should be noted that it did not imply on Cartellier's part any retraction of his opinion on the event of La Salette. By allowing him to write it, the bishop respected his dignity much more than Cartellier had respected the dignity of others.

> By attacking the fact of the apparition, I did not intend to attack the La Salette devotion. I will obey the pronouncement of November 4 completely and will not seek to spread my report. In humble submission I accept the official condemnation of my report; I wish to submit to all the administrative acts of my bishop. I have reported the facts contained in my report in good faith, but I repudiate and condemn all that is untrue and incorrect, still holding to my opinion on La Salette. I repudiate, deplore, and condemn all the expressions in my report which could have caused pain to Bishop de Bruillard and to all the priests who are referred to by the bishop in his pronouncement.

After having received this declaration on February 26,1855, Bishop Ginoulhiac communicated to Father Cartellier that he considered the matter concluded, in order "to give to the Cardinal a sign of deference to his wishes and to Father Cartellier one more proof of his own fatherly kindness and of his extreme respect." Was this to be the end of the controversy?

Publicly, Cartellier avoided compromising himself. But his opinion on La Salette was so passionately held that it was impossible for him to contain it either in his letters or in his conversations. What he could not say openly, he confided to his diary: the footnote history of people related to the event, the sarcasms provoked by articles in Le Siècle, or the miraculous, sudden changes in the Curé of Ars. The rest of his life was spent feeding this obsession: La Salette is harebrained nonsense. All that happened had confirmed, as far as he was concerned, that he was not mistaken. He died at Vichy in 1865.

Déléon had a longer career as part of an opposition in which he did not believe. What Bishop Ginoulhiac wanted from him, a change of behavior, he was unwilling to grant. Whence came resentment and invective spread over some twenty years, each manifestation different from the other in its effrontery, all desperately monotonous in their repetition of the same sophistry. Suffice it to recall only *La Conscience d'un prêtre et le pouwir d'un évêque (The Conscience of a Priest and the Power of a Bishop)* in 1856, and *Le Dernier mot sur La Salette (The Final Word on La Salette)* in 1872.

In the first piece, Déléon presented himself as the victim of fanaticism. After a long letter to Cardinal de Bonald, he lectured his bishop on the theology of Christ and of the Virgin. Bishop Ginoulhiac saw fit to point out a few of these aberrations. His circular letter of September 19, 1857 destroyed the credit Déléon still enjoyed among a few carping critics, and dispelled the uneasiness brought on by the verdict of the Court of Appeals which a few months before had rejected Miss de Lamerlière's plea of defamation of character.

Le dernier mot sur La Salette (The Final Word on La Salette) is the final cry of a condemned man who curses his judges. In 1870, Bishop Ginoulhiac succeeded Cardinal de Bonald. In Lyons he was informed that nothing of what had happened in Grenoble was forgotten, and that, in 1857, he had attempted to slander an innocent man after having tried to corrupt him on the subject of La Salette with the collaboration of the timid Father Cartellier who had offered his submission as an example. Cartellier, an accomplice of Bishop Ginoulhiac! This last detail is surely the most original touch in the whole work.

Still, the poor man was yet to experience a time of grace. In 1883, Déléon was 85. He had survived all his adversaries and felt alone to face the final struggle. The ordinary of Grenoble, Bishop Fava, offered the Church's pardon, and the old man readily admitted his erring ways throughout 29 years. "I regret," he declared, "having written against La Salette, an event protected by diocesan authority. As a man and as a priest, I also repudiate in my writings whatever has been hurtful toward the bishops of Grenoble, their administration, and some of my colleagues." **(8)**

Restored to good standing the old adversary did not hide the fact that La Salette had never been other than a pretext. "I did not attack La Salette in itself," he wrote to Father Bertrand.

> *I used it in an attempt to show the bishop's shallowness, the idolatry of his power, and the defiance his words provoked. I had only one purpose: to seek out and highlight all that was not perfectly accurate in the pronouncements. My method was simple and I adhered to it against Bishop Ginoulhiac as against his predecessor, and for the same motive.* **(9)**

There is more to this story. The grace of La Salette was reaching him also. Toward the end of his life, he was meeting at the rectory of Saint-Ismier with Father Maron, a young Missionary of La Salette who was a native of the parish. At their last meeting, it was agreed that the young religious would bring the old adversary incognito to La Salette. Déléon had long wished to make this pilgrimage. Only the fear of being recognized had prevented him from going. But death itself intervened and led him to the Reconciling Lady (1895).

If Déléon had been alone, we could confidently dismiss objections he himself never believed in, despite the noisy claims that surrounded them. But Cartellier maintained his stand to the very end. In his official act of submission he professed his good faith. He may have repudiated "all that is false or inaccurate," but he insisted on maintaining his opinion on La Salette. Father Burnoud, the first superior of the Missionaries, had spoken in a promotion piece of Cartellier's "retraction." Cartellier quickly complained to Bishop Ginoulhiac of the inaccuracy of the term and succeeded in having the piece withdrawn. Such a persistent conviction deserves at the least a summary analysis.

What could the *Mémoire au Pape* have revealed to discredit Bishop de Bruillard's pronouncement, as Cartellier claimed it had? All the objections brought forth in the 1847 Commission surfaced again in the Report, but without variation and with no attempt to make them serve a coherent explanation. In his eyes the children remained liars, and this accusation rested on the same reasons that the majority found wanting in 1847: the citizens of Corps are opportunists, neither better nor worse than before the event; the Pastor of Corps sequestered the children and was involved in the sale of miraculous water; the Lady's discourse is inane and trivial; her prophecies have not been realized. All this is heavy with insinuation, but the mystery remains: who then first conceived this story coming from the lips of two ignorant children? If there is any hint of progress in the restatement of these old criticisms, it lies not so much in the explanations they provide as in their newly-acquired assertiveness. Bishop de Bruillard is depicted as a gullible and tyrannical old man. He is described as immensely naive. Cartellier's so-called "good taste" sometimes borrows some of Déléon's glib rudeness.

The newly-minted objections are listed under four headings: the retraction at Ars; the de Lamerlière caper; the shepherd's present conduct; the testimony of early narratives which would destroy the official version as well as the substance of the bishop's pronouncement.

We have seen enough of the Ars incident to assess Cartellier's judgment in the matter. The de Lamerlière fable needs no further discreditation. To those who believe it on the faith of such as Salomon Reinach **(10)** or Renan **(11)** or some distinguished lecturer, we confidently state that Déléon's plot is pure fiction.

One day, the parish priest of Saint-Ismier, Father Jayet, said to Déléon: "Now tell me, did you ever believe that Miss de Lamerlière had been the heroine of La Salette and that she had been the one who appeared to Maximin and Mélanie on September 19, 1846?"

"Of course not," Déléon replied. "I never believed that. It was a crazy story that someone told in the course of a meal at Albenc. I recorded it in my journal. The de Lamerlière family was furious and took me to court." **(12)**

But how could Cartellier, who knew Déléon well, have picked up such an insipid story and included it in his report to the Pope? Submitting himself to his bishop he wrote: "I have recorded the facts in my report in good faith." In fairness, one must note this, but clearly his good faith admitted everything that concurred with his version of the truth and nothing that contradicted it.

Cartellier's systematic prejudice appeared as early as the meetings of 1847. The reports of the bishop's commission mentioned one opponent who was more intractable than the others. One voice alone refused to concede that the children's stories were in agreement with one another as well as with the official report. One voice alone disagreed with the topography of the site of the apparition as presented by the investigators. Is it rash to presume that this is the voice of our perennial skeptic? Yes, the children made up this story. Yes, they learned it from someone concealed somewhere near the fountain. All assumptions are allowed, even contradictory ones, as long as they do not say that the children have seen the Blessed Virgin.

The prejudice was fully visible in the report and, at times, it confused the author himself. The Ars incident seemed to have settled the question in his mind, but he still had to cope with the de Lamerlière story. To introduce it, he was forced into a subtle exegesis aimed at harmonizing it with the categorical statement he attributed to the Curé of Ars: "The child has seen nothing, neither white nor black, neither man nor woman."

"Taken literally,"—Cartellier is speaking—"this means: I have seen no one. I saw nothing at all." "On the other hand, it can mean I have seen nothing supernatural, nothing that I have tried to make you believe." "I have seen nothing" is therefore not opposed to any feeling." "It could mean anything. What is clear in what Maximin has said, what is unquestionable, is that he has not seen the Blessed Virgin and that what he has told is a well-learned fable. As far as the rest is concerned, one could say that there was a lady there, without contradicting what was said at Ars."

But there is no longer one lady. There are now three in Cartellier's overly exhaustive report. Before crowning Miss de Lamerlière, he introduced two Bohemians and seriously added: "These two women, one of them especially (Larivière), could have played the La Salette role." Even this did not prevent him from concluding the de Lamerlière story with more gravity: "A lawyer said that to bring a verdict in a case the courts needed only prove Miss de Lamerlière's *apparition*."

Did Cartellier believe his own proofs? What is certain is that he had not established a single one. Even if, in good faith, he was duped by Donnadieu, in the end, his system can be summed up in a few words: anything goes.

Such deep hostility must have stemmed from beyond the ideas he expressed. It brought to the fore the deep-seated options that Pascal calls "reasons of the heart." We are allowed to see in a few telltale lines that Cartellier's attitude toward La Salette predated any type of reasoning. This is the least that can be said.

Before the imperial court of Grenoble, on April 30, 1857, his lawyer, Farconet, was into his summation: "Religion can only suffer from this story of La Salette. In this century, the Divinity manifests Itself in such great marvels: steam is harnessed to man's chariots, carrying him with the speed of the wind; electricity communicates his very thought with lightning speed. These and other marvels speak so well of His bounty and goodness that to mention *yellow stockings, dialects,* and *butter in soup* amounts to a veritable profanation." **(13)**

This short burst of eloquence deserves closer scrutiny. But no one need be fooled. The inspiration was not the speaker's alone. The details of the apparition are too precise, too well chosen, the ideas too similar to Cartellier's to conceal their source. Throughout the entire report, he bemoaned the minor role he played in the councils of Bishop de Bruillard. His attitude, indeed, was hardly conducive to finding the truth in the miraculous events before him.

The accusation of evolution in the presentation of the La Salette story would be serious if it could be proven. We recall the categorical statement of the two investigators appointed by the bishop in 1847: "All those who, from the very first days after the apparition, had interrogated the children and had taken notes, did indeed testify to the children's constancy in giving to all the very same account, without variation, either in form or in substance." We know that the bishop's verdict rested on the report of his two commission members as well as on the strong majority approval given him by the general meeting of 1847. But according to the *Mémoire au Pape*, some versions written much before Rousselot's would attest to progressive phases in the composition of the Lady's Discourse. "The hand of man might be in evidence," insinuated Cartellier. "Is the hand of the Virgin as clearly there?"

To understand the precise nature of these accusations, one must illuminate Cartellier's half tones with Déléon's harsh coloring. The man who "breathed life into the report" with an introduction entitled *La Salette face au Pape* had no qualms about openly naming his victims. He clearly accused Rousselot of having written an adulterated report; Mélin, pastor of Corps, of having prompted Maximin; Lagier, the judicious Lagier, of having produced an apocryphal report, the Pra narrative, "because La Salette will become a mini-California for his region as well as for his family." All this was included in the *Mémoire au Pape*, but in well-couched implications. A kind of osmosis had taken place between the two works in which each author would have been hard put to distinguish his own arguments from those of his colleague.

The person principally accused is the bishop's official advocate. He is accused of adding and subtracting elements from the Discourse as contained in certain accounts, of mentioning a secret that would be of interest to the public precisely where the same accounts had contained wise counsels given to the shepherds. The prophecy concerning grapes and nuts was allegedly added later. The expression "next year" relative to rotting wheat was left out, Déléon explained cynically, because in May 1847 the wheat was growing well while almost everywhere the vines and the nuts were diseased. Then a letter arrived from Corps for the Bishop of Grenoble, said the accuser, stating that the white Lady's prophecy extended also to nuts and grapes. This prophecy was first mentioned in May (the Long narrative). Moreover, this Long document which passed from the hands of the justice of the peace to those of Rousselot was published by the latter only three years later. "No document he has touched can offer a serious guarantee."

To firm up this pitiful fiction, one must eliminate the documents on which the advocate's version is based, in particular the Pra account, the most embarrassing one because it is the closest to the origins. This is why Lagier was attacked, since his is the only report containing the Pra version. And since the children's progress had to be specifically accounted for, Father Mélin became the object of mocking calumny.

Said the *Mémoire au Pape:*

> According to Messieurs Day and Guillaud, Maximin didn't know how to give his narrative. This is confirmed by the following incident. A highly placed official of the University, being in Corps, wanted to see the heroes of La Salette. He went to their convent-residence. He was not alone when he entered and found still more strangers inside.

> Before this entire gathering, Maximin recited his story. He spoke glibly, like a schoolboy who had learned his lesson well. "My child," asked the man we alluded to, "did you know it in the beginning as you know it now?"

> "No, sir."

> "How did you come to remember all this?"

> "It is the parish priest."

We are not rehearsing this old controversy to add more fireworks to the many already lit by the adversaries. We merely want to show that

The kitchen of Mr. Pra's house in Les Ablandins where
the children first told the story of the Apparition

fireworks are not an argument. We want to take the occasion of this controversy to show that the version of the La Salette event held by Bishop de Bruillard's delegates can well withstand the test of historical criticism. The importance of this question goes well beyond the refutation of past arguments. We therefore ask the reader's indulgence as we proceed to a somewhat technical discussion.

When we described the mission of Fathers Rousselot and Orcel, we pointed out the sources that justified the adoption of their text as well as the key statement: "the two children have always told the same story." These sources rely on the testimony of those who first heard the story as well as on three accounts that can be termed privileged because they were written under the children's dictation. These are the Pra, Lagier, and Lambert narratives. To this group of truly reliable texts the bishop's staff added the deposition of Monsieur Long, substitute justice of the peace in Corps. This document was still unknown to the bishop's delegates at the time of the inquiry. It came as another confirmation of their critical sense. The bishop's delegates made no mention of an account written by the haberdasher Laurent, which reproduces Mélanie's narrative almost exactly, and thus completes the cycle of privileged testimonies.

We have also alluded to other narratives of lesser value. Many ecclesiastics rushed to the mountain in October and November of 1846 and kept notes on what they had seen and heard, or corresponded with friends. They interrogated the children but did not always understand the answers given in the local dialect. They took a few hasty notes, editing them from memory many days later. Critical judgment would advise cautious use of these notes. The investigators were aware of some of these accounts. They rightfully preferred the narratives of the first group.

When he condemned the *Mémoire au Pape*, Bishop Ginoulhiac had all the earliest narratives before him, those of the first as well as those of the second group. He noted that neither group presented important variants concerning the *externals of the apparition.* This agreement on so many details is impressive. He had no difficulty showing that the variations in the discourse, so often underscored by the adversaries, were insignificant when we consider the better narratives.

The prophecy concerning nuts and grapes was included not only in the Long narrative but much earlier also in Lagier and from the very beginning in Pra. The phrase "next year" should perhaps have been kept in the definitive account since it appears in Pra, but its suppression does not really alter the general sense. In its context, the mention of rotting wheat can only refer to the following year's harvest. *"The potatoes will continue to spoil and by Christmas time this year there will be none left. If you have grain, it will do no good to sow it."* There are other differences between the secondary narratives and the official one, but one statement must be singled out as simply false. Cartellier pointed out this sentence which had been rejected by Rousselot: "The Blessed Virgin said that young people were making bad confessions and that they even went as far as to have meals brought in at the dance hall." He was advised that this reproach "was not found in any narrative, not even in Mr. Day's, but only in a paper written by a woman, and of no value whatever."

There remained the phrase concerning "the stones thrown at girls" which Cartellier still insisted on debating during the meetings of 1847. Bishop Ginoulhiac quickly summarized the explanations provided by his Commission and concluded: "It must be understood that this accretion is of little importance and does not justify the insults the boy received because of it." Regarding the secret that had allegedly changed in nature, and which now concerned the public instead of the children, it would only be fair to note that the qualifying term "wise counsels" represents the personal opinion of clerics, "the children having remained inscrutable on the contents of their secret."

After all of these explanations, the bishop could rightfully give these adversaries, whose prejudices could no longer remain concealed, a lesson in critical fairness and loyalty.

> *It is easy to understand, dear Colleagues, why there is no mention in the "Mémoire" of the narratives of J.B. Pra, of Fathers Lagier and Lambert, of the Justice of the Peace of Corps, that is, of the earliest or of the most official of the accounts.*

> *It is also easy to understand that when the testimony of other narratives is invoked, these are not referred to as stemming from one account only. When it is referred to, its true nature and character are glossed over. These omissions, which cannot be set aside as merely accidental or caused by an inadequate critical sense, helped spread doubt concerning the integrity of the primitive version.*

The Bishop's pronouncement made one point clear: the diocese's official version, whose authenticity was questioned, stemmed directly from the very first account. All five of the critically "privileged" versions—Pra, Laurent, Lagier, Long and Lambert—attest to this. These versions can withstand detailed comparison to one another. The basic elements are the same in all of them. These elements are narrated in the same order, with variations limited to differences of expression. It is true that the framework of narrative and descriptive passages is not found in the Pra account, and that the Laurent narrative which provides them is of later vintage (November 27). Many of these missing links were provided by the secondary narratives. Father Mélin's letter, dated October 4, already contained the principal events surrounding the apparition as well as a general description of the Lady. Information was gradually added and specified according to the curiosity of the investigators.

We are well aware that children tend to shorten and to summarize when asked to describe an event. Their evaluation of details is not the same as an adult's. Particulars which are important to a grown-up are of no interest to them. They must be interrogated further. The children's spontaneous accounts were naturally brief, but when they were questioned patiently, one could draw out, as Lagier the inquisitor did, much extremely precise information. When all the versions, the principal as well as the secondary, are compared, there is no doubt that all the details harmonize well with one another. This has never been contested.

Can we then conclude that the problem of concordance among the narratives is solved according to Rousselot's own terms? Is it so very certain that Maximin and Mélanie never differed in their accounts? Are we sure that as they came down the mountain on September 19, 1846, they narrated the very same story that Orcel and Rousselot heard them recite the following month of August? In Mélanie's case there is clear evidence of this, since the Pra narrative (September 20) was drafted under her dictation and agrees with the four others written under the same circumstances. This, however, cannot be said of Maximin.

The first account that we can consider authentically Maximin's own is the one Lagier took down at the end of February 1847. It conforms in every way to the accepted details of the apparition as well as with the Lady's discourse. But up to that time, his account had come down only through the confused allusions contained in narratives we have called secondary. In narrative and descriptive detail, we know that these stories agree with the principal versions, but their handling of the discourse is subject to caution and cannot guarantee that in the beginning Maximin recited it as Mélanie did.

Written proof and detailed notation are lacking on this point. This should cause no alarm if we recall that all the primitive accounts, the principal as well as the secondary, had purely random beginnings and that the bishop's office initiated no formal inquiry until August 1847. Until February 1847 no one had thought of taking down and passing on Maximin's own exact report of the events. This should not reflect against him. Prudence demands that we fall back on the global assurances of those who had heard him: Selme, Pra, Peytard, Mélin. It is nevertheless essential that we examine the problem placed before us. "According to Mr. Day and Mr. Guillaud," as the *Mémoire au Pape* says, "in the beginning Maximin did not know how to tell his story." Bishop Ginoulhiac did not answer this objection because he had not undertaken to refute the *Report* to the very last iota. We, however, cannot cut short our examination of such a crucial difficulty.

What do Guillaud and Day actually say? Not quite what we would have them say, nor perhaps what they wanted to say. They simply copied Perrin and reproduced a perplexing paragraph which they probably did not understand. "This entire narrative is very faithfully given by little Mélanie, and although Maximin was unable in the beginning to give it in the same order, he still corroborated Mélanie's story when he heard her tell it." So say all three men, the copiers and the original author of these lines. Perrin is most certainly at the origin of this statement. As he sent his requisitioned text to Bishop Ginoulhiac, Day said clearly that it was copied from Perrin, even partly written in the latter's own hand. Guillaud likewise intimated that he copied a text placed before him at the rectory of La Salette. "When I wrote this I had only Maximin with me. At each sentence I would ask him if this was his account as well as Mélanie's and he would answer yes."

What did Perrin mean by this mysterious sentence that the adversaries so quickly seized upon?

Let us begin by saying that it is never a good idea to interpret a text contrary to the general intent and spirit of its author. This Father Louis Perrin, whose testimony the adversaries sought without even naming him, had always been a dedicated servant of the new shrine until the Missionaries' arrival on the mountain. He

Fr. Joseph Perrin, M.S. (1836-1913), fourth La Salette Superior General founded the Archconfraternity, was the first to bestow on the Virgin of the apparition the title of Our Lady of La Salette, Reconciler. But the ardor of the believer replaced in him a very systematic doubt. "When I arrived in the parish, this event had penetrated every family. Every day travelers were going up the mountain.... Immediately and at every occasion I sought information.... My very definite intention was to uncover a hoax in the story that the two shepherds were telling." **(14)** If Maximin had not been reciting the words of the Virgin in the same manner as Mélanie, can we imagine such a priest overlooking this flaw? The same can be said of the many priests who had interrogated the children during the fall: none of them alluded to it.

We reopen the manuscript where the new parish priest of La Salette recalls his first steps in the parish and we find the circumstances in which he drafted his own narrative.

> *Ten days after having been installed as pastor of La Salette, I brought Mélanie with me and I visited the site of the apparition for the first time. As we were leaving Les Ablandins, I interrogated her on her story and I noted all her answers. Above the village of Dorsières three priests joined us: Father Cat, pastor of La Mure; Father Chevanas, assistant pastor at Corps; and another priest unknown to me. When we arrived at the site we were approximately thirty people. Mélanie explained to us in detail the different phases of the apparition, repeated all the Virgin's words, and retraced her steps up the path. After hearing this account at the site, I rectified many omissions I had made while coming up the mountain with Mélanie.*

What Perrin does not say here but what he writes in his account and reaffirms in later correspondence is that Maximin was also with him. When exactly did he interrogate the boy? Since Maximin was from Corps, he was very probably accompanying the assistant pastor of Corps and the other clerics. Perrin's curiosity turned to him only after he had questioned Mélanie. This alone interests us. The mysterious sentence becomes clear when we place it in this set of circumstances. The day he interrogated the children, he was seeing them for the first time. Was he qualified to state that "in the begin-

The hamlet of Les Ablandains, near the hamlet of La Salette

ning" Maximin could not tell his story as clearly as Mélanie did? In his understanding, the expression "in the beginning" would not mean "at the outset," or "in the early days following the apparition," as the adversaries would have it, but "at the beginning of this interrogation to which I have just subjected him."

What can we conclude? Only this: the boy's narrative did not make the sequence of facts as clear to him as did Mélanie's account. Having reached the site of the apparition, he even had to correct Mélanie's prior explanations. As we reread the passage revealing his intention, is it not clear that his main purpose was to re-enact the event on the site itself and that this is how he expected to expose the hoax? "Hearing her account on the site of the apparition, I corrected many omissions I had made as I came up the mountain with her." He is not correcting the order of the Discourse, since this is not the order of the narrative that Mélanie dictated to Pra, then to Laurent and to all those who agreed to take things down as she said them. He is not preoccupied with the order of the Discourse but with the proper sequence of facts, like his colleague Cat, who also was looking for "circumstantial details". We need not be surprised at Maximin's inferiority on this point. Only total inexperience with regard to children would cause one to wonder why Maximin did not follow the natural sequence of events: they had slept, they had picked up their lunch bags, the Lady was seated, then she stood.

Everyday experience shows that an eleven-year-old boy does not relate a sequence of actions with the ease of a fifteen-year-old girl. Perrin himself felt this to be true when he wrote very calmly and without a hint of skepticism or scandal: "When he [Maximin] heard Mélanie tell the story, he always said that this was indeed the way it had taken place."

No historical document allows anyone to infer that the boy needed special tutoring to confirm and put in order what he had seen and heard the first day. The assurances given us by those who first heard the children are still fully valid. Even all the other faulty narratives, as long as no more is expected of them than they mean to convey, likewise show that Maximin's story was substantially the same as that of Mélanie.

Cartellier's exegeses are not overly meticulous but a close scrutiny will show their critical value. His anecdotes all come from the same source. The story he tells to confirm the statements of Guillaud and Day is suspect. The highly placed official remains anonymous. He is accompanied by "certain" persons and meets a "certain" number of strangers. We are not told the date of this memorable incident, but two queries will be enough to obtain an answer and prove the thesis, with a little comedy thrown in: It is the pastor! Indeed, it would be difficult to think of a more childish answer. In view of this grave accusation against Father Mélin, the critical reader would be entitled to equal time from the children themselves. But whoever takes the time to look into the sources will find to his or her amazement that this incident is also found in La Salette devant le Pape, which precedes the Mémoire and which Déléon also takes up briefly in La Salette-Fallavaux, published two years previously.

We know, and Cartellier more than anyone, what Déléon's anecdotes are worth, but this one happens to serve the purpose and braces up a cherished contradiction. As we observe the intellectual methods of these adversaries, we can agree with Bishop Ginoulhiac when he writes in his circular letter, dated September 19, 1857, against Déléon: If anything besides the proofs of the apparition itself could bring about belief in La Salette, it would be the way it was attacked!

For the benefit of future generations, here is the most specious of all their objections.

What the children became in 1854 is so unedifying, they utter such stupidities, that the whole story that made them famous deserves to be discredited.

"It is a tree bearing bad fruit because it is a bad tree. The waters are muddy because the source is dirty." We have faithfully just summarized the last argument worthy of note in the report. It has not lost its virulence and, even today, undiscerning people deride La Salette under the pretext that Mélanie and Maximin cannot be considered saints.

Bishop Ginoulhiac's response to this is to restate the truth of the teaching as well as that of the facts. In the minds of people, the witness to an apparition must be a saint and must remain so by a kind of continuous miracle. Against this notion, the bishop presents the traditional teaching of the Church: "It is well known that this kind of grace, as all theologians agree, and according to the Gospel itself, can be granted to people unworthy of it, especially when its main purpose is not to sanctify those who receive it, but to warn and teach others. We also know that we can abuse divine revelations, even those that concern us personally, even when they have been received in the time of one's youth and accepted with a pure heart. They still do not prevent even the most dreadful moral collapses. Solomon's example is a well known case in point and suffices for our purpose."

The Most Reverend
William Ullathorne,
Bishop of Birmingham, England

He then reminds his readers that the moral character of the children plays a very secondary role in proving the

240

truth of the apparition. This proof resides in the total incongruity between the children's story and "their coarseness, their eccentric behavior, and their ignorance." A consideration of their character is relevant only inasmuch as it stresses this incongruity. Here, the Bishop of Grenoble contributes the remarkable observation of Bishop Ullathorne of Birmingham [England]:

> *While they were intent solely on giving the details of the apparition as well as showing the part they had played in it, they unwittingly, truthfully, and in such detail displayed their character, their short-comings, and their qualities, that it is impossible not to accept that they have seen and done as they have said.*

We could state, in sum, that the strength of the proof rests on the contrast between what they are and the event they report. If this is so, then what they became after the apparition is still less important than what they were at that time.

The *Mémoire* gives such a negative and false impression of their conduct that the bishop saw fit to bring the facts into proper perspective. This he did not only to do justice to the children, but also to offset the damage inflicted on La Salette by those who twisted their every word and action. They would even accuse the children of being constitutionally prone to lying and seeing visions. We recognize here the strategy Cartellier used earlier in 1847.

With the perspective acquired from his own research, Bishop Ginoulhiac could then properly evaluate the statements made against the children and, through them, against the apparition itself. Maximin was not the inveterate liar nor the herald of falsehood he was made out to be. Neither did Mélanie preach heresy. But the bishop became aware that, of late, both had drawn too much attention to themselves. Maximin had taken to prophesying, Mélanie to occupying center stage. Such were the consequences of inordinate and exaggerated adulation lavished on the Blessed Virgin's privileged children. It had not been so with them at the beginning. This particular moment in their lives, these events, with all of their foreseeable consequences, are of such crucial importance that we must try to explain them with the same integrity that the bishop himself brought to the task.

Maximin's oracles were those of a young idiot. After the Ars affair, he told the followers of Richemont to warn their leader: "You must tell him to trim those (his sideburns) because his life is in danger." This type of remark made in the company of adolescent seminarians can make for amusing conversation. Bishop Ginoulhiac saw fit to bring order and quiet to this situation and he tells us that his warnings were heeded. It is essential here to identify the point of deviation. The bishop uncovered it in the tactics of Maximin's entourage of visionaries who tried to have him say that his secret concerned the

Jacques-Marie-Achille Ginoulhiac (1806-1875), Bishop of Grenoble

Baron of Richemont. We saw how they schemed to bring about the trip to Ars. It is also worth pointing out the unsettling influence on Maximin of a man like Antoine Gay, whether he was possessed or not. As early as 1847, they had come to Corps and had been disappointed by Maximin's ignorance of Louis XVI, Louis XVII, and Louis XVIII. He had heard only of Louis-Philippe. They could never obtain a particle of Maximin's secret, but their visionary dreams finally colored the young boy's impressionable mind. Bishop Ginoulhiac wrote,

> They had not succeeded in stealing his secret, so they confided to him the prophecies it was supposed to contain. Even as late as 1851, Maximin had not imagined the role they would have him play. But, charmed by the flattering content of these prophecies, he finally succumbed to self infatuation. Finding peers and other people willing to listen to him, he confided these so-called prophecies to them. He was actively pursuing this course of action when we were informed of it and had to take severe measures to withdraw him from it.

Mélanie's case was perhaps more pathetic. The adversaries, as well as the whole diocese, knew of the failure of her first attempt at religious life at Corenc. It is well known that she claimed to be favored with mystical gifts. When she met with opposition she resorted to childish behavior. Déléon gleefully describes a morbidly angry scene that became the talk of Vienne. Cartellier, meanwhile, labored hard to condense Mélanie's predictions into a clearly heretical proposition linking La Salette to the Vintras sect. Neither one of these men approached her case with a minimum of understanding. In their opinion all of this came as the conclusion from a principle: the root is evil, so the fruit is already condemned.

The Bishop made a serious attempt at tracking down the beginnings of these tendencies in Mélanie that were so contrary to the children's original message. He traced the time of their origin to the novitiate of Corenc and very discreetly isolated the causes capable of producing them. The La Salette event predated these tendencies and is of an entirely different order.

While Mélanie did not undergo the same trials [as Maximin], she was subjected to temptations capable of firing the most dormant imagination and of trying the most proven virtue. Ever since September 19,1846, a large number of people, some of them influential and well known, showered adulation and consideration upon her, bordering on a kind of cult. For many years this had little effect upon her. But would it not have been surprising had she not finally let herself be convinced of her own importance? This is one of the great dangers facing people who are favored with extraordinary gifts. This self-importance and the peculiar behavior resulting from it caught our interest as soon as we were informed of it. Even if the Community praised her piety and her zeal for the religious instruction of children, we felt it our duty not to admit her to temporary vows in order that she might be more effectively trained in the practice of Christian humility and simplicity. These are the necessary and sure safeguards against the illusions of the inner life.

Mélanie, pressed as much as Maximin to reveal the mysteries of the future supposedly contained in her secret, received the confidences of sick and anxious minds who believed that they had uncovered it.

It would seem that before leaving Corps for the first time, she heard of some of the popular predictions of events that were to mark the end times: the coming of Antichrist, his origins, and the wonders he would perform to seduce even the elect. She may have been persuaded to believe it all. In a dream (it could only be a dream, as is clear from the statements made for us under oath) she would have uttered a part of the sentence that has since become notorious, that "some apostles" or "the apostles would rise from the dead."

She energetically and categorically denied having stated that the original apostles of Jesus Christ would rise from the dead and preach a new Gospel as the "Mémoire" would have it, in order to prove La Salette false. Her religious superiors, her mistress of novices, her novitiate companions, the chaplain, the Missionaries who saw her and received her confidences also protested unanimously with her. We have spoken to all of them and we are convinced, after all the information we have gathered, that the predictions attributed to Mélanie have no foundation, because like those of Maximin, they were made after the fact and are unrelated to it. Dear Colleagues, this is certainly all we need to know about the children of the apparition.

Some people are still amazed at Bishop Ginoulhiac's quiet assurance. Many of the faithful who had believed would come to be definitively alienated from La Salette by Maximin's extravagances as well as by Mélanie's published assertions that these predictions were in fact her secret. Father Thurston, an esteemed historian, could not hide his discomfort in the face of the children's disappointing careers. "Bishop de Bruillard published his doctrinal pronouncement in 1851," he wrote.

At that time, the children were still young. Mélanie was twenty and Maximin sixteen. Life was opening up before them. No one could foresee what turn it would take for each one of them.... I dare say that if the Bishop of Grenoble and the members of his commissions had been able to foresee what the children's lives would become, he would have hesitated much longer before pronouncing himself in their favor. (15)

Certainly, impressionable people or amateur psychologists whose judgments depended on the latest views about Maximin and Mélanie did not enter deeply into the bishop's thinking. The real issue is not what they assumed it to be. If they insisted on pursuing this path, one fact remains clear: the children's testimony always remained the same relative to the apparition of September 19, 1846. The force of this truth emerged with the passing of time. It had deeply impressed Bishop Ginoulhiac.

> The dealings we have had with the children bring a remarkable fact to light. In spite of the measures we have taken in their regard and which may have seemed severe, in spite of our public statement that a retraction on their part would be of little concern to us, in spite of the broad freedom allowed them in their normal relationships and in their travel, in spite of all manner of provocation and of endless opportunities to contradict themselves, they have remained consistent in their testimony about La Salette. They have never uttered a word that would betray an absence of conviction.

Bishop Ginoulhiac's observation suggests another. When he published his own pronouncement in 1854, it could not be said of him, as it was of Bishop de Bruillard, that the children's careers were an unknown quantity. More than anyone, he noted the banner-waving tendency which would be the root cause of all the errors of their later years. At Corenc the bishop had read the first rough outlines of Mélanie's troubled writings: the secret and the autobiography. In any case, he knew them in substance. But he still saw a sign, more favorable than all the worrisome ones: the conviction of these two youths was just as strong then as it had been in their childhood. This was all he expected of them, but it provided him with a foundation for his own belief and allowed him to propose it to others. The meaning of their account remained the same in the face of many mood changes and character variations. It would be superfluous to rehearse Bishop de Bruillard's reasons for belief, but for his successor the proofs contained in the event and in its consequences were so established that he did not fear even the children's own denials. He freely confided their future to the Virgin's care.

His doctrinal pronouncement was viewed as diplomatic hypocrisy.

Talk of this nature was so rife among the clergy of Bordeaux that he forwarded a strong letter of protest to Father Fonteneau, the archbishop's secretary, authorizing him to make his true opinion known throughout the archdiocese. A few months later, on September 19, 1855, on the mountain of La Salette he preached before some eight thousand pilgrims. On that occasion he solemnly proclaimed his conviction and gave a clear expression of his thinking with regard to the two shepherds.

We are not here to crown the Blessed Virgin, [he said]. We confidently hope that, in the near future, a delegate of the Holy See will crown her in the name of His Holiness.... Reassure everyone about the truth of our Mother's apparition here. Proclaim our own belief in it. Let everyone know our innermost conviction.... The shepherd's mission is ended. The Church's mission begins. They may now leave, go into the world, even become unfaithful to this great grace. Mary's apparition will remain unchanged because it is true. Nothing coming after it in time can affect it. (16)

Clearly, this confidence in the future was not arrived at lightly. It came from a resolute man, thoroughly convinced of the value of the principles that had guided him to the truth. Now that the careers of the two shepherds are an open book before us, we might ascertain, for those who are troubled by them, whether something new has emerged to weaken the bishop-theologian's thesis as well as the supernatural foundation of La Salette. This writer finds in these careers (they will be treated in the next chapter) one more way of stating, as Maximin said the morning after the apparition, that La Salette could not have been invented.

What does emerge from a comparison of the arguments of the adversaries with those of the canonical authority is the solidity of the latter and the vacuousness of the former. The specious quibbling of the *Mémoire au Pape* cannot withstand Bishop Ginoulhiac's critical grilling of the facts. He traveled to Rome and repeated the same arguments there.

Writing to Father Fonteneau, he declared:

*I made it known to the Pope that after having examined La Salette
conscientiously and at length, I found all the hypotheses that others
presented and that I could conjure up to explain it other than supernaturally to be without foundation and probability. All the proofs
in its favor fulfilled the conditions needed to justify and maintain a
holy and praiseworthy devotion. What I said to the Holy Father I
had previously told His Eminence the Archbishop of Lyons. I repeated it afterward to His Eminence the Archbishop of Bordeaux.* **(17)**

The Holy Father, the archbishop of Lyons: what a setback for J.-P.
Cartellier! And what a rectification of any mistaken notion that such
a bishop could stoop to play politics.

-11-
Charism: Gift or Guarantee?

There is no denying it, people have a problem accepting a theologian's distinction between sanctity and the privilege of communicating a message from heaven. Were not the children chosen by the Virgin changed forever? Does not the honor they received make them ideal guides on the paths of grace? This was Cartellier's logic. Friends of the children of La Salette also reasoned in this way. When Bonnefous brought a possessed man to have Maximin read into his soul, he counted on him to accomplish great things. And Mélanie became the victim of a type of spiritual direction which assumed that consummate virtue was hers already.

We do not plan to review the children's entire careers. It would be a lengthy undertaking and is quite another subject. We simply want to show that from two lives filled with frailty and illusion came a force which did not destroy their original testimony but paradoxically strengthened it. To assess the import of their witness after their mission had ended, we must look at it from the viewpoint of an authentic theology. What is the meaning of an apparition such as that of La Salette in the teaching of the Church?

The realm of grace is complex but ordered. Saint Thomas Aquinas often repeated that it would be a mistake to exclude from it the principles of hierarchy and subordination that govern all of creation. The supernatural order, as well as the natural, is maintained by the subordination of means to ends and by the divinely organized collaboration of creatures pursuing together a common goal.

Human beings are meant to come to rest in God. This is the final end, the greatest means to which is sanctifying grace. But people are not left alone. God views all of humanity returning to Him as an endless climbing line of people struggling in solidarity, where it is in the nature of things that some give and others receive. On some

persons He bestows gratuitous blessings
without proportion to individual merit, supernatural gifts not meant for their
recipients, and which do not sanctify them,
but which they must simply place at the disposal
of their brothers and sisters. In theological parlance
these are called graces gratuitously given. In the language of Saint Paul they are the charisms that were
so prominent in the early Church. The Apostle's
word is more readily usable when we know what
it covers. In the forefront of these gifts come the
strength of the miracle-worker and the light of
the prophet. In this way, by the ministry of a few
exceptional people, the climbing ranks of humanity will be sustained at critical turns and in times
of need.

Sanctifying grace is the greatest means of union
with God. Charisms may be given to a few for
the good of all, but they are meant to bring
sanctifying grace to those who take advantage of them. The order of means demands
this. Belief in miracles and apparitions would
be pointless if it did not predispose us to conversion and growth in grace. On the other hand, we cannot invoke
the pretext that the messengers God uses lack inspiration. We cannot
expect from them anything more than a credible witness, because
revelations are not given to reveal the holiness of the messenger but
to bring us to holiness.

These are the principles enabling us to properly assess the role played
by the messengers between the Virgin and her people. This is the
Church's traditional doctrine on the matter. Those who are familiar
with Saint Thomas will surely recognize his teaching. (1) Even before
the advent of systematic theology, the Apostle Paul told the Corinthians that charisms must not divide people. Their one purpose is to
make of all our brothers and sisters members of Christ's body and to
enrich the life of grace that everyone draws from the body. (2)

The theologian can be sure that the grace given to Maximin and Mélanie is a charism when he learns that the two children were bearers of a revelation meant for the Christian people. Inspiration is not granted to anyone for personal advantage but for the good of the Church. Throughout his work this is Saint Thomas's constant teaching. (3)

All the features of a charism are radiantly present in La Salette and unmistakable. *"If my people will not obey"* are the opening words of the beautiful Lady's message. She is dealing with her people. Her grievances, threats, and promises are addressed to her people. Through the children she challenges her people almost constantly. Her very language makes clear her intention to be heard and understood by all her people. Except for the recommendation to the children to pray more, nothing in the discourse concerns them directly. They are to be merely messengers as the injunction makes clear: *"You will make this known to all my people."* It is clear that the grace they receive has an eminently social character.

Furthermore, the gift is gratuitous, with no bearing on the development of their spiritual life. In the case of Maximin and Mélanie, history confirms this. In her later years, Mélanie indulged in the fiction of her marvelous childhood, but she could never revoke her simple answer to the beautiful Lady's question: *"Do you say your prayers well, my children?"* "No, Madame," she said, "hardly at all." It is known that she did not pray. Jacques Pra and Maman Caron paid her no compliments on this point, and as long as humility gave her a grip on reality she admitted it. "Isn't justice served," she wrote in 1854, "that I, the least of all creatures, who did not begin to pray until the age of 15, suffer more and am more humiliated than others?" (4)

Finally, the grace of La Salette is supernatural and determined by this fact. It is an expression of God's special will, when it pleased Him to intervene into the established laws of nature with a proof of his power and love. The story that Maximin and Mélanie brought home from the mountain one evening did not gush forth from the depths of their subconscious selves. They could never have understood any of it. But in one hour, heaven gifted them more effectively and more happily than would have been possible in years of normal instruction. For what purpose? To provoke admiration? Or a senseless, idolizing curiosity? The Lady who sent them to us requested one thing: conversion. *"If my people will not obey, I shall be compelled to loose my Son's arm.... If people are converted, the rocks will become piles of wheat."* Ever since Paul, this has been the Church's constant voice: the charisms of some become sanctifying grace for others. With singular clarity Saint Thomas comments: "God's power will interrupt the laws of nature only for a greater good, that is to say, precisely a good that is related to grace, or eternal glory." **(5)** The only adequate and true response to God's call at La Salette is a renewal of heart. To expect this response to be maintained through the lives and example of the shepherds is wishful thinking.

Was Bishop Ginoulhiac adapting his teaching or harmonizing Bishop de Bruillard's own pronouncement? There is no mention of the children's conduct in the preamble to Bishop de Bruillard's own document. The gratuitous nature of the favor they had received must have been clear to him. Reading official reports, he learned that before the apparition Maximin lied and swore, Mélanie already was sulky and moody. Father Mélin, the parish priest of Corps, a discerning observer, kept his bishop informed of the children's conduct after the apparition. As early as September 1847, Father Mélin expressed in layman's terms what Bishop Ginoulhiac would later phrase theologically. Speaking to Mademoiselle des Brulais, he said: "Many people would like to see the children more mystical, at least more perfect. But the Blessed Virgin has left them their own natures and there is nothing we can do about it. What has been confided to them, it seems to me, can be compared to an orange in a jar. The orange does not change the jar, will not make it crystal if it is simple glass. But the jar lets us see the orange as it is." **(6)**

No one has defined his mission and reckoned his own indebtedness to the apparition more accurately than has the much-slandered but good-natured Maximin himself. On September 19, 1871, he was repeating to pilgrims on the holy mountain the same message he had been proclaiming since this date twenty-five years before. Father Bossan was there and noted that "Maximin always had the tone and bearing of a child." He recorded the following "When he had finished, he added: "Then the Blessed Virgin went in this direction (indicating the slope she had climbed). From there, she rose into the air, disappeared, and left me with all my faults."

Two days later, the same Father Bossan visited Maximin in Corps.

Father Bossan: "What must we say," [asked the merciless questioner,] "to those who accuse you and Mélanie of having faults?"
Maximin: "You should ask them which faults."

Father Bossan: "They say you are flighty and unpredictable."
Maximin: "These are not faults."

Father Bossan: "They are not vices, but they are faults."
Maximin: "I am like everyone else. I am not perfect."

Father Bossan: "I always say you are a good Christian because that is the truth...."

After a few moments the interrogator persisted:

Father Bossan: "Hasn't the apparition produced something special within you? I mean, hasn't it brought you a particular grace to improve you, to inspire you to live in a saintly way?"
Maximin: "I can't say that. I never felt anything special. But the Blessed Virgin did grant me the grace of a very Christian education with the good Sisters of Corps. She surrounded me with very edifying priests. My childhood and youth were spent in a milieu that encouraged me to do good and to avoid evil. Without the apparition I could have strayed far from God and become really bad. I might even have become a member of the '*Internationale*', or the '*Commune*'. By keeping me in this milieu and giving me the religious convictions I still have, she bestowed a wonderful gift on me."

Father Bossan: "These certainly are special graces. But many unthinking people would like to see you a saint and not simply the Christian you are."

Maximin: "Well, they are idiots. We can't reason with them. The apparition and I are two different things. I was only an instrument. Water can flow through a silver or a gold pipe, it will never become wine. No more than by flowing through a wood or a clay conduit. The grace of the apparition has gone forth through me but has not changed me."

Father Bossan: "Are you absolutely convinced, that you have been only an instrument in the hands of the Blessed Virgin?"

Maximin: "Yes, absolutely. We have been only conduits, only parrots who have repeated what we have heard. We were stupid before the apparition, we were stupid after, and we will be stupid all of our lives." **(7)**

It is difficult to speak more candidly. At 36, after failing in all his business ventures, Maximin no longer dreamed of advising the great of this world. Nor did he complain any more of being uprooted. The hardships of his unstable life disappear before the incalculable benefit of the Christian education he had received as a result of the apparition. He thus recognized quite clearly what the grace of La Salette had meant for him. What he did not say, and this is a credit to his modesty, was that an extraordinary Providence had helped him retain a childlike heart.

Mélanie was more subject to illusion. From the time of her departure from Corenc, all her life was characterized by the self-importance that prompted Bishop Ginoulhiac's decision not to admit her to religious profession. "The idiosyncrasies naturally flowing from it" achieved notoriety through the publication of what she called her secret and, more mysteriously, **(8)** by the story of her "marvelous youth," which, according to Léon Bloy, placed her "light years away from the legend of the rough-hewn and unintelligent peasant girl." Whatever the personal or external causes might have been, it is certain that she never agreed with her bishop's decision concerning the limits of her mission. Her followers venerated these idiosyncrasies and bemoaned the Church's refusal to accept them. Others, on the contrary, found the exaggerations scandalous and wondered if the mind that conceived them might not also have invented the story of La Salette. Between these two extremes, the bishop's position seems all the more justified by the exigencies of theology as well as by the facts of history.

"The shepherds" mission is ended, that of the Church begins," proclaimed Bishop Ginoulhiac in 1855. By this he meant that the Church approved La Salette as announced by its messengers and that by so doing she became its authentic interpreter to the faithful. If in the future, additional material or secondary changes unconfirmed by the Church were brought to their original narratives by the children, the faithful would have to discern prudently the value of these variations. The Church would perhaps need to pronounce itself on the matter. As the Church examined the La Salette event, there was no indication that the children had any further word from the Virgin to her people. In any case, any additional material would have to be treated as new revelations, and, as such, would have to be cleared by the Church.

Some individuals have difficulty understanding that the Church is a better judge of revelations than even those who have received them. But Christian piety is too involved and faith itself too intimately implicated in a matter of this kind to be left to the whims of personal interpretation. The ease with which humans commandeer the divine to appropriate it and deface it is a matter of common experience.

Authentically inspired people can fall prey to the same failings, and the deposit of faith entrusted to the Church to be preserved in its purity would be endangered if manifestations of the Spirit were to escape its jurisdiction. But, in reality, it is the same Spirit who raises up inspired people and designates their interpreters. The hierarchical organization so essential to the unity of the Church is itself quickened by the Spirit. According to Saint Thomas Aquinas this organization is an ongoing charism which discerns temporary charisms. If one still assumes that theological reasoning has fashioned this doctrine by dint of logic, he or she should re-read Saint Paul. He is the first to speak of charisms and to underline their usefulness for the Church. Yet he subordinates them to the hierarchical organization.

MAXIMIN 1846 MAXIMIN 1846

THE WITNESSES OF THE APPARITION

MAXIMIN
PAPAL ZOUAVE

MÉLANIE
AT PALERMO 1896

255

"Clearly, he did not attribute his own teaching and governing authority to the abundance of charisms with which he had been gifted, but to the apostolate Christ had called him to exercise. The officials he [Paul] established in the churches he founded or those he established through his deacons, presbyters, and overseers (Acts 14:22; Pastoral Epistles) comprised in reality a hierarchical institution, not a charismatic one." **(9)**

Simple submission should therefore constitute the Christian's only response to the Church's decisions regarding Mélanie's secret. We merely recall them here. The Holy Office reacted promptly after the publication of Mélanie's booklet. The Secretary, Cardinal Caterini, communicated to his Excellency Bishop Sarnelli of Castellamare, to Father Archier, Superior of the Missionaries of La Salette, and to Bishop Cortet of Troyes, "that the publication of this book had not pleased the Holy See. It therefore orders that inasmuch as possible, copies of this work should be withdrawn from the hands of the faithful." **(10)**

In 1915, the war had given rise to a renewed outbreak of apocalyptic literature centered on the secret of La Salette. The Holy Office was compelled to intervene more energetically. A decree dated December 21 was addressed to the Bishop of Grenoble "ordering all the faithful to abstain from treating this subject under any pretext and in any form whatsoever.... However, this decree is not delivered against the devotion to the Most Blessed Virgin invoked and known under the title of Reconciler of La Salette."

Finally, in 1923, a new edition of Mélanie's booklet, buttressed by supporting documents, was simply consigned to the Index of Forbidden Books by an order dated May 9. **(11)**

These are clearly drafted decisions. They assure the right-minded Christian that the new revelations coming from Mélanie and her commentators add nothing to his or her piety. They also stress Rome's desire to dissociate the apparition of La Salette from "the *so-called* secret of La Salette," according to the telling expression of the decree issued in 1915. This document specifies that the devotion to Our Lady of La Salette, Reconciler, remains authorized and the clear implication is that the fact itself, in the terms of the Encyclical, *Pascendi*, is credible through human faith. This question of the event was never canonically judged in Rome, but rather by Bishop de Bruillard, with Rome's full cognizance. And Rome, always seeking to safeguard the faithful from the contaminated version of the secret, continued to point to the apparition as a blessed fountainhead. Whoever wanted to see the Virgin triumph, instead of some particular view of the supernatural, could not ask for more.

But in the presence of Mélanie's new revelations, the Christian people's most common reaction is neither admiration nor blind faith. For most people, a few lines or a few words are enough to create the impression of strangeness, of a sudden introduction into an unreal world. The general reaction is not to escape the Church's verdict, but to include La Salette in this kind of revelation and to respond to it with suspicion and disapproval. This is an extreme response, which takes neither history nor psychology into account.

The La Salette narrative is attributed by some to the same dispositions that led Mélanie to produce writings which even the most benevolent critics labeled illusory. But is there anything in her actual childhood pointing to this tendency to confabulate? Not a thing. Eyewitnesses describe her as timid, sulky, and withdrawn. Poverty, early servitude, and a denial of her right to a childhood can very well account for these character traits. These may have formed a background conducive to the dangerous imaginings of later years, but such imaginings postdate the apparition by at least five years. Meanwhile, Mélanie made some progress in mastering her moods. **(12)** As long as she remained under Sister Sainte-Thecle's guidance, she could struggle successfully against vanity, an inevitable failing in an adolescent girl who was so swiftly raised to high honors and adulation. The well-known praises of her simplicity and her childlike spirit remained appropriate until the end of 1850 (approximately, 1851). In 1850 she kept a private journal in which she noted her own thoughts "prior to becoming a religious." In it, she reveals her choice of religious life as the surest way to salvation. Faced with a variety of apostolates, she deliberated and finally leaned toward the Christian education of children in mission lands. She copied a passage from a missionary publication ("Our Indians were no less happy than their missionaries to have their own prayer hut"), as well as a conversation, real or imagined, with her mother who advised her to remain a lay person. Romantic dreams of martyrdom did not prevent her from keeping both feet on the ground. Absolutely no trace of fabrication or of mystical pretension can be found during this period. **(13)**

Her tendency toward the spectacular and toward grandiose thinking was first noticed at the novitiate of Corenc. Bishop Ginoulhiac vainly attempted to correct these inclinations, which eventually succeeded in severing, more or less, her contact with reality. This was to be expected. The trial she underwent was such that it prohibits us from judging her and from bringing her past into question once again.

This flood of veneration, penetrating even the novitiate grillwork, had its inevitable perils. The chaplain, Father Gérente, told Father Bossan that he had seen priests taking down every word Mélanie spoke as if she were uttering oracles.

> *"A pastor from the south of France had already written three pages of his conversation with Mélanie. I said to him: "My good Father, what on earth are you doing?"*
>
> *"I am writing everything she is saying. It is so very edifying. I will read all this to my parishioners next Sunday."*

He said this in Melanie's presence. I saw priests, generals, ladies, officers, people of high rank standing before Mélanie as if in the presence of a great personage, speaking to her in humble tones, having her autograph pictures or anything else, only to have something from her hand. People engaged in all kinds of nonsense on her account." **(14)**

During this period, Mélanie avidly read lives of the saints, mystical writings, and revelations of doubtful authenticity. Said Gérente to Bossan: "She has read much. She could have taken from her readings all she wrote after the apparition." When her imagination was fired up, the only guide available to her was the blindly tender mistress of novices, who affirmed and approved illusions that Mélanie herself perhaps only half believed. All the documents of this period agree that Sister Thérèse de Jésus, the mistress of novices, seemed to be the affective point drawing out all of Mélanie's mystical confidences and provoking her strange behavior. Soon after Mélanie left Corenc, Sister Thérèse herself left the convent. The following excerpt, probably from her hand, gives us an idea of the quality of her guidance.

> *"During recreation sometimes, postulants and novices surrounded the young shepherdess, urging her to tell them about Our Lady of La Salette, about the site and various details of the apparition, and about the life she led before this extraordinary event.*
>
> *Sister Marie de la Croix [Mélanie] said the most amazing things, but with such conviction that no one thought of doubting her, not even the mistress of novices who had been advised by the Superior to treat Sister Marie de la Croix's declarations as pure fantasy and to keep her informed of the extraordinary things occurring in Mélanie.*
>
> *One day, the child of Mary, answering her companion's eager questions, told them that she sometimes missed her life as a shepherdess, when she led her cows into deep woods, and enjoyed the comforts of solitude. She said that she never met anyone but was able to enjoy the company of wolves, foxes, snakes, and other denizens of the forest with whom she organized beautiful processions, singing the praises of God. A wolf would carry the cross."* **(15)**

We remember how Bishop Ginoulhiac intervened. But there were priests who made light of the bishop's warnings. Like Bishop Ullathorne, he feared that the novice of Darlington might be "walking dangerous paths" which he wanted her to avoid. He confided to Bishop Ullathorne what he had not been able to say in a public pronouncement.

"After long reflection on the child's conduct, I refused to admit her even to temporary vows against the virtually unanimous vote of the Community. Later, for the same reasons, I forbade her to enter the house of Corenc where her eccentricities were a cause of distraction and disorder. I assigned her to the house of Corps, where I knew she would be supervised with a firmness that had now become necessary.

These precautions seemed wise but were rendered partly useless by the blind confidence some priests placed in Mélanie, particularly the Superior of the Missionaries of La Salette. **(16)** They viewed these measures as persecutions. They told her this, and attributed my actions to a lack of interest in La Salette. They could not separate the event and the children's original testimony from illusions provoked in the children at a later time by various circumstances." **(17)**

There had therefore been a turning-point in the life of Mélanie. We can see its origin and follow its path. History assures us, however, that the young girl who came down the mountain with her companion bearing a message that neither one of them understood was at the time incapable of contriving that message.

But archives and libraries cannot explain everything, any skeptic will say. When abnormal behavior appears in someone, can we always succeed in tracking down its distant source or even the many unsuspected consequences that might flow from it? How can we be sure that La Salette does not lie somewhere within this series of unknown factors?

There is an easy way of arriving at an answer. After Mélanie had crossed the threshold into illusion, all her revelations could be traced to rearranged events of her own life or to her own reading. The style is composite in character. If the apparition story stemmed from her personality, why can she no longer provide us with even a sampling from the same lode? One can select at random from any of the works produced after the years of change and compare them to the message and the story we have studied. The comparison is conclusive. In the former, we see the ubiquitous imprint of her personality. In the latter, there is only the dignity of the Virgin, and nothing in the children's ignorant, candid selves can explain what they have seen and heard. Father Loew, among others, recognized in the message of La Salette an indefinable something that the spirit immediately perceives. He writes with enlightening humor: "The grandeur of Our Lady's style seemed a guarantee of authenticity. Priests can't speak that way. *'If my people will not submit… It is so heavy… How long have I suffered for you! … You paid no attention… No matter how well you pray in the future…'*" **(18)** We can add in all certainty that Mélanie herself did not speak that way either.

There is an equally conclusive second proof. Instead of speculating on the arcane resources of abnormal behavior, we might consider its known consequences. Mélanie's resentment against Bishop Ginoulhiac was often expressed with distressing violence in her writings. While prohibiting her from publishing her new revelations, the bishop never required her to sustain at all cost her original testimony on La Salette. On the contrary, he let it be known to her "that any denial on her part would be of no importance to him." In the face of "provocation" the rebellious girl of Vienne or Darlington never retracted herself. Would not a reaction contrary to this have been expected in such a case?

There is more, and it has been pointed out by Father Bliguet, O.P., an expert in apologetics. "This half-spontaneous, half-provoked delirium in which the poor woman seemed to have ended her troubled life should normally have altered the wording of the secret as well as the history of the apparition. This would be the expected result. Nothing like this happened." (19) In fact, the themes of Mélanie's inspiration follow the whims of her imagination, and especially of her affectivity. Some of the visions of Corenc or Darlington were never mentioned again. She returned to others when she was told to write her autobiography, but then she again rearranged them and placed them in another chronological period of her life. Her contradictory statements relative to the secret are without number. The so-called definitive version of her secret that she wrote in 1879 is a considerably expanded version of her previous one. A few embellishments attempt to rectify the image of an unrefined country waif who did not know her prayers. She tells how she built a small shrine with Maximin and how they both raised their souls to God at the sound of the Angelus bell. But fabrication comes to a halt at the threshold of the apparition itself. Her description of the words and actions of the beautiful Lady is identical to the 1846 version. On this point it seems impossible for her to say anything different from what she had originally seen and heard. In her strange psychology, the event story of the apparition will stand like an immovable rock in the midst of the fluctuations of her troubled existence.

When the Virgin sought messengers, she was pleased to discover the candor of Maximin and Mélanie. She would make use of this quality, but without committing herself to keeping it unscathed by the thousand natural shocks that flesh is heir to. She knew each one of the children's weaknesses and how she would intervene, on occasion, to correct an error with typical discretion and absence of show. The presence of the divine is conspicuous in the very beginnings of their testimony. They labeled themselves "little nobodies," and it is this recognized and avowed nothingness that convinced Church representatives to give them a hearing. Adulation and admiration would later breach the absolute simplicity that Bishop Dupanloup spoke of, but the miracle had been engraved in their souls. Their errors and shortcomings would even serve to set it off the more clearly.

What we have said of Mélanie is no less true of Maximin. To the end of his life he remained volatile and unpredictable. At 11 years of age or at 35, all who met him described him in the same way: he is a child. He was by turns a theological student, an official in a home for children at Vésinet, a medical student, a Papal Zouave, a liquor merchant (in this case he lent his name to a swindler). In the end, ill and debt-ridden, he supported as best he could his adoptive parents, the Jourdains. Such a life-story is no model of the bourgeois virtues or even of the so-called rational virtues: discipline, foresight, and the proper care of his own health were foreign to him. But it is precisely his fickleness that most confirmed his testimony. In this alone was he earnest and reliable. This was the only matter he ever took seriously.

In order to exorcise definitively the memory of Ars, we can recall this fidelity as it was professed amid hopeless entanglements and as it stood, finally, on the threshold of eternity.

The publication, La Vie parisienne, in an issue dated November 11, 1865, carried a humorous piece about the Shepherd of La Salette. A few lines suggest the tone of the whole article: "You have to see him holding his sides with laughter when he happens to spot the plaster facsimile representing him and his sister standing before this good Virgin clad in an Auvergnat dress." Maximin responded with a very well written booklet: *My Profession of Faith in the Apparition of Our*

Lady of La Salette. Showing little interest in polemics, he presented his own case as an argument that adversaries would understand and which was touchingly personal.

> *People make me out to be clever enough to invent a hoax like this one, yet dumb enough to turn it against my own interests. This is like trying to link shrewdness with rank stupidity. We know these two will never wed. I did run after fame, fortune, and pleasure, and I lost myself doing it. I found none of these things, and I have no regrets. I would even say that the mission of spreading the message has always been the cause of all of my vicissitudes. I wish I had remained in the mountains. I would have had a more peaceful and more joyful existence. I never would have had the experience of living as a stranger among my own people. In my own village, I would not have gone without black bread as often as I went without the more refined foods of great cities. And I would be wealthy by now, had I been weak enough to deny everything. Had I invented all of this, would it have been so impossible for me to come forward and tell the truth, especially when I could have reaped the benefits of a huge scandal and lent my name to all types of publicity? The people who accuse me of so many vices surely cannot think that I would abhor scandal.* **(20)**

And then there is his testament. His daily existence tended to blur and disfigure the thrust and meaning of his entire life which was deeply anchored in the presence of God. We see our scatterbrained incorrigible child transformed in the end by eternity into his very self.

In the name of the Father, and of the Son, and of the Holy Spirit. Amen.

I believe in everything the Holy, Apostolic and Roman Church teaches, in all the dogmas defined by Our Holy Father the Pope, the august and infallible Pius IX.

I believe firmly, even at the cost of my blood, in the famous apparition of the Most Blessed Virgin on the holy mountain of La Salette, on September 19, 1846, the apparition I have defended in word, writing, and suffering.

After my death, let no one say that he has heard me deny the great event of La Salette. By lying to the whole world, he would also deceive himself.

In this spirit, I give my heart to Our Lady of La Salette. **(21)**

How do the faults people accused him of compare to this manifesto and to his unchanging testimony (the Ars incident does not really count)? "He drank a few glasses of wine," said his friend Minder, the surgeon. Could one not find some excuse for this failing, which was never excessive and which never brought a single inappropriate word to his lips? The education given him by Giraud the wheelwright, perhaps?

Surely, one can point to the inexperience of a simple, candid man and to the abyss of misery he skirted all his life. If one insists on seeing some evidence of the grace he received reflected in his behavior, one might consult people who knew him in preference to newspaper columnists. "Some have gone so far as to say that he was not prayerful," said Father Archier, Superior of the Missionaries, to his companions. "Nothing could be more unjust nor further from the truth. Many times I was a witness to his piety: I tired of praying, while he never did." His friends from seminary days, those from the Papal Guard, as well as acquaintances from the medical school were unanimous in their praise of the moral purity of Maximin's life. After leaving the seminary, he arrived in Paris without means, "took on a porter's job and many others to make ends meet. He slept on the ground or anywhere he could." **(22)**

In medical school his friends cruelly led him into compromising situations, but he was able to resist all temptations of the flesh. At Frascati, his friend Le Chauff de Kerguenec, who later became a Jesuit, was amazed at his sensitivity and modesty. "I know him thoroughly" said de Kerguenec, "and for methis miracle is even more miraculous, if I can so express myself, than the miracle of La Salette." **(23)** There might be a strong element of enthusiasm here, but the value of the testimony is undiminished: it is simply not true, legend notwithstanding, that the Shepherd of La Salette was the *bon vivant* whose moral behavior betrayed his lack of faith in the apparition.

Both Maximin and Mélanie had their detractors and their defenders. What we say of them is based on history. We feel no iniquitous joy in diminishing them, but neither do we feel the need to embellish their personalities in order to make them more worthy of an apparition. Were we to weigh and compare the losses and the gains resulting from their mission, we would find, without burdening the truth, that the sum of good far outweighs the sum of evil. Thus the Virgin's influence in Maximin's life was deeper and more lasting than it would at first appear. Hidden virtues are worth more than appearances, no matter how respectable.

Mélanie's illusions necessarily provoke some question as to her humility. Still, when Bishop Ginoulhiac confided her to Bishop Ullathorne he was not judgmental. "She continues to behave in England as she did here. The same propensity to illusion governs her, *perhaps without her being aware it.*" Greeting her at the Shrine of La Salette in 1867, Father Giraud also avoided judging her. He was frustrated at his inability to reach her. "How the poor child is to be pitied" I thought her somewhat gifted, but she is in fact quite limited intellectually." To what degree was she aware of the deplorable path she had taken? After the imprudence of those around her, can we fault her will or her lack of judgment? No one can answer these questions. We believe, in any case, that in the strange world in which she moved, genuine virtue cohabited with illusion. There is no doubt that Mélanie led a pious and austere life, that she had no love for the world. Her most extravagant writings resonate with constant and edifying references to eternal truths. The persistence with which, in her correspondence, she spoke of servile work on Sunday, of blasphemy, of irreligious behavior, showed how deeply the beautiful Lady's reproaches had affected her. This is of some consequence when we attempt to assess her spiritual indebtedness to the apparition. Even if these virtues were more perfect or purer, to what degree could they determine our belief in La Salette?

In reality, the life of the shepherds in its connection to La Salette can offer only a secondary proof of the judgment already arrived at. The motives inspiring this judgment cannot be other than those of the canonical judge. When Bishop Ginoulhiac declared the children's mission ended, he implied that they had fulfilled it well enough to enable the message to stand on its own without them. The disparity between them and their message would constitute an indelible signature and authenticate the message forever. What can we who examine the remainder of their lives rightfully ask of them? One thing only, that they not obliterate this signature. If they were to tell us "We have heard and seen nothing on the mountain" and offer us a plausible explanation for their false story, we would have to bow before the evidence.

Likewise, if this same explanation were to come to us as a result of their behavior. This is why we accept them as they are, with their qualities and shortcomings. We scrutinize their words, writings, and actions for the flaw that would explain that avidly sought-after hoax or fabrication. But their entire checkered career only adds to the impossibility of impugning their original testimony. Mélanie invented a whole mystical childhood for herself, a fiction of her real childhood. But under the superficial and shifting first stratum of her thinking, when we reach bedrock, we find the unchanged, unchanging, and unchallenged reality of the apparition. Maximin's inconstancy is pitiable, yet in the midst of the trials of poverty he was forever ready to defend his conviction "to the shedding of his blood." If doubt persists, these elements should persuade. By means of their enduring testimony, the Lord strengthened the foundations he had laid.

Some critics require holiness as a seal of divine missioning. What would this holiness prove? It would show the children's heroic fidelity to their personal grace, but it would not prove that they have brought from God a grace destined for the Christian people. Revelations must be judged by proofs belonging to their category, and these are to be evaluated according to the theology and the traditions of the Church.

"You expect me to believe that this girl has seen the Blessed Virgin? She doesn't even say her prayers!" The very idea of such a gratuitous selection scandalized young Pra, but Saint Thomas Aquinas would not have found her unworthy of divine wisdom which weighs, measures, and balances all things.

"Divine discernment," he says, "regulates the charism of revelation: it is not given to all, not even to those whom we would think disposed to it, for one reason or another, but only to those whom the divine will has chosen. And these are not considered good or very good in themselves, but only relative to the prophetic function that divine wisdom judges them capable of fulfilling." (24)

According to this teaching, neither the recognition of past merits nor the expectation of future ones, but the ability to bear witness is the quality that recommended the two shepherds to the Virgin. She chose them, in preference to so many other children, that they might contemplate her glory and her tears.

The tradition of the Church rests on this theology. There is no need to read volumes in order to understand this. All the officially approved apparitions of the last century stand before us. What does the canonical judge look for in these cases? He examines the credibility of the witnesses and the event they proclaim, as well as the signs of God (miracles and graces) surrounding the event and confirming its credibility. The messengers interest the judge because of the trust that their prophetic mission calls for, not for their personal worth before God. On this essential point, the case of Lourdes casts a decisive light. When Bishop Laurence recognized the authenticity of the apparitions to Bernadette, he clearly could not invoke her holiness as a proof. His pronouncement is modeled on Bishop de Bruillard's. His decree is written in practically the same terms and rests on the same preamble. Was this document then found lacking? Even if Bernadette had not become the lovable saint we know, would Lourdes have been any the less a heavenly grace?

All apparitions are a poem from heaven whose words are ever new. We can understand why it is that at Lourdes, where the smile of the ideal Woman outshone all of earth's ugliness, the Virgin would choose a witness raised by grace to a special holiness. Why should we be surprised that the Mother of La Salette, who weeps over the indifference

of her people, would choose messengers who forever represent that very indifference? Maximin and Mélanie remained ordinary, simple Christian people. By their shortcomings—and they are not among the worst—the children remain close to us, telling us that the tears of the Virgin concern us all, that no one can do without Redemption, and that no stricken human being need ever lose hope. "She left me with all of my faults," said Maximin, as if he were already aware of God's strategy.

As we ponder the mystery of grace and freedom, of the number of refusals each person can oppose to God's will in one lifetime, it remains true that the future of these children was present before God when He chose them. Finding ourselves on the threshold of a century which has forgotten the true measure of the human person, which believes so little in the need for a Redeemer, can we not imagine that the children's faults are intended to remind us of our own broken-ness? "I have not come to call the just...." The grace of La Salette, like that of the Gospel, demands that we undo the Pharisee within us."

-12-
The Grace Bestowed Upon The Christian People

*I*n spite of brazen cynics and the timidity of good people, in spite of all obstacles, the great news of La Salette has managed to come down to us. Indeed, it has reached the ends of the earth. The Curé of Ars had been right: "If this is the work of God, no one will destroy it."

People alone could not save it, not even the critical historians and the valiant champions. All the conflicting material spoken and written about La Salette should normally have inspired nothing but frustration, but the mountain draws people to itself and the message goes forth. Indeed, originating within the event itself there is an immense stream of grace whose waters have filled the world.

The call of the Virgin, the moving scene of a mother overwhelmed by the burden of our sins has shown the path of Redemption to Christians once again, and helped them return to the Creator. This has been happening now for well over a century. Bishop Ullathorne said that La Salette is a new grace bestowed on the Christian people. This is the secret of its expansion and of its enduring quality. Beyond Maximin and Mélanie, this grace is what the merciful Virgin wanted. Once more the divine origin of La Salette is proclaimed.

The authenticity of the apparition is ratified by this very consideration. The canonical judge understood it this way when he said: "We believe that the immense and spontaneous gathering of the faithful at the site, the many wonders that have occurred *because* of it have contributed an added measure of credibility to this apparition." Opponents attempted to neutralize this reasoning by invoking the argument of "error in good faith." "Praying to Our Lady means praying to the Blessed Virgin. These are not two persons. The one who is called upon is the all powerful, all merciful Virgin. La Salette is only a help.... People are granted what they petition even if they believe in La Salette, not because they believe." **(1)** Bishop Dupanloup's intellectual criteria were stringent with regard to La Salette; he never hesitated to invoke the argument of efficacy in order to buttress his early conviction. During his second pilgrimage to La Salette in 1872 he confided to his personal journal:

> *I have reread what I wrote* **(2)** *and it is still quite convincing. To-day, I would add:*
>
> *1. Why all these proofs? What would one have gained? Faith, piety, communions, honor to the Blessed Virgin, the glory of God given in an extraordinary measure?*
> *2. It is difficult to believe that this great movement of people throughout the world should have been inspired by a hoax.*
> *3. It is again difficult to believe that sacrifices of all kinds should not have been inspired by graces and genuine miracles.* **(3)**

Written over a century ago, these words have lost none of their import. Since that time the impetus born of La Salette has grown steadily. The quality of that movement is especially striking. The conversion of sinners, inner growth, and an extraordinary spirit of repentance are the typical results of prayer to the reconciling Lady of La Salette. Afflicted people beg to be relieved of their burden or to grow through their suffering. Instinctively, people turn to her when threatened by cholera or by war; but no one would dare beg for power in this world from a Mother who comes offering hope with her tears and a Crucified Son on her breast. At this point, the skeptic's positions become less and less convincing. Assuredly, Mary's only source of grace and mediating power is Christ himself and not some personal title. This title of Mary, however, has indeed channeled a river of grace to her people. God's providence, simplicity, and truth would not tolerate a hoax mediating supernatural goodness.

So many people have fallen under the reconciling Lady's influence that we would like to see them all come together in some vast spiritual study conducted with the subtle touch of a new Bremond. Bishop Giray's work on the miracles already contains a rough outline of such a study. Our purpose here in writing about the grace of La Salette is different. Historically, we will only seek out the features that best characterized the devotion to Our Lady of La Salette from the beginning. Then, we will try to define that devotion so that the theologian may find satisfaction and the faithful Christian a path that will never stray from the only way, Christ himself.

"The Virgin of Converts": this was how, thirty years ago, Stanislaus Fumet described the Virgin of La Salette's special role. Events proved him right. Writers, artists, scientists, inspired especially by Léon Bloy, began to heed the sobs of the weeping Virgin. "One cannot imagine," said this lover of the *magnetic mountain*, "the preeminent role played by Our Lady in the spiritual rebirth so often spoken of today. I mean the return of intellectuals to God. No names need be mentioned. Suffice it to say that the Virgin of La Salette has never been at work more efficiently than in these times." (4)

The converts form a brilliant company around Our Lady of La Salette. They draw the most attention. The first to appear are those mentioned by Fumet and their features show either the first impact of grace or the painful uprooting that almost always follows it.

We meet Ernest Psichari as he rediscovers the straight path he will walk until the holocaust at Rossignol:

> As he entered his tent the thought of his friend Pierre-Marie and the picture of the Virgin in tears suddenly came to him. He had received it long ago and the desert wind had swept it far away. He felt a dreadful sorrow, a sorrow he had never known. His heart forever destined to remorse experienced a new, unspeakable suffering, where in a single cry heaven mingled with earth. Maxence had wept much for himself. But on this day he could not turn his gaze from this faraway Lady who wept over the sins of the world. (5)

Huysmans speaks of his painful journeying:

How they were filled with her, these high alpine mountains of La Salette, this great white guest-house, this vaguely Byzantine, vaguely roman church covered with yellowing mortar. And the narrow cell with its plaster Christ nailed to a black wooden cross, the small room, whitewashed and so tiny that one could not walk two steps in any direction. How they were filled with Her!

Surely she returns to assist the hosts, in spite of the seeming abandon. At night as we sat in front of a candle, she seemed so near to us, so watchful and so sad, that the soul burst like a pod sowing the seeds of our sins, the grains of our faults. Repentance, so long in coming, so hesitant, became tyrannical, so absolute that we fell on our knees by the bed, choking with tears, sobbing, head buried in sheets.

They were mortally sad evenings, and still, so exquisite! We savaged ourselves, stripping away the very fibers of the soul, but we felt the Virgin close by. She was so compassionate, so maternal that, after the tears, she held this bloodied soul in her arms and lulled it to sleep as she would a sick child.
(6)

Spring which has flowed continuously since Apparition and involved in many healings

Those who have experienced miracles at La Salette are legion. Besides those who impress us by their power of expression, we cannot overlook those who have been led discreetly into the Church by her maternal hand. The Lemann brothers, for example, made the journey from Judaism into the priesthood. William Butler, who taught at the Rondeau minor seminary was a former Anglican minister. From the most distant past to the present time, we learn that mercy reaches out to all.

A man walked to the communion rail in Father Mélin's little church at Corps. It was Maximin's father, Giraud the wheelwright. No one had seen him do that in twenty years. He had been feeling uneasy since Maximin had told him, "But father, the Lady also spoke about you." The next day, he allowed his family to go with Maximin to the site of the apparition. A few weeks later, he went up the mountain himself pleading to be rid of asthma. He was cured and his eyes were opened. One Sunday in November, he boldly received Communion in a parish where men performed their Easter duty in hiding. From then on, he assisted at daily Mass, to compensate, as he said, for all the Sundays he had not assisted, for not having sent his hired help or for not having allowed them to go. He could not read so he prayed the Rosary.

Six years later in the same church, Father Mélin opened the month of Mary services and asked his parishioners for special prayers. "The fruit of our prayers is always assured," he had told them, "even if it often remains hidden. At other times, God encourages us by showing us exactly what our prayers have done." Early in the morning of May 2, as he entered the church for Mass, he saw another priest kneeling before the altar. The priest followed Father Mélin into the sacristy and, without introduction blurted out: "I want to change my way of life." Father Mélin knew him well. It was Father Viollet, the official pastor of Corps under interdict by his bishop. He resided in the parish and inevitably caused much alienation among the people of the village. Father Viollet received the Sacrament of Reconciliation and the next morning received Communion as a lay person. On May 25, as he journeyed to the mountain to lay the first stone at the shrine, Bishop de Bruillard granted Father Viollet priestly reinstatement. "He is no longer the same man," said Father Mélin. "Grace has made a new man of him. Having known his inflexibility, his fits of anger, his hatreds, I can say that this is the most powerful grace ever to come upon my parish since I have been here. I thank God each day and much of my gratitude is directed to Our Lady of La Salette." (7)

Besides the outstanding examples history has preserved for us, we also look at the anonymous crowd. By the grace of a pilgrimage, a mission, the Virgin has led many good sinners to reconciliation. They rise from sin leaning on her for their first halting steps. There are people who are just beginning to respond to God, who want to follow him more faithfully. Her special gift, noted Fumet, is to turn these people completely around.

In 1851, Bishop Ullathorne presented the conversion of the Corps region as Our Lady of La Salette's greatest miracle. But Bishop Villecourt, Father Rousselot, Father Doyen, together with the first historians of La Salette had felt the wave coming from the mountain, spreading through France and into Belgium. The diocesan archives of Grenoble carry a note from Canon Rousselot relative to his inquiry visit: "In 1847, the Cardinal Archbishop of Cambrai told me that during that jubilee year eighty thousand people of his diocese had returned to religious practice. He attributed this to the knowledge (as yet incomplete) that people had of La Salette."

In 1850, in Rome, Cardinal Lambruschini, whom Rousselot considered prejudiced against La Salette, summarized his own opinion: "The Virgin of La Salette has become for our era a universal missionary." By recourse to the tears of Our Lady, priests were said to have obtained the resurrection of defunct parishes. A case in point was Father Lemoisin who founded the shrine of Baraques (Bleriot-Plage) where crowds now come from all over the Pas-de-Calais.

Pilgrimages! The automobile sometimes brings tourism and mysticism together in strange combinations. Times have changed since Thiers categorically declared from the podium of the Chamber: "Pilgrimages are no longer part of our customs." But the traveler registering for a trip to La Salette doesn't know what awaits him. A tête-à-tête, unexpected as it is, with this woman who is weeping is enough to cut through a lifetime of pettiness and sin. Priest-observers are quick to assert that the daily wonder of this place is the change of heart that takes place in the people.

We can take Father Veillard's word for it. He was a former rector of the Basilica of La Salette and met crowds of pilgrims during the centennial year.

The feeling of the first Missionaries of La Salette is identical to that of my happy colleagues who minister to pilgrims during the summer season. A few hours in the confessional here bring us to an awareness of Our Lady's profound influence, of the sureness with which she brings about that greatest of all miracles, the conversion of the heart. We don't know the name of the inspired pilgrim who gave Our Lady the title of Reconciler of Sinners. I would think it might perhaps be a priest who had been ministering the Sacrament of Reconciliation.

Without jeopardizing sacramental secrecy in any way, priests in the ministry of reconciliation will tell you that their ministry is often distressing and difficult in other places and in other circumstances because of the lack of proper dispositions in the penitent. At La Salette, this sacramental ministry is much easier to perform and is a great comfort to the priest. What is it that brings about a sincere reconciliation and a contrition coupled with strong resolutions? By her tears, her rebukes, her warnings, and especially by her maternal kindness, Our Lady has touched the heart and moved the spirit. The priest has only to pardon. We could see what the grace of La Salette means to a sinner only if the walls of the confessional could speak.

They are rare indeed the people who escape the magnetism of the reconciling Lady. I could name sightseers who came up to the shrine with nothing else in mind but to enjoy a few days in the mountains and who, within a day or two, were changed into veritable pilgrims, unable to thank the Virgin enough for having won them over. I could name young people who could not receive the sacraments even on the holy mountain. But once back home, they became active Christians and transformed dechristianized parishes through the grace of La Salette. They have drawn friends to the Sacrament of Reconciliation and to the Eucharist. Young women followed suit. Now, amazed parish priests are distributing up to forty communions at the parish Mass when last year only one young man performed his Easter duty there.

Needless to say, after celebrating reconciliation a pilgrim naturally wants to share the Eucharist. Isn't the purpose of any sacrament union with God through the Bread of Life? The action of Our Lady of La Salette reaches its fulfillment as an act of the Church.

But conversion, wonderful as it is, leaves us only on the threshold of the devotion to Our Lady of La Salette. To plumb its secrets we must seek out experienced and tested Christians. We must look for saints.

There are many examples from which to choose. One pilgrimage in particular reflects the compelling warmth of the Virgin's interest in her people. We speak here of the visit of Mother Marie of Jesus (née Deluil-Martiny), who was then founding the Society of the Daughters of the Heart of Jesus. She was to die assassinated by a demented person. In 1868 she was a pilgrim at La Salette.

> I went [she writes] to the site of the apparition. My God! How moving it was! The sight of the weeping Virgin is heartbreaking! I attended the liturgy and received the Eucharist. With the Lord within me I knew she had to receive me and listen to me. I surrendered myself to her completely, together with all her future servants in the Order. I prayed near the statue of the weeping Virgin. On a small sheet of paper I wrote down my intentions for the present as well as for the future, for the souls I usually recommended to Jesus, and I slipped the paper onto the knees of the Blessed Virgin I also implored her for my own conversion! I surely believed I was one of the causes of her tears.
>
> I made a second station near the statue of the Conversation where the Blessed virgin revealed her secrets to the two children and I asked her to tell me some also. Here is what she told me deep in my heart: "my secret is made of threats and promises." I understood that if her people did not want to obey, the threats would become reality, and that if her people did obey, the promises would become blessings. The Blessed Virgin wants victims to step into the breach between the crimes of people and divine Justice, in union with her own pierced heart and with the sacrificial Jesus.
>
> Our Lady of La Salette made it known to me that in the future Institute, the Holy Sacrifice of the Mass would more than make up for the physical sacrifices that ill health would no longer permit. (8)

People in active life agree with the mystics in their understanding of the tears of Mary. The origins of social works are revealed in an unusual light when their authors or founders speak about founding inspiration. "How happy I am to see you at La Salette," wrote Léon Harmel to Father Charcosset. "I would want to have you come here and be all taken up with the tears of the Blessed Virgin. The La Salette spirit is a spirit of reparation. It is my ideal." **(9)**

This spirit of reparation so highly prized by Léon Harmel is surely characteristic of the devotion to the Virgin of La Salette. It is expressed in various forms. There is the self-offering of heroic individuals and there are collective movements. Sometimes this reparation is expressly sponsored by La Salette, and at others it spurs on a more vigorous following of the Christ who is an integral part of La Salette.

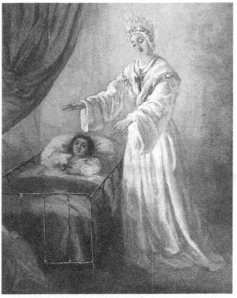

Ex voto painting given by Louis Marie Charles Aberille in 1861, commemorates the healing of a young girl through the intercession of Our Lady of La Salette

Bishop Ginoulhiac did not overstate the matter in his doctrinal pronouncement of November 4, 1854. Speaking as a spiritual leader, he was aware of the signs of the times. He associated with La Salette "the general spiritual movement in France toward atonement." "What people do not know," he pointed out with a hint of sorrow, "what we have not been sufficiently aware of, is that this movement finds its most powerful source in the words spoken on this far-off mountain on September 19, 1846."

In this general trend he certainly included the well-known archconfraternities, such as that of Saint-Dizier, founded by Bishop Parisis in 1847 to atone for blasphemy and the profanation of the Lord's Day, and the Archconfraternity of Our Reconciling Lady of La Salette in his diocese. But he was also thinking of less well-known and more mystical initiatives, more compatible with the sorrowful themes of the Lady's discourse.

One point in particular deserves attention. It is fascinating to discover in the course of history the ties between La Salette and the Eucharistic renewal.

In a preceding chapter we spoke of Sister St. Pierre, a Carmelite nun of Tours. Her collaboration with Father Dupont and Bishop Parisis is well known. We recall how the Archconfraternity for the Atonement of Blasphemy and the Profanation of the Lord's Day was born of a convergence of her revelations with the message of the apparition. The latter eliminated all the bishop's doubts and hesitations. There must have been great rejoicing in the Carmelite monasteries where the privileged nun's communications had an eager following, when news arrived of the apparition she had foretold. It was not surprising, then, to see in 1848 the Carmel of the rue d'Enfer in Paris return to the idea of atonement in another form. Mother Isabelle, the Prioress, was directing a new candidate, Miss Théodelinde Dubouché. Together they drew up plans for a third order dedicated to the adoration of the Blessed Sacrament. On August 6, the women recruited by Miss Dubouché for this purpose met for the first time. At the outset, it was only an association of pious women who took turns, at certain times, in perpetual adoration of the Blessed Sacrament. But in 1850, Father Eymard invited them to Lyons to found a similar third order and helped them become a religious congregation.

A few people practicing contemplation frequented the Chapel at the rue d'Enfer. Among them was a musician recently converted from Judaism named Hermann Cohen (the future Father Hermann). The new convert became envious of the women who were permitted the honor of watching with Christ. He met Father de la Bouillerie, Vicar General of Paris, who, in 1846, had founded a home nocturnal adoration society. With his backing, Hermann Cohen gathered a few men of good will in his apartment at 102 rue de l'Université. Nineteen members were present at that first meeting on November 22, 1848.

Father de la Bouillerie presided.

The minutes of that gathering clearly reveal the spiritual climate created by the recent apparition of La Salette. Those present were gathered together, said the minutes, "to found an association whose purpose would be the nocturnal adoration of the Most Blessed Sacrament and the expiation of offenses against it, in order to draw blessings upon France and to divert from her all the scourges that threaten her." They scheduled their first nocturnal adoration on December 6 at the shrine of Notre-Dame des Victoires, around the altar of the Most Holy and Most Immaculate Heart of Mary. This unusual activity in such a crowded shrine caused some inconvenience. They asked the Marist Fathers for the use of their chapel on the rue Montparnasse, the present site of the church of Notre-Dame des Champs. This is where the devotion grew before finding its permanent home at the Sacré-Cœur of Montmartre.

Another leading advocate of Eucharistic devotion, and the most eminent, was Saint Pierre-Julien Eymard. At the time of the apparition, the founder of the Priests and Servants of the Most Blessed Sacrament was still a Marist. On December 8, 1848, he wrote to Father Mélin to report the miraculous cure of one of his spiritual daughters, Miss Marguerite Guillot, and he declared: "I have searched, I have seen, and I have believed." When the Ars affair threatened to sweep everything in its wake "like a storm from hell," he encouraged Canon Rousselot. On August 18, 1852, he wrote in the shrine visitor's log: "If I did not have the good fortune to be a Marist I would ask my bishop, as a special favor, to dedicate myself body and soul to the service of Our Lady of La Salette." That is ample evidence of his fondness for the Virgin Reconciler. There is also this startling coincidence: he celebrated his last Mass at Grenoble, in the chapel of Our Lady of La Salette which is dedicated to perpetual adoration. It is obvious that his life was dedicated to atonement.

We read in the *Annales de Notre-Dame de La Salette*: "On August 1, we had the good fortune to hear Father Eymard, founder and superior of the Priests of the Blessed Sacrament. It is interesting to learn that this holy religious first conceived the idea of founding his recently

approved Congregation here, at the feet of Our Lady of La Salette."
(10)

The work of Father Eymard is known especially in his *Revue des Oeuvres eucharistiques*, founded in 1866 and revived by Father Philibert Vrau in 1876. It was a harbinger of Eucharistic congresses.

Did Father Eymard have wellsprings of inspiration other than La Salette? Indeed yes, as would any person whose life is centered on a great idea. He appears indebted notably to Marie Eustelle, the "angel of the Eucharist." According to Father Grenot, a Marist, the reading of her *Lettres eucharistiques* convinced him to leave the Congregation of Mary and to found that of the Priests of the Most Blessed Sacrament. This intersecting of various influences is part of any life. However, within the *Lettres eucharistiques* we again find reference to La Salette, together with a number of facts demonstrating how the idea of atonement informed the thinking of these leaders of the Christian people. The writings of Marie Eustelle were published by Bishop Villecourt shortly after he himself had authored *A New Account of the Apparition of the Blessed Virgin in the Alps*.

This Bishop, we know, was the very first to align himself with those who believed in the apparition. He later supported Bishop de Bruillard's doctrinal statement. He was also in communication with the Carmel of Tours. The coincidence of the apparition with Sister St. Pierre's revelations explains, in all likelihood, his prompt commitment to La Salette. In his mind, the message of the Virgin only lent more urgency to the idea of atonement through the Eucharistic devotion. In this, his conviction concurs with that of Bishop Parisis, the founder of the Archconfraternity for the Atonement of Blasphemy and the Profanation of the Lord's Day, who had written to Bishop de Bruillard: "It seemed to me we could not satisfy the Lord quickly enough for the two great crimes mentioned in the children's declaration." **(11)**

All these endeavors and devotions highlight one fact: the spirit of La Salette profoundly marked the spirituality of the nineteenth century. This spirit is as old as Christianity itself. At the time of the apparition, many religious communities lived it and promoted it.

The already flourishing devotion to the Sacred Heart embraced this spirit as the fruit of a grateful love. But this spirit did not have the clear shape that it has today, and it remained the special preserve of the spiritual elite. Shortly after the apparition the spirit informing La Salette appeared in the many different practices of popular piety. The faithful were, so to speak, forced to acknowledge a long-overlooked value of their faith. The new climate in mid-nineteenth-century France was dominated by the idea of atonement. It filtered in everywhere and in the most varied forms. The Pope and the bishops had cleared a path for it by calling attention to a need that had been greatly overlooked until then. Still, the welcome the idea of atonement found among Christians can be attributed in great part to the apparition of 1846. To be convinced of this, one need only examine briefly the mass movements clearly traceable to La Salette.

Many people, deeply affected by the reprimands voiced by the Mother of Mercies on the mountain of La Salette and justifiably frightened by the ills she has foretold, are eager to enter into the spirit of this miraculous Apparition whose purpose is to restrain the Lord's anger by a sincere return to the commandments of God and of the Church. They have gathered together in an Association of prayer and good works, under the title of Our Lady of La Salette, Reconciler.

Father Burnoud, the first superior of the Missionaries of La Salette, wrote these words in a petition to Bishop de Bruillard to obtain canonical status for the Archconfraternity of Our Lady, Reconciler of La Salette. In point of fact, the Archconfraternity had existed with Bishop de Bruillard's authorization since May 1, 1848. It had been Father Louis Perrin's desire to make of his La Salette parish a center of prayer and conversion. He had founded the Archconfraternity and had directed it with this in mind. When the Missionaries arrived, he had already recruited fifty thousand members. Thus, what Pius IX approved on September 7, 1852 was in reality a popular movement, authentically directed toward atonement. Today, thanks to the spread of the Missionaries of Our Lady of La Salette in various countries, the confraternities of Our Lady of La Salette form a network of reconciling prayer spanning the globe.

Moreover, the "*Oeuvre dominicale de France*" (*a Sunday observance society*), founded by Count Louis de Cissey in 1873, was very characteristic of the era. This was not a replica of the Saint Dizier confraternity. Since that time, especially since the Commune, French Catholics had found that economic liberalism had erected social structures that made the practice of Sunday observance impossible. Louis de Cissey advocated a kind of social action geared to the goal he had set. To this end, he fostered consumer education to free the merchant. He placed petitions before the National Assembly to obtain passage of a law establishing Sunday rest. Finally, in 1879 he founded an association which eventually grew to 200,000 members and which exerted a decisive influence on public opinion.

But this work was essentially supernatural in its inspiration. In 1891, long after Cissey's death, the diocesan sector of Mans offered 1,400,000 acts of atonement for the religious observance of Sunday. At Annonay, the devoutly Christian wife of a noted industrialist dedicated her efforts to the revitalizing of Sunday observance in her township. Her prayers were heard and the mills of Annonay closed on Sunday. The founder of this movement gave all the glory to the Blessed Virgin. When people called him "founder," he gently corrected them: "Our Lady of La Salette is our founder, as she is of the Archconfraternity of Saint Dizier."

The National Shrines of France also owe their inspiration to La Salette. As the horrors of the Commune subsided, Father Thévenat, curate of St. Gervais in Paris, journeyed to Ars to pray at the tomb of the beloved Curé. There, he remembered with how much disdain the warnings of the beautiful Lady had been received. He conceived the project of a national pilgrimage to the place where the Virgin had wept over her unfaithful people. In his *Echo de Ste. Philoméne*, he later wrote: "Isn't the mountain of La Salette the place where the most important and the most relevant event of our time occurred?" Too busy with his ministry, he confided the organization of the pilgrimage to the Assumptionist Fathers.

On August 19, 1872, seven-hundred and fifty pilgrims knelt to pray at the tomb of the Curé of Ars. Then more people joined them in

Lyons. Entering Grenoble, their numbers had swelled to over one thousand. This was so unusual for the time that they were jeered as they crossed the city. This very incident prompted Thiers to declare in a session of the National Assembly that "pilgrimages are no longer in our customs." Enthusiasm and faith proved stronger than hatred, however. At La Salette, 7,000 pilgrims from the south had joined the northerners. This shared experience of like-minded people convinced the organizers that the pilgrimage should become an annual event. Before leaving the site, they called the first meeting of the Council of Pilgrimages. The seed had been sown.

The following October, the religious and the Third Order of St. Dominic, 70,000 strong, gathered at Lourdes for the Rosary procession. La Salette, of course, will never see such numbers. At an altitude of 6,000 feet, accommodations and lodging become difficult. Still, organized pilgrimages always include La Salette in their itineraries. Having inspired a movement of penance and prayer, La Salette would well cherish these two spiritual priorities. The General Council of Pilgrimages recognized its debt to La Salette in a short article in the newspaper *l'Univers*, dated June 23, 1875:

> *The pilgrimage movement was born at the tomb of the Curé of Ars, at the altar of St. Philomena, and at La Salette.... We wish gratefully to acknowledge our origins. This year we would like to invite a few people to come with us on the Holy Mountain to pray. We have always found much grace and consolation there. However, we would not want to be too numerous....*

We remember, of course, that the Pélerin was a means of publicity for the pilgrimage movement and that it paved the way for La Croix at the Bonne Presse publishing house.

Clearly, Christians lived the devotion to Our Lady of La Salette under the sign of atonement. The testimony of the crowds and of the outstanding leaders of the time proves this. Still, there was need for a master of the spiritual life to gather so many scattered aspirations into one body of teaching. The people who answered the call of La Salette's mysterious helplessness, who offered to fill up in their own flesh what was lacking in the sufferings of Christ, needed a sure-footed guide. The life and the work of Father Sylvain-Marie Giraud answered the need.

Only Providence can account for the affinity between Father Giraud and La Salette. On November 13, 1858 Sylvain Giraud, a young priest from the diocese of Aix, came to the house owned by the Missionaries of La Salette in Grenoble. No human ambition drove him there. He was a learned professor and a popular orator who could easily have had a brilliant career in the diocesan clergy. He was well aware of the problem. facing the young congregation. Venerable and respected counselors had warned him against impulsive action. Still, he was guided by the conclusion he had reached during his retreat of discernment at La Salette more than a year before. "The most Blessed Virgin, my mother, wants me to become a missionary of her tears and of her sufferings. I am deeply convinced of this. I am very serene about this. All my doubts are gone. And so begins a future filled with the work, suffering, and trials spoken of in my ordination promises... I am accepting this wonderful grace free from all pressure, I assure you. I have absolutely no doubt that this is my vocation. In spite of misgivings about tribulations to come, I leave a most comfortable situation in order to embrace the new mission Mary has given me." **(12)**

Here, one senses, is an uncommon man. Will his generosity stand the test of daily life? At the very first, he understood what others, the good priests appointed by the Bishop of Grenoble to minister at the shrine, had overlooked, namely, that to enter into the ministry of La Salette, one needed self-denial. On his own initiative he asked for a novitiate year. "Consider me as clay and mold me as you see fit," he told his Master of Novices. But the rigid potter was to be Father Bossan and the new priests joining Father Giraud were stifled by the ascetical practices of the Desert Fathers. Yet Father Giraud always saw God in the man. "One must let go," he advised. "It isn't up to the victim to argue about the means employed to lead it to its goal of total self-denial." Thus, in a less than perfect setting and through his daily conversation with his Compassionate Lady, he struggled toward the ideal of self-denial. He well knew that for his Community in the grips of growth pangs, this was the only salvation. There was no illusion, no concession to a maudlin sadness guiding his steps, but rather an absolute conviction of the value of sacrifice in the light of the Gospel. "I feel that if the grain of wheat (I mean myself) falls into the ground and really dies, much good will be accomplished." To one of his former classmates whom he wanted to draw to La Salette, he wrote:

> *You would be a thousand times happier (more at peace) with the Capuchins or the Trappists. What we have here is agony. It is the immense suffering that weighed on our Mother in her Apparition. Come without fear. I will be indulgent toward you; but in the early stages of any foundation, there is no need of a great theologian or a great preacher. What we need are people who have died. The one who has given us life by his death stipulates this as a condition for any work.*
> (13)

Fr. Sylvain-Marie Giraud (1830 - 1885), La Salette Superior General, 1865-1876

Father Giraud's entire career can be summarized by his own formula: life given for others to the glory of God by death to self.

In 1865 he was elected superior of the Missionaries. For eleven years he carried what he called "the heaviest cross in the community." At the same time he was the rector of the shrine. He became the founder and editor of the Annales de Notre-Dame de La Salette. He spent the winter months preaching. In the respite left him during the preaching season, or when confined by sickness, he still found time to write. His pleasant disposition allowed him to deal with many seemingly incompatible tasks. People who came to him left with the impression that they had been his sole concern. To certain confidants he expressed his fatigue: "My life is cut to pieces by these good people who come to see our Mother. Night comes and I still haven't had a moment to myself...."

The ideal to which his Compassionate Lady drew him was so lofty that it could be reached only through constant openness to God. Along with service to the neighbor, Father Giraud regarded events as masters come from God's own hand, molding him into the likeness of "the one who has given us all by his death." Never perhaps did he reveal his own grace more clearly than in these magnificent words sent to a nun stricken by illness:

> Reflecting on your suffering, I remember St. Augustine's great doctrine founded on the teaching of St. Paul. It has pleased the Father that Our Lord should suffer in his natural body as well as in his mystical body. These two kinds of suffering were necessary for the perfection of our redemption. But Our Lord could not suffer certain pains and certain infirmities because of the dignity of his adorable humanity. This is why he is suffering them, since he has gone to heaven, in his mystical body, which is his body as much as the one he received from the Virgin. This total sum of suffering and pain is foreseen and fixed. The world lasts until it is complete. By our suffering we share in its completion. You see how important this participation can be!

Father Giraud generously gave his share to complete what was lacking in the sufferings of Christ. Physical suffering was his lot as soon as he reached the holy mountain. Exhausted from work and prevented by illness from reaching his religious house, he died in a hospital, after having preached a priest's retreat. He was 55 years of age. The moral suffering which was his lot until the end would have broken many lesser spirits. One day during his novitiate, he assisted at the missionary departure of a priest who was, like himself, a native of Aix, and he cried out: "For me, inasmuch as I can possibly say, I will be with La Salette until death." Fifteen years later, after the elections that seemed to have sealed the failure of his efforts to breathe into the Institute a spirit worthy of the apparition, he confessed:

> What would you expect? I so often expressed our need of a spirit to undergird this work and so often repeated that this was to be a

spirit of Victim and Sacrifice for us, that the good Master has tested me a little. That test was terrible at times. But my soul has now reached a deep serenity.

Not content with the ordeals the Master saw fit to send him, he plunged headlong into a darkness that could be labeled excessive if one did not realize that only a mediocre love avoids excess. Thus, in obedience to his superior and to oblige those around him, he altered his preaching style, abandoning what was called the grand manner. He avoided even the popularity he might have gained through parish retreats to dedicate himself almost exclusively to conducting retreats for religious and priests and to spiritual direction. Choosing privacy and silence, he wrote the works by which he communicated to the world the light he felt he had no right to withhold from it.

In such a master the ring of truth is heard when he suggests to committed people the prayer-life he himself embraced.

> *Whoever you may be, victim spirit, follow your Mother's example simply and lovingly. Live affectionately close to her engaging mystery. Love her tenderly and strongly and you will readily understand that for you this mystery is one of light and consolation in the committed life you have chosen. It will capture your spirit and perhaps completely possess it. It is powerfully attractive. Its sweetness and its sorrows are of a sort that leaves one unable to drink from any other stream. You will indeed live within this ravishing mystery as in a sanctuary, or on an altar, where your life as a Victim will be lived out in suffering, prayer, and love.*

> *The apparition, this great and glorious and beloved apparition of Our Mother (let no one condemn us before having experienced and tasted what love leads us to say here), the apparition of Mary, Victim of atonement, will be your spirit's all! Indeed, you will find the weeping Mary and the crucified Jesus to console, God our Father to serve, to praise, to appease, to love. And people to save! Really, this is everything...* **(14)**

Even before coming to La Salette, Father Giraud's spirituality was oriented toward the notion of Christian sacrifice. Father Olier deeply influenced him during his seminary years. He was later directed to Condren and this influence is especially felt in his great work, *Priest and Sacrifice*. He was familiar with the whole Oratorian school. Henri Bremond Considered him the progeny of the French spiritual theologians of the 17th century. Father Giraud had many other sources, especially the Church Fathers, to whom he liked to attribute whatever was harsh or shocking to modern sensibilities. Still, whatever may have been the mainstays of his thought, his principal, and in a sense his only, inspiration was the Virgin of La Salette. The others were adopted because of her, their lights blended with hers. To an abstract body of doctrine, she gave life and motion. Through her he went beyond commonly held opinions (for example, the notion, with its consequences, of the ongoing Sacrifice which Christ offers in heaven), and he embraced, with the energy of a trailblazer, some more secure truths: the mediation of Mary, the kingship of Christ. His contemplation of her burst forth in strains that critics have praised as "utterances of great beauty and solid doctrine, brief and burning as angelic song." **(15)**

Unfortunately, Father Giraud's beautiful texts on Our Lady of La Salette are scattered throughout his works, in his correspondence, and in the outlines of his homilies. He never had the time to collect them into the "summary of mystical theology" he had discovered in the apparition. But one page from his first book convinces us that in La Salette the whole mystery of the Virgin is offered for our contemplation. He entitles it: "The Excellence of the Devotion to Our Lady of La Salette, Reconciler."

> *The devotion to Our Lady of La Salette is the devotion to Mary. Here, in one word, lies an infinity of great and comforting truths. Here, and wherever her children love and bless her, she is Mary our Mother. She is the one we love in all her shrines as in all her mysteries. Always and everywhere, she is our life, our sweetness, and our hope.*

> *Surely, this would be enough to set our hearts on fire for the apparition, but let us go further. With devotion and gratitude let us appraise what is singularly admirable in the La Salette miracle.*

An examination of various apparitions of the Most Blessed Virgin shows the following: this wonderful Mother normally revealed herself to people in order to fulfill one of those missions she has received from God and that the Church constantly calls to mind in her invocation "Refuge of Sinners, Consolation of the Afflicted, Help of Christians, pray for us." At other times she recalls a simple event of her earthly life or a mystery in the life of her Son.

In all of these instances, an apparition does not take on a universal character and the devotion born of it remains specific and local. But universality seems quite clearly to be a special characteristic of the miracle of La Salette. Twice, the Virgin says that the news of her merciful visit and the message of her teachings and warnings must be announced to all her people. Her word has spread throughout the world. Secondly, and more relevant to our piety, is the consideration that at La Salette the Virgin does not only recall a mystery of her early life. She is not simply fulfilling a ministry of charity and mercy. In one single event she seems to recall all her mysteries. She also appears with all the humility of her earthly existence and with all the glory, the power, and the authority that crown her in heaven. Mary at La Salette (if we may be allowed to say so) is the complete Mary shown us by Catholic tradition and theology. In a word, here she is as God wanted her to be in the incomparable role she plays in his divine plan.

Consider this holy apparition for a moment. First, we note the Virgin hidden from the eyes of the public, a humble, modest, Mary of Nazareth speaking a people-language, wearing a simple dress, preferring the company of humble, helpless, and poor people.

We also recognize, in this weeping Mother wearing the cross of Jesus, praying without ceasing for her guilty children, the afflicted Mother of Calvary. The Church shows her in the mystery of sorrow, all in tears. The Fathers say that she alone was the true cross, the real altar on which Jesus was being sacrificed, and who becomes, on this day of our Redemption, our own Mother, the Mother of the just and of sinners.

And then, isn't she here as she appears in tradition, after the Ascen-

sion, filled with concern and charity for the Church, her people?

Finally, here we see our Mother as the angels see her in heaven, the powerful Mediatrix, always interceding for us, the divine keeper of heavenly gifts, the generous giver of graces, the world's gentle providence, the merciful Queen, making her own all of her children's concerns, those of this life and those of eternity.

All this is amazingly beautiful and we have mentioned nothing that does not come, in a striking and wonderful way, from the apparition itself and from the words and actions of our Mother. This simple event that has so forcefully echoed throughout the world is perhaps a lesson given to us by God to deepen our knowledge of Mary and to develop our theology of the Mother of God. In this apparition, Mary certainly reveals a new plan Jesus has for the world.
(16)

If we wish to give to our attraction to the Virgin of La Salette an orientation toward divine mystery and a dynamism essential to a genuine devotion, then it is good to be led by such a guide as Father Giraud. From his very first article he feels that to reach that goal we have to view the apparition from a certain vantage point, free from the control of our own personal interests. Then it becomes more than a pious story, a miracle of the Virgin proclaiming lavishness toward her devotees. It is a window onto the entire mystery of Mary and at the same time into the depths of the Redemption, onto the unity of the mystical Body, and onto the role given each one of us to play in conjunction with our sorrowful Mother. From the visible to the invisible, from the incidental to the eternal, the law of ascent to higher things must accompany any devotion, but especially one born of an apparition.

Theologians note that faith in the apparition and the faith which inspires our devotion differ in kind. The faith by which we believe in the apparition is human. The faith which inspires devotion is of God. The first implication of such a distinction is that the apparition is only a means to an end.

An apparition of the Blessed Virgin either at La Salette or anywhere else is not and can never be an object of faith. But our devotion, if it is to increase our life of grace, must have as its object a reality that is in the order of faith. In the movement drawing us toward the Virgin of La Salette or of Lourdes or Fourvières, we must go beyond the event that bears its name. When we deliberately limit our vision to the event, we do not make a single step toward God. Not that looking beyond the event is difficult. In fact, it is difficult not to do so. It is the person of Mary we wish to love at La Salette or at Lourdes, with her merits and privileges and the place that is hers in the plan of salvation. Viewing her mystery from this choice vantage point, we hope now to discover new perspectives in the total mystery of faith. From her power we await the grace to raise our life to the level of the realities we contemplate. Very surely, our devotion leads us on an authentic path to God.

This is an elementary reminder and we would like to believe it superfluous. Nevertheless, certain forms of popular devotion limit their horizons to a chapel, a stream, to sacred places hallowed by a pious tradition. It would be wise to suggest politely that the venerated saint is actually not here. What is more important is to follow him. Intemperate devotees admittedly do not help us understand the mystery of Mary when they draw exaggerated attention to some peculiarities of the apparition. To have held Mélanie's famous secret as an article of faith was especially wrong. It does not possess enough credibility to warrant even human faith.

Such apparent disregard of the event might shock some people. Still, all the documents of the magisterium support this approach. The encyclical, *Pascendi*, previously alluded to states clearly the Church's traditional position on this subject:

> *With regard to the judgment to be rendered on pious tradition, here is what must be kept in mind: the Church exercises such prudence in the matter that she does not allow these traditions to be published in writing unless it be done with great caution and after including the directive prescribed by Urban VIII. She does not hold herself guarantor even after having acknowledged the veracity of the event. She merely does not prohibit belief in matters not bereft of the mo-*

tives of human faith. The Sacred Congregation of Rites decreed this thirty years ago (May 12, 1877).

These apparitions or revelations have been neither condemned nor approved by the Holy See which has merely allowed them to be believed with a purely human faith, on the strength of the traditions that pass them on, corroborated by works and trustworthy witnesses. Whoever holds this doctrine is secure. A devotion that springs from an apparition must always be founded on the undeniable truth of the fact and it must always look through the particulars of the miraculous event to this truth. **(17)**

The Church never loses sight of the distinction between the event and the devotion, as the history of La Salette consistently shows.

"To establish a new shrine in honor of the Blessed Virgin one needs only a probability, since there is no question here of canonizing the Blessed Virgin," said Monsignor Frattini to Father Rousselot. "La Salette is founded on a multitude of probabilities, or in other words and using the expression of the Promoter himself, it possesses all the characteristics of truth." **(18)**

At La Salette we find the Blessed Virgin. This is basic and can never be too strongly highlighted. And the Virgin we find is the one we see in the Gospel and in tradition, the same person who lived on earth and who reigns in heaven, who is the object of our faith.

To underscore the credibility of the miraculous event is hardly the last word. Is there no other scope to the work done by historians and apologists than to establish authenticity and reach a more or less firm assent on the strength of proofs and evidence? After a long inquest conducted according to all the rules of prudence and near enough to us in time to exclude suspicion of its methodology, the bishop's approbation clearly confers a moral certainty. This approval must have some bearing on the way we live our life. It would be easy to say that the more certainty there is in an apparition, the more the faithful are prompted to invoke the saint in question with confidence. This, of course, goes a long way in developing devotion to him and, indirectly, to God. But in the case of La Salette this kind of answer does not go deep enough.

"If my people will not obey.... How long have I suffered for you...." The specific details of this event almost compel our faith, like Mary's majesty and her heart-rending pleas, her concern about a meaningless conversation that so overwhelmed Maximin's father, and her tears— tears that could make even an unbeliever weep. What more could our faith tell us about the mystery of Mary? Is the theologian telling me to keep the La Salette event, so rich in religious meaning, out of my devotion? Practically speaking, this is the question the faithful are asking.

To draw such conclusions is seriously to misread the spirit of theological analyses. To distinguish in order better to unite and so sustain the rhythm of life could very appropriately become the motto of such anatomists of devotion. When the Virgin herself gives every sign of opening a school of piety, no theologian will want to close it. One wishes simply to please oneself in that attitude required for true progress in her ways.

Certain apparitions contain valuable teachings which allow us to penetrate the mystery of Mary. One of the masters who has most deepened this topic explains:

> *They [apparitions] are not binding in faith, true, but many of them come to us with such sureness that even the most demanding theologian cannot avoid taking them seriously. Some visible signs, at least, of the invisible motherhood must appear; some impact on earth of the intercession she exercises in heaven must be felt. It must be said, though, that these are necessarily very imperfect, very fleeting signs, able to yield only a weak notion of heavenly reality. Nevertheless, from these signs, the most rigorous and the wisest Christian thought can rise to higher levels of contemplation. Thus it is meaningful and truly revealing for what pertains to the state of glory, that in different ways Mary can manifest herself with equal truth. At Lourdes, she assumes the appearance of a young lady (Bernadette called her "Damizella," I believe) dressed for betrothal when she had just been seen at La Salette in the austere bearing of a woman in mourning. Here, her age and appearance suggested*

compassion; at Lourdes, they indicated the Annunciation. There is great truth in all of this! **(19)**

Indeed, the translation of the mystery into human language is so faithful, so simple that the theologian, putting all excessive wariness aside, can only join the common folk in admiration.

This woman, seated and overcome with grief, alone in this deserted place and weeping [wrote Father Lemonnyer] even if we never knew who she was, is a soul-wrenching sight to behold. She touches especially the soul of the people, so eager to open itself to the feeling of human solidarity in the face of misfortune. But it is heartrending to realize that this woman, seated on a stone and overcome with tears, is the Mother of God. The theologian is speechless, intellectually bewildered before such a scene. After the initial surprise, the lay person is immediately won over and profoundly moved. **(20)**

The Magisterium clearly acknowledges that an event such as an apparition can inspire a devotion. In his pronouncement on the apparition of La Salette, Bishop de Bruillard declared: "We are authorizing the devotion to Our Lady of La Salette. We grant permission to preach it and to draw the practical and moral conclusions from this great event."

He himself led the way "Since the main goal of the apparition was to bring Christians back to the practice of their religious duties, to divine worship, we entreat you, dear Brothers, in your own spiritual and earthly interest, to consider this seriously."

The history of the devotion to Our Lady of La Salette clearly highlights the mystery of Mary. The devotion associated with it springs from that very same mystery as she so lovingly and attentively brought it to us at La Salette, and not from theological discussions. The first act, the earliest form of the devotion in honor of Our Lady of La Salette, was the confraternity established in 1848 by the pastor of the parish for the conversion of sinners. Its members were invited to recite each day the invocation, "Our Lady of La Salette, Reconciler of sinners, pray without ceasing for us who have recourse to you." This is how a humble country pastor, searching for the deeper meaning of the drama experienced by the two children, found a title that is truly one of Mary's spiritual attributes.

Theologians will not deny it, but they would never have made a devotion of it. The importance of it escaped them. In order to bring us to focus on it and to nourish our lives from it, the Virgin opened our eyes to the spiritual wealth of this title through all the phases and symbols of her apparition. Following the lead of Father Perrin, millions of people have invoked the Virgin under the title of Reconciler. Contemplatives have come to see her in this new light. They have had a fresh look at the mystery which has always been hers, the reconciliation of us all. They have examined the various aspects of this mystery, so to speak, in its earthly and eternal elements.

Father Giraud especially was struck by Mary's role as victim with Christ before God. Léon Bloy was fascinated by the earthly aspect of this mystery of unfathomable Compassion. In reality, the reconciling Virgin brings these points of view together in herself. One thing is certain: people who are nourished by La Salette are fed by the authentic spiritual truths contained in the words and images that were heard and seen in the small vale of the Sezia. Moreover, the canonical title by which Rome encourages the devotion always mentions the event that gave birth to the basic mystery: Our Lady of La Salette, Reconciler. The event itself should guide us, we are given to understand, if we are to practice the devotion well.

The Church and its theologians remind us that if our devotion is to be valid, it must look beyond the event of the apparition. Yet, we are not dissuaded from reflecting on the event and all its circumstances as an introduction to the spiritual truths our faith will encounter. Indeed, we are encouraged to do so. Enfleshed in symbols and images, otherworldly realities become more accessible and moving to the earthbound beings we are. But these images and symbols must be reliable. They should not make a travesty of the lofty notion we have of the divine mystery. Canonical approval guarantees that this is so for La Salette and for all that it contains.

The golden rule to follow is to use the authentic facts of La Salette as a system of symbols designed by the Virgin to guide us on the path of her true mystery. Prudently, the theologian must refer to the Church for the interpretation of the more obscure signs.

As a matter of principle, a solid and effective devotion must rest on a central mystery capable of shedding light on other truths of faith. All the great devotions in the Church are like that. If the devotion to La Salette is to be special, if it is to galvanize our spiritual energies, and lead us to embrace the mystery of Mary and through it, the mystery of God, it must focus on essentials. It must have, in Scholastic terminology, a formal object.

A rich, lived tradition consecrated by the Church has designated the Virgin Reconciler as the object of our devotion. Christian intuition was not misled when it focused on this perspective. It brings us to the heart of the mystery of Mary. Her day's visit to La Salette means that the Queen of heaven in her glory is always and forever concerned with reconciling her people. In the apparition's system of signs there is a central scene of critical importance: the Conversation wherein Mary shares her great news and beseeches her people's attention permits us to understand the other two phases of the seated Weeping Virgin and the Assumption. To highlight her role as Reconciler, Our Lady shows herself as a woman of Compassion living now in the glory that awaits us. She teaches us also in other ways. Her dress and its ornamentation contain lessons for everyday living. The interpretation of these signs will be credible inasmuch as we stay close to the essential teaching.

When the symbolism of the apparition is reduced to its most general and undeniable elements, and when the ministry of reconciliation is acknowledged as unifying principle, one is surprised to see how the Virgin's pedagogy resembles that of the Church. The parallel asserts itself with regard to the sacraments and the entire liturgy.

"O Sacrum convivium, (O holy banquet)" do we sing of the Sacrament in which we receive Christ and venerate the memory of his Passion and in which we are filled with grace and given the pledge of future glory.

Likewise at La Salette, when the Virgin brings us the grace of reconciliation she compels us to venerate the memory of her compassion and gives us, as a pledge of future glory, the radiant image which Mélanie contemplated and which Maximin reached for, as it hovered between heaven and earth.

Let us ponder the meaning that the Church gives to the season of Advent. Between the first coming at Bethlehem and the final coming at the end of time, she points to the daily coming of Christ in people and urges us to receive Him. She is telling us that the present pertains to the past and to the future. Today, Christ offers us his grace but there was a time once on earth when He brought this gift by His crèche and by His cross. And there will come a time of reckoning because of the price He paid for the gift. Whether past or future, God's word always touches eternity. All things considered, is this not the vision suggested by the three phases of the apparition of La Salette?

These correspondences capture our attention. Is this sheer coincidence or are all the expressions of the Christian mystery really linked together? When a heavenly being wants to give us an idea of the value of the action it is performing for us, it must demonstrate in the course of time a few of the qualities that constitute its eternal state, especially those that are the basis of its power. The symbolism of La Salette is indeed clear. When we try to insert timeless realities into the dark glass of our own present moment, we are brought deep into the mystery of Mary.

The first scene of the apparition shows the beautiful Lady overwhelmed by a sadness that brings to mind all the lamentations of Scripture: "He has left me desolate, in misery all day long" (Lamentations 1:13b). This is an image, but the reality it portrays is powerful. "A weeping, suffering, blessedness! This boggles the mind. How can anyone imagine such a thing?" Léon Bloy wondered.

What is there to say in the presence of beings freed from the categories of time? When the Virgin speaks to us of her tears in the present tense, when she assures us that these tears are shed for us, she must be believed with outright simplicity, without wondering how, in the presence of God, she could shed such tears as we do.

"Forever have I been suffering for you!" These are real tears. They are real

on earth and real in heaven. More precisely, they are an earth reality
borne into heaven. It is as if she had learned a heartrending melody
in this valley of tears and were eternally singing it in a heavenly key.

The tears of Our Lady are an earthly reality

They have fallen from the eyes of this woman called Mary on a day
in time, this continuous time which is part of the fabric of our lives.
They have streamed from the most maternal, the most afflicted heart
that ever was, from the holiest and the most adoring heart outside
that of Christ himself. At the foot of the cross she was the only one
to feel that she was losing her Son. She knew with the clear insight of
innocence that the humanity that came before Him and after Him,
the whole of humankind including us was rejecting Him. This was sin
on a massive scale. How could she withstand it? The evangelist shows
her standing and sharing in her Son's struggle. He does not say that
her eyes were dry. He mentions nothing — this was their own secret
— of the storm of tears, of the flood-release of pain when, after the
secret burial, he brought to his home the one who had drunk deep
from the chalice of suffering reserved for mothers.

The tears of Our Lady are a heavenly reality

We believe in the merits of the saints and we ourselves want to gain
some. Many people imagine them to be external to us, things we will
hold in our hands to offer to God. A merit is not a possession, but
rather a quality of our being laboriously acquired. It is an expression
we have given to our spiritual appearance during this pilgrimage
through time. The tears of Mary are a merit inscribed in her being
forever. But they do not disfigure her beauty. They soften it and cause
it to glow. They do not lessen her joy but strengthen it, always renew-
ing and nourishing it.

The remainder of the apparition has made us very sensitive to this transfiguration of tears that takes place in glory. Mélaniehad closely observed the beautiful Lady and she assured us that the tears never fell to earth At knee-height they would blend with the glory and nourish the brightness that eclipsed that of the sun. It is good for us to think of earthly trials as the sustenance of eternal joy, of darkness and night destroyed by light. But it is so only if our tears do not become stagnant pools within us, only if they change us, only if they become part of our growth in grace.

The beautiful, weeping Lady of La Salette does not mislead us. Whether they be heavenly or earthly, her tears fall upon us and should sear us. In heaven her suffering has come to an end, but not her love. Released from pain, she has not freed herself from offering on our behalf the inexhaustible intercession of her tears. "I am obliged to plead with him without ceasing." And if, impossibly, this intercessory resource were to be taken from her and she were again reduced to manifesting her affection in our human terms and symbols, we would see her exactly as Maximin and Mélanie saw her, or the Apostle John on Good Friday evening, eager to clothe with tenderness the Child of her flesh and the children of her love.

Yet this ability to leap over centuries and transform each of our sinful lives already belonged to the earthly tears and the very heart's blood of Our Lady. A loving intention cannot be constrained by arbitrary divisions of time. It was the will of the new Eve that her tears be shed for all peoples, for all generations. In intent, her tears flowed down the course of centuries and back through expired time and touched the brow of every person coming into the world in order to bring about a rebirth originating not in flesh and blood but in God.

Did not all the sins of the world provide the spark to ignite such an intense suffering and love in a human heart? There is a direct proportion as well as a strict correlation between these two forces: our sins, her tears. Whoever adds to the one, adds to the other and whoever takes away from the one also takes away from the other. Saint and sinner alike are surely aware of this. The communion of saints is indeed powerful. Mary's mediation is a profound mystery. I can choose at this very moment to commune with the most compelling and purifying tears of this most motherly of all women. When she evokes for our own generation her travail on Calvary, when she insists, "Forever have I been suffering for you!" she is not playing on words. It is that she has really been waiting for us, overwhelmed with sadness, for two thousand years. Perhaps you can do something for her. You may have something to tell her. The little boy who saw her was a scatterbrain, but he still managed to say the decent word: "Do not cry, Madam, I will help you."

Unable to find the words to say to her, you might stay away. You may not hear her beckoning maternal call. In your own suffering you believe God has turned his back on you. You are in mourning. You feel betrayed. You are hemmed in by loneliness. Until now, you could drink from the cup of the Son of Man, but this last drop has made you turn away. Your prayer has become a reprimand: "Why, Lord, have you forgotten what a creature can bear?"

Come near to this weeping Lady. Say nothing. Her presence will envelop you. In the stillness you wait for surrender's first step: suffering does not last, but having suffered lasts forever. Later, in God's own time, you will understand. Christ once said to Saint Thérèse: "I would rather overturn heaven and earth than allow one person I love not to suffer." You will then receive this word with a worshiping heart. To redeem people, you see, the Son of God could not escape the necessity of suffering nor of seeing His own mother undergo pain.

An even more bitter experience awaits the saintliest of people: the dark nights of faith. With utter simplicity, Saint Thérèse of the Child Jesus described the silent, closed heaven under which she ended her pilgrimage on earth. She leads us into the forlorn, desolate atmosphere that conceals truths of the faith even for one who has never ceased clinging to them more than to life itself. The dark nights of faith experienced by the disciples are an extension of the dark depths the Master himself plumbed. "My God, my God, why have you forsaken me?" No one comes closer to knowing what this cry means than the Mother of God. Having shared with her Son the ordeal of the sixth hour, she is qualified and appointed to complement the silences of God.

Father Giraud certainly did not escape the trial of such darkness. He told a confidant about his painful experience and the ultimate refuge he found in Mary.

> You have no idea what my interior life is like! There is almost perpetual desolation. Our good mother continues to be my only felt comfort. Except for her there is nothing or almost nothing that sustains or enlightens me. I find at the feet of Mary a strength and a peace that Our Lord apparently does not want to grant me, even in the Eucharist. Our Lord reduces me to this state of weakness and interior sadness no doubt so that He can become in Mary my only life and my only strength. I rest confidently in this thought.

The Weeping Virgin. One could listen forever to these sobs that still echo after twenty centuries. As long as there are sinners to save, Jesus will be in agony and His Mother will be at the cross, waiting. But each person rightly keeps for himself his mother's confidences as well as his response to her. Popular piety is looked upon with apprehension, and sometimes rightly so. But there is little to fear at La Salette. The humblest Christian, pausing before this Woman in tears, cannot avoid recognizing her spiritual message. He will see in her not only the Lady who appeared at La Salette but also the Mother who shares the cup of her Son, a mother whose tears are mysteriously caused by our sins. Both extremes of excessive asceticism and complete flight from pain are purified in the fire of her own sacrifice. The only logical result of an encounter with the compassionate Lady is the reconciliation of the sinner by means of the saint's self-offering for the Mystical Body of Christ.

Mary speaks during the second phase of the apparition and makes the meaning of the opening scene totally explicit. My compassion is only a memory for you, she tells us, but for me it is a reality inscribed in my everlasting existence. It gives me the right to speak to you as I do. "How long have I suffered for you! If I would not have my Son abandon you, I am compelled to pray to Him without ceasing; and as for you, you take no heed of it. However much you pray, however much you do, you will never repay the pains I have taken for you." Her abundant tears bring home the truth of these words. With human words she attempts to bring us closer to her Son by seeking out whatever can still respond in the most barricaded heart. To bear the Son's punishment would be painful, but to be abandoned by Him would be worse still. We have seen how this discourse was worthy of the Virgin. But, a superficial reading will never reveal how practical it is for anyone's growth, how it leads to the heart of the Christian mystery. How can I relate to a blaspheming cart driver?

The Christian instinct chose aright the title it gave to Our Lady of La Salette. It was well aware that the apparition of September 19,1846 had become a visible manifestation of the invisible and ongoing role that Mary plays in heaven—our very reconciliation. Nevertheless, the traditional invocation, Reconciler of sinners, has something misleading about it. We could easily fail to grasp the mystery of Our Lady and overlook an essential aspect of Christian belief. Its formulation was influenced by the individualism of the time, and could perhaps be corrected. In any case, it has to be well understood. When we recite it we should add mentally: Reconciler *of the sinners that we are,* as we say in the *Hail Mary.* Otherwise, we appear to limit Our Lady's clientele to a single category of Christians, quite distressingly for those who believe they *are* sinners, and quite smugly for those who do not. Does not the collective expression *my people* which she repeatedly uses suggest the unity of Christ's Body? It is worth noting that throughout this long message she never declares having come for sinners only. Her first sentence as well as her last encompasses us all in a like reprimand and a like compassion. *"If my people will not submit...* *You will make this known to all my people."* Inveterate sinners are certainly the most directly concerned here. However, the solidarity that unites the members of the same Body is so irresistibly suggested that our indifference to sins committed around us should give us pause.

It is also quite possible that the ingratitude which gives rise to our small faults is greater than that of the blasphemy of the cart drivers.

The Virgin's ministry involves us all

Some are more specifically summoned to reconciliation, others to expiation. If all do what they must, that is, what their present gifts empower them to do, then salvation will be assured in collaboration with the Virgin who is mandated to pray without ceasing. It is pointless to ask whether the Virgin of La Salette is more properly the Virgin of converts or the model of people dedicated to expiation. In the framework of redemption and the communion of saints she is the Reconciler of her people. Given our solidarity with Adam as well as with Christ, it behooves the Handmaid of the Lord to model her ministry on that of the Master. Necessarily, she sees us in the unity of the human race. (This does not prevent her from seeing each one of us individually, as she saw little Maximin on the road to Corps.) As we respond to her we become aware of this oneness and of its endless implications. The most beautiful and the most convincing prayer with which we can "repay" the concern she has had for us is surely this cry of the Church in the Christmas antiphon: "Come to help this people forever falling and forever seeking to rise again. *Succurre cadenti surgere qui curat populo. (People who strive to assist the fallen to rise.)*"

The social sense that this startling discourse rekindles in us is, after all, nothing but a keen appreciation of the mystery of Redemption which the mystery of Mary reflects as light from a distant star. And the question arises whether the message of La Salette can still be of some use after more than a century. Do Christians today better appreciate the personal and social dimensions of Redemption? We must acknowledge as fact that in our world the idea of sin is seriously eroded. People are effectively convincing themselves that they no longer need redemption. The Christian who has heard the Virgin of La Salette will counter the mounting refrains of the prevailing goodness and greatness of human nature with the words that accurately describe the wound in Mary's heart "How long have I suffered for you! If I would not have my Son abandon you, I am compelled to pray to him without ceasing."

This message of La Salette is endlessly rich

In the main, Our Lady claims the privilege of advocacy for her
people. She also reminds us that she is mother of God and of grace.
She is queen over people and over elements. The whole spectrum of
her mediation takes its meaning from her coming as Reconciler. All
her virtues come to light when she wants these obstinate peasants
to understand the meaning of a bad harvest. There is something for
everyone. One may believe that at La Salette certain things were said
in vain, or that they have now lost their meaning. One may think
that some of the Virgin's reproaches to her people no longer apply,
because today vices are more refined or more monstrous. Consider
then that these very objections are the reason she continues to pray
that her Son not turn his back on us.

God is never the first to break a relationship. The first and essential
condition under which He will continue to call us His people is that
we ourselves not sever our relationship with Him. When a people as
a whole neglects the minimum of religious practice required in strict
justice—making holy the Lord's day, respecting His name, praying
observing prescribed penances, it is close to abandoning God. What
then can hold back the rising tide of barbarism? What then can unite
people in a common and meaningful fellowship? For an individual, there are worse things than missing Mass. For a people, there is
nothing worse than to proclaim that God is dead. This is the extreme
situation the Virgin wants to avoid when she attacks the blasphemy
of the cart drivers, and when she asks innocent children to say their
prayers morning and evening. If we as a people had a sense of our
identity as Christian Community, we would find such counsels and
such reprimands most useful. But centuries of individualism have
blinded us with pride. Whether it be at the parish sermon or in listening to the La Salette discourse, all too often people are bewildered
by the insistence on fidelity to Sunday Mass. Such a detail! And no
one sees that spurning this detail leads to millions of apostasies. It is
now time to begin in earnest to follow the one who is mandated to

pray without ceasing. We must learn anew, with her help, our spiritual solidarity and the importance of the virtue of religion.

The People of God: this is the title of a book in which Dom Vonier tries to capture the characteristics of what can properly be called such a people. It is amazing to see how these meditations conducted completely apart from La Salette coincide with the teaching Mary gave her people on the mountain.

Religion [says Dom Vonier] is really part of the virtue of justice, its highest expression, its most sacred manifestation. Through it, people give to God what belongs to God. It is also through specific acts of religion that a superior kind of life is maintained among people. The practice of religion also comprises a considerable amount of external action: no one can be religious if he or she is satisfied with a solely internal relationship with God. Submission to the will of God by men and women in the virtue of religion affects all of creation. In human beings the world does homage to God. It would be simply disastrous for Christians to limit the loftiest part of their life to interior acts of worship, to a purely cerebral relationship with God. Under these conditions no people of God could exist. A people of God needs a voice, a song, an altar, banners, holy places. It needs holy days when it can proclaim with one voice what it actually is: the people of God.

We can easily note the principal acts of the people of God throughout the centuries. First and foremost, there is the Eucharistic sacrifice. Then there are the holy days, the Sundays and feasts of the year whose observance constitutes a sure barometer of the faith in a given epoch. Then we have the whole realm of prayer. Finally, there are certain bodily acts which are clearly acts of divine worship, such as fasts, abstinence, bows and genuflections before God and His altar, the sign of the Cross. The people of God has always excelled in all of these practices. In the eyes of the world these are the acts which constitute Catholicism; they distinguish the people of God from any other people. Through these acts, a sense of unity and brotherhood flows throughout the powerful body which is the Christian people. Whoever performs them is known as a citizen of *this powerful realm.*

These requisites of the Christian ideal indeed justify the La Salette discourse. We can almost hear, in another key, the very complaints of the beautiful Lady. But at the theologian's every sentence there is a choked sob. *"Only a few older women attend Mass. During Lent, they go to the butcher shop like dogs. Ah ! my children, you must say your prayers well...."*

Astonishingly, the Virgin in this apparition asks nothing for herself. There are no requests for a chapel, no special acts of devotion in her honor. Her roses symbolize the Rosary and discreetly invite us to compensate for the suffering she has endured for us. With regard to strict obligation she requests only the minimal religious practices required of any Catholic. Her Son, she reiterates, is offended because His rights are disregarded. She refers everything to this Christ resplendent on her breast. If her pleading is heard she will have prepared, as John the Baptist had done, a perfect people for God. There are other failings besides the missing of Mass. This Virgin whom nineteen centuries of sinners have hailed as their refuge is well aware of this. Innovations in this area will not surprise her. Modern times cannot claim new developments in the realm of either the grotesque or the sublime. It is important that people be allowed the possibility of repenting in an atmosphere of ideas and practices proper to the people of God. A fallen person can rise again within a religious environment. In order to break the shell of self-complacency, a Christian needs to see around him waters that wash and heal, to see a child saying his prayers, to see his own people at Sunday Mass. To be immersed in an irreligious society might well seal the fate of those alienated from God. "The people of God," notes Father Vonier, "is certainly not without sin and should therefore always be ready to repent. In this way, sorrow for sin becomes a springboard to greater fidelity. What most afflicts the Christian character is not the occasional fault but the absence of repentance."

We note the spontaneous agreement between this theologian and the Lady of La Salette on the merciful aspect of temporal punishment: "In the presence of sin, a just retribution from God will help the people to redirect its conduct on the path of holiness. It will even be the characteristic gift of the people of God to understand how such a trial is just and wise and to be endured with patience and humility. Even if this people were to be completely the prisoner of God's justice, it would nonetheless remain God's people. Only in the case of open revolt, of blasphemy, would it become a nation not only of strangers but also of outlaws."

It is precisely this terrible predicament that the beautiful Lady wants to spare her people. *"I warned you last year with the potatoes but you paid no heed. They will continue to decay, so that by Christmas none will be left."*

The purpose of the discourse at La Salette is to safeguard a religious people for the Lord, a people He can truly call His own. From this viewpoint, nothing is insignificant. This Lady who speaks in dialect and wears a long colored apron has shocked some sensibilities. Still, she places within reach of the humblest people what deeply religious men and women have understood from her very first words: *"If I would not have my Son abandon you, I am compelled to pray to him without ceasing."* The people of God is made up of peasants who will stop blaspheming and of children who will say their prayers, as well as of heroic victims roused by their example. Praise and expiation will be in proportion to the grace of each person. But all these voices will sing of the Redemption in the same concert to which the Son and the Mother will respond in heaven. The Son is himself, according to Father Olier's striking expression, *"le grand religieux de son Père (the great religious of his Father)."* Indeed, it is difficult to imagine a nobler use of human language than to give everyday words so transcendent a meaning. Instead of being shocked by this familiarity, we should receive it as a valuable lesson. "To go to the people," we used to say. This means that we had not been with the people, nor of the people. We must live with them, never stop speaking their language and sharing their concerns. This is the challenge presented to the disciple by this Lady from heaven dressed as a handmaid.

To live with the people? This is the whole problem of today's ministry. We cannot ignore the fact that since the apparition of La Salette, the insubordination that the Virgin complained about has taken more critical forms. Religion is questioned at its very root. We congratulate ourselves that we have severed the tie between Creator and creature. There has been Karl Marx and his justification of apostasy for the benefit of the working classes. And there has been Nietzsche and his terrible mockery: we have killed God!

What a setback it would be for the priest and for the active Christian to embrace a purely humanistic ideal in the pursuit of their people's cause. What a failure it would be to silence the Good News while striving for legitimate, worldly goals. We must acknowledge the danger of an excessively human compassion and not underestimate the strength of a trend which, from the suburbs of great cities to the African bush, seeks to base human fellowship on shared possessions.

Still, Christian compassion cannot be a cerebral, fleshless reality. It is completely impossible for one who loves people coldly to dissociate eternal salvation from the temporal well-being of a human person. A person is a whole. Time is eternity already begun yet still not completely visible. The conflict will be resolved if Christian apostles learn to live with their people while remaining present to the Lady who, with her Son, weeps over both the death of souls and the death of little children. "Lady of heaven, empress of earth." Through the Virgin Mediator and Queen, apostles will find a balance between the demands of heaven and those of earth.

Father Giraud, who had received from his masters of the French school of spirituality a keen sense of the majesty of God and of the creature's nothingness, came to learn compassion at the school of the Virgin. According to his biographer, he was aware of his discomfort in preaching to lay people. He would ask his brother priests to alert him if his preaching and his reprimands became too vehement.

People ask if La Salette is still relevant

We can say that it enjoys the privilege of that which is authentically religious. It teaches the people of today, as it did those of a time now past, how to couple human compassion with theological charity.

The image of future glory is shown us in the third phase of the apparition.

We are not overly concerned about this glory while we are plunged in the struggle of daily life. We think that we have understood the fundamentals, such as the Gospel and the Church. However, we should not overlook the reality of future glory. To do so could mean that we end up living like the slave who turns the grinding wheel. To look at the sky refreshes and purifies us. It is a form of hygiene as well as a duty. We should no more turn away from the virgin of the Assumption than Maximin and Mélanie did, if we want to catch her parting secrets. She looks up at heaven and ceases to weep, embraced as she is by glory. She lowers her eyes toward the southeast where the Pope toils in Rome, and she meets Mélanie's gaze, her face expressing infinite compassion. Each of these actions marvelously beckons us to a life of deeper faith.

Not all Christians believe in an afterlife. In many minds, the certainty of future rewards is dulled by mental reservations and practical doubts which a true Christian finds disconcerting. "Yes, perhaps. We can only hope." But we too quickly conclude that God has spoken his final word of judgment here on earth. "I would be ashamed to treat a mangy dog the way God treats me," wrote Léon Bloy one day. Anyone who would live the mystery of La Salette needs above all to believe with unshakable faith in an afterlife. If you accept to be treated by God as he treated his Mother, you must discern, as you step into life's incomprehensible crucible, the final purpose of the divine Alchemist.

People want to rediscover the meaning of their daily actions. "God will wipe every tear from their eyes." We try to believe that. But we just barely manage to hope in some image of salvation, where life on earth is irrelevant because time and eternity are strangers one to the other. Nevertheless, the purpose and sense of time is restored to us when we see that tears are absorbed in glory—our last glimpse of the Lady. That purpose is to fashion with the grace of Jesus Christ the kind of person we will be throughout eternity. The rush-hour people who race through traffic away from plant, shop, and office, the elderly who feel useless and yearn for death, the orphans, the widows, all those who toil and weep—if only we could convince them that Paradise will be shaped by their toil, their exhaustion, and their tears as well as by their joy. How their lives would change if only they could believe without hesitation that the Almighty is more concerned with the smallest act of kindness than with the correct trajectory of the stars.

Besides, it is good to gaze at heaven with Mary and it is good to look upon this lovely mountain statue cast in the heavy bronze needed to weather the harsh alpine climate. Heaven seems closer, more accessible, and more hospitable when we see it reflected in the Mother whose concern constantly seeks us out. The Pope about to be exiled, little Mélanie on the threshold of her dangerous mission—these are only the representatives of that vast throng which with good reason we call the Church Militant. These very eyes that learned compassion from her Son's suffering now rest on countless children and could help them carry their crosses if only they raised their eyes to her. This could happen for us at any instant, at any point of our pilgrimage where we choose to meet her merciful gaze. In eternity she is rich with a credit acquired in time which she uses for our benefit without ever exhausting it. The purest and most tested of all creatures has become the immeasurable power supporting the action of the Almighty. Such is the mystery of Mary. We find in her the most faithful reflection of Christ. Her mystery of Reconciliation allows us to anticipate in utter confidence the hour of that Judge she knows so well how to appease. Through this same mystery, we await the revelation of the Infinite Being in whom justice and mercy are so perfectly reconciled that he has given us his only Son.

Are these truths supernatural enough to be proposed to the eye of faith as such? Are they connected enough to act together and not scatter our spiritual energies, to stamp our inner life with a certain spirit and our ministry with a specific style? Are they pivotal enough to provide a vantage point from which one can embrace the entire Christian mystery and come before the throne of the all-holy God?

If so—and we believe it is, the devotion to Our Lady of La Salette deserves to be fostered. It will become food for prayer to all who have understood it.

We have heard the Church's urging to go beyond the fact of the apparition which is not of faith in order to venerate in the person of Mary the prerogatives that belong to faith. With regard to critical theology, is it necessary to justify the privilege of Reconciler which we see as the axis of the La Salette devotion?

The privilege of Reconciler is only one aspect of the universal mediation of Mary. If she has merited for us all the graces that her Son gained in strict justice, the gift of conversion is necessarily the first one.

Now, though the mediation of Mary is not a dogma of faith, the awareness of this role has grown in the Church through recent theological investigation and more so through liturgical prayer.

> The universal mediation of Mary [notes Father Garrigou-Lagrange] has been far less opposed than the Immaculate Conception and the Assumption. In the ordinary Church magisterium, it is already quite certain, and we can only hope for a definition in order to promote the devotion of all toward the one who is really the spiritual Mother of us all and whose vigilance is constant. (21)

Understandably, we cannot examine all the arguments and the problems of theologians who attempt to articulate the concept of mediation. But how can we avoid noticing what Tradition has to say on the subject? The most beautiful texts describe Mary as Reconciler and refuge of sinners. In Saint Bernard this theme sings:

> Blessed Virgin, may you draw us near to your Son. May your abundant love cover our many sins. O Sovereign Lady, our Mediator and Advocate, reconcile us to your Son. (22)

> Surely, Christ Jesus is the completely faithful and all powerful Mediator between God and people, but His divine majesty fills them with a reverential fear. In Him, humanity seems absorbed by divinity, not that there exists a substantial change, but because all His

acts are divine. We do not sing only of the mercy of Christ but also of His judgments. Indeed, through suffering He learned the compassion that made Him merciful but He remains nonetheless our judge. We do not look, then, upon the role of the woman blessed among all women as superfluous; she has her designated place in this reconciliation because we need a mediator to go to Christ Mediator and we cannot find a better one than Mary. **(23)**

Here is the same idea in a more lyrical form:

You would fear to approach the Father. Only hearing Him you are frightened and you seek cover in the bush. He has given you Jesus as Mediator: what would not such a Son obtain from such a Father? His petitions would be granted because he made them, for the Father loves the Son. But does the Son also frighten you? He is your brother, of the same flesh. He has undergone all, except sin, to learn mercy. Mary has given you this brother. Perhaps in Him would you fear God's majesty, for although enfleshed, He remains God. You want an advocate before Him? Turn to Mary. In her, there is nothing but pure humanity, not only because she is exempt from all taint, but also because in her there is only the one, human nature. And I do not hesitate to say that she also will be granted what she asks, because of herself. The Son will hearken to the Mother and the Father will hearken to the Son. My little children, this is the sinner's ladder, my supreme hope. What then? Would the Son refuse His mother or allow that she be refused? Can He refuse to hear her? Could He himself not be heard? Clearly, not one of these instances could happen. **(24)**

Saint Albert the Great has lately been denied the authorship of the *Mariale*, the great work accrediting him as the doctor of Marian mediation. Still, by the whole of his work and with the unknown author of the *Mariale*, he remains a witness to the common belief of his era.

"She is the Advocate of all her people," says the *Mariale*. "As the mediator of reconciliation she has gathered together all that is beneath the fullness of her grace." **(25)**

Contemplating the Assumption scene, Saint Albert discerns the purpose that concerns us all: the reconciliation of sinners.

The Blessed Virgin rose above all the choirs, to intercede as a gentle mediator for sinners. But in order that the intercession of the Son with the Father and that of the Mother with the Son be more efficacious, we must offend neither the Son nor the Mother. With confidence, the sinner can begin doing penance when he believes and hopes that Mary, the Mother of mercy, will not reject the penitent, but will even be always ready to intercede for the guilty. **(26)**

He knows under what title she exercises her immense power of intercession. He shows us the Virgin in heaven in the accustomed attitude that has often inspired artists.

Her two hands come to the help of her prayer. One appeals to her Son's compassion. She shows Him her breast, her arms, this entire body, which was, is, and will be the temple of divinity. And this gesture stuns any adversary. The other hand reaches out to the poor who are imploring her who is filled with the lavishness of grace. **(27)**

Need we fear that such a succinctly formulated teaching be only a pious elaboration of the Latin Middle Ages? It would be easy to show its continuity in the Orient as well as in the West from a parallel drawn by St. Justin and St. Irenaeus between Adam and Jesus, Eve and Mary. The gordian knot of rebellion has been cut by the sword of obedience. In this bold move, Mary is associated with Jesus. This is one of the seminal themes of the Apostolic Fathers which Christian reflection over the centuries has appropriated. The privilege of being a Reconciler is implied in the merit of the New Eve. This is what two saintly Eastern doctors have felt.

St. Ephrem is famous in his praises addressed to the Virgin: "You alone, Lord, and your Mother, are beauty unsurpassed. There is no stain in you, Lord, no blemish in your Mother." **(28)**

Still, in the mind of Ephrem, this unrivaled purity should not discourage the sinner. On the contrary, nothing can better convince him that his advocate's requests will be granted.

"Hope of the desperate," he prays, "by you we are reconciled with

Christ your Son. You are the one advocate, help of sinners and of those who are bereft of all help."

And again: "Hail, refuge of sinners, true home where sinners eagerly come." **(29)**

St. John Damascene locates the source of Mary's mediation in her extraordinary union with her Son. All their treasures are held in common.

> It was proper for the Mother of God to share her Son's wealth and be honored by all creation as the mother and handmaid of God. The inheritance of parents goes to the children. Now, today, as a wise man has said, the sacred rivers run upstream, for the Son of Man leaves all his wealth to his Mother. **(30)**

St. John Damascene prays to her in every circumstance:

> Theotokos, Mother of God without blemish, pray your Son and my God to have pity on me because your supplication powerfully draws out the Master's clemency.

But he believes that the most desperate sinners are the choice clients of God's mercy. To St. Mary of Egypt he attributes this moving prayer:

> Virgin Mother of God, who conceived the Word made flesh, I know, yes I know that it is not becoming but embarrassing for me, who am so unclean, so soiled, to contemplate you, who are ever Virgin. In the presence of your purity it is only proper that I should be despised and rejected. But the God who was born of you has come to call sinners to penance. Help me, for alone I am helpless. Command that I be allowed to enter. Do not deny me the vision of this wood of the Cross on which was nailed the flesh of the God-Word you conceived and who gave His blood for my sake. **(31)**

The prayer of the Church, according to the adage, Lex orandi, lex credendi (the content of prayer expresses the meaning of faith), is for everyone the easiest source and strongest witness to consult. Anyone who has some feeling for the liturgy cannot avoid noting the grandeur of an offertory prayer such as the one for Our Lady of Seven Dolors. At the moment when all the offerings have been gathered and are made one with the Sacrifice of Jesus Christ, the Church sings as if these gifts and prayers had to be presented by an all-powerful advocate: "In the presence of God, remember, Virgin Mary, to speak in our behalf, that He may turn His anger from us." It is a remembrance of her role on Calvary and of her ministry in heaven. A recent text echoes it: "Look with mercy upon the fallen children of Adam; by your prayer, may your Son set aside His avenging anger." **(32)** The divine office always ends with an antiphon to the Blessed Virgin. Be it the *Alma Redemptoris* or *the Salve Regina*, the *Ave Regina Caelorum* or the *Regina Caeli*, they all express in similar terms the "hope of rising from our iniquity with the help of her intercession." The humblest of the faithful, those held, like Maximin and Mélanie, only to the *Our Father* and the *Hail Mary*, cannot ignore Mary's most characteristic response, when they make this one petition: "Pray for us, poor sinners. ..."

All that the devotion to Our Lady of La Salette offers us then, is worthy of the faith. Indeed, no doubt could be raised concerning the compassion and the heavenly glory of Mary. Considering its elements abstractly, we can actually sustain the devotion without necessarily involving the phenomenon of La Salette. Paradoxical as it may seem, this is the best guarantee of its orthodoxy. Would it then be helpful to us, under the pretext of going directly to Mary, to disregard the system of signs that make up her apparition? For over 150 years, the faithful have admiringly perceived in it the depth and breadth of her mystery. In effect, such a bypassing would constitute a misunderstanding of the demands of theology and the intentions of God.

The apparition and the devotion are not linked of absolute necessity. There is, though, a historical relationship. The devotion to the Reconciler was born of this apparition and not of speculative theology. Surely, the doctrine was received and the title proclaimed. But its value had never been assessed. No theologian, no bishop, had imagined that the proclamation of the powers of Mary could release a stream of grace. In her apparition, Mary had to inform Christians to what degree she was their Reconciler. The faithful invoked her as the Refuge of Sinners, but they could not imagine her seeking out the sinner avidly, with an eagerness proportionate to her suffering. This title bestowed on her by an ancient tradition was now filled with a new meaning. Together with the apparition's historical role of stimulating people to an awareness of the revealed truth, this is one fact that demonstrates the usefulness of the La Salette event in the practice of the devotion.

Furthermore, if the devotion had been developed by some theologian, it is not certain whether he would have advised linking Mary's reconciliation to her compassion as to its point of origin and to the glory of God as to its final purpose. He might perhaps have spoken dispassionately of her divine motherhood and of her motherhood of grace. The most concrete and dynamic relationships might have escaped him. Following in the steps of the one who spoke to us on the mountain, we can delve more deeply into divine mystery. We will know how invigorating it is to reflect on the nearness of Mary and of heaven, and on the importance of compassion as the crowning glory of her life. And we will know that our sufferings here below are as nothing compared to the glory that awaits us [St. Paul].

To understand the mystery of Mary as Reconciler, there are two points that need to be stressed in the marvelous symbolism of La Salette. In preparation for the reconciling work begun over 145 years ago, the Virgin sat overwhelmed on the shepherd's rustic stones, her face in her hands. She was prolonging or recalling what seemed, to the two children, her agony on Calvary. At the very moment of her apparition, the Church prayed in memory of her sorrows. As real as her compassion is, and precisely because it is real, there still is the happiness of discovering how closely associated it is to her work of mercy. Those who speak of automatic absolutions, of confessions absolving the sinner with impunity, are not aware of the power of these tears over a heart filled with pain.

We know well that Mary is the refuge of sinners, but in coming close to her and seeing what that title has cost her, we see the aspect of sin change from trifling to terrifying. The tears of the Mother help us to understand the blood of the Son. There is no denying, in the presence of over 145 year's experience, that the privilege of Reconciler, coupled with compassion, possesses an unsurpassed effectiveness. It does not allow anyone to play with God's forgiveness. It prevents us from making any magical or poetic use of the cross. We find here the antidote for any superficial sentimentality that can contaminate true devotion.

The challenge of Mary's sorrow provokes resolutions that transform us. The marvels of La Salette are not told in books, say generations of Missionaries and chaplains. There is no doubting the dispositions of kneeling penitents. The merciful hands of the Mother of grace, the weeping Mother, have touched their hearts.

The reconciling mediation of Mary touches us all. This is the second aspect of the mystery, and the light of La Salette clarifies it more than does any speculation. She presents this revelation of her sorrow to the just and the unjust. It is already a plea heard by the children and interpreted in their own way. "I wanted to tell her: "Do not cry any more, Madam, I will help you," said Maximin. In response to this silent invitation, some of the faithful understood that they could be associated with Mary's mission. But the discourse addressed to the entire people of God is more than an invitation. *"If my people will not submit, I shall be forced to let fall the arm of my Son."* Sinners are denounced with severity, yet all, even little children, are included in the threatened punishment. This fact certainly points to the unity of the Mystical Body and to the mutual responsibility we must have for each other, and it calls all sinners, those of today and yesterday, to repay the concern she had for us. *"No matter how much you pray, how much you do...."* This challenge is not reserved for a select few who, because of their exceptional fidelity to grace, would respond of their own accord. It summons the people of God as such to work in solidarity for salvation. In this sense, the challenge cannot be accepted because in a social body there is always an incredible waste of energy. It should be understood at least that every person's basic duty is to reassure the weak and the humble of this world of the possibility of Redemption in the spirit of the people of God and that the ideal would be to imitate Mary in her self-offering and unceasing prayer.

La Salette A Very Biblical Message

The biblical flavor of the La Salette discourse has often been noted. Mary is speaking to all her people, in reality the people of her Son. This is to be expected, but it is very enlightening for us to see how her ministry as Reconciler shares in the sweep of the Redemption. Salvation is personal, but it is also social. "Whoever gives even a cup of cold water to one of these little ones in the name of a disciple— truly I tell you, none of these will lose their reward." If this is true of a glass of water, how much more is it true of the quiet sharing of the spiritual alms of prayer? "May I not be guilty, my Lord, of the blood of souls," prayed the great Newman. Could Christians find a simpler and more apt way of discovering the meaning of their mystical unity than through the apparition of Mary at La Salette where the words of the Reconciler echo those of the Redeemer?

We can now understand the power and impetus the apparition can have in a well-balanced devotion. And we are not referring to its affective overtones. "We devoured her words," said Maximin to express what he felt as he listened to the beautiful Lady. How can we not feel something akin to that when we realize that each of her words, each of her actions, springs from a heart that seeks us as it weeps.

No, the power of this event, unusual but explained by love, is not spent. The grace of La Salette will go on penetrating stubborn hearts and quickening the self-giving of committed people. It will continue inspiring apostolic initiatives and societies of atonement. We hope especially that Christians will rediscover the supernatural laws of solidarity and reparation that maintain the balance of the mystical Body. They will strive, under the Reconciler's inspiration, to return to the social conditions worthy of a people belonging to God. In this way, it will be granted to the weakest among Christ's brothers and sisters to see the cross and to feel the cleansing blood that the Redeemer has shed for them.

Our Lady of La Salette asks nothing for herself. But what a wholesome atmosphere she creates at the foot of the cross! Committed, admirable people come to La Salette, especially those who desire to help reconcile their brothers and sisters to Christ. La Salette is their special mountain, not only because the Virgin speaks their language and dresses like them, but because she is their accredited Reconciler before God. They will learn from her by watching her. For the little they ask, they will receive much. The woman in tears seems austere, but let none be afraid to approach her. She holds the secret all people want to learn. She knows better than poets or statesmen, better than a loving sister or anyone in the world, how tears can be turned into joy.

Endnotes

Preface

1. Unless otherwise indicated, all quotations from Sacred Scripture will be taken from the New Revised Standard Version (New York: Oxford University Press, 1991).

2. See Albert Chazelle, *Au service de la Vierge en pleurs: Le Père Jean Jaouen* (Shrine of Our Lady of La Salette, 1978), 75 photocopied pages.

Chapter One

1. In the region of Corps everyone had a surname, used more often than his own, but whose origin was lost. The Pra family's was Caron and Selme's, Le Brouit. Mélanie was often called Mathieu in memory of her father. Her real name was Calvat.

2. "It was wrong to remove me from my original way of life," Maximin told Father Barbe in 1858. "I had no resources and did not feel called to the priesthood, as my benefactors had hoped. I now find myself in a very critical situation and the future seems bleak indeed" (*Manuscrits Bossan*). *In these endnotes, the translator will provide English translations of source-materials for the reader's convenience, but will leave the titles of sources in the original French because the sources themselves have never been translated in their entirety.*

3. As of the present translation, one hundred and 152 years.

Chapter Two

1. Letter from Peytard to Bishop Villecourt, reproduced by the latter in his *Nouveau Récit de l'apparition de la Sainte Vierge sur les montagnes des Alpes.* 2nd ed. (1847), p. 200. Peytard is the mayor of La Salette. A year after the fact (October 2, 1847), he narrated the event for the benefit of the Bishop of La Rochelle who had visited the area in July of that year and wanted to know more.

2. Letter from Father Louis Perrin to Canon Rousselot, dated July 6, 1848. *Dossier de l'évêché de Grenoble* in Bassette, *Le Fait de La Salette*, (Paris: Editions du Cerf, 1955), p. 172.

3. Letter from Peytard to Bishop Villecourt, in *Nouveau récit*, p. 200.

4. Ibid.

5. In his letter to Bishop Villecourt, his memory fails him on one point: he states having interrogated the two shepherds for the first time on Sunday, September 20, at Les Ablandins. But it is an undisputed fact that Maximin had returned to Corps that very morning. In 1848, Father Louis Perrin, pastor of La Salette, asked the mayor for more details on this point. Peytard replied that, in fact, his first interview with the boy had taken place on Monday the 21st. After a year's time, the mayor's error is understandable, since on the following Sunday he had again questioned the two children on the mountain and had stopped at Les Ablandins to bring Mélanie with him. An error in detail does not invalidate an overall impression: from the very first, Peytard clearly believed that the accounts of Maximin and Mélanie were identical.

6. The Pra account was preserved in a copy made by Father Lagier on February 28, 1847 (now in the Archives of the Missionaries of Our Lady of La Salette). Father Auguste Veillard, M.S. examined the authenticity of this document in an article published in the third *Cahier Notre-Dame de La Salette* (edited at the Shrine of Our Lady of La Salette).

7. From October 1853 to March 1856. Father Champon's work appeared in part in the *Annales de Notre-Dame de La Salette* from 1881 to 1888 under the title *Récits de Maximin*.

8. Champon, *Récits de Maximin*, in *Annales* (December 1881). Maximin's disclosure is certainly belated but it corroborates what he had said from the beginning to Marie des Brulais: "I was eight days without seeing Mélanie." See *Cahiers de Notre-Dame de La Salette*, Vol. 2, p. 22.

9. Dated October 4, 1846. Bassette, *Le Fait*, pp. 1, 2.

10. Father Blanc's account, in *Annales de La Salette* (June 1909), pp. 24-25.

11. The Cat Report, dated October 23, in *Dossier de l'évêché*. Text reproduced in *Cahiers de Notre-Dame de La Salette*, Vol. 2, pp. 14244.

12. The seminary professors also received an account from Father Guillaud, professor at Notre-Dame in Grenoble: it is measured in tone, but has some weaknesses. All these early reports have been published in *Cahiers Notre-Dame de La Salette*, Vol. 2.

13. Text of their statement in Rousselot, *La vérité sur l'événement de La Salette*. See Bassette, *Le Fait*, p. 101, note 5.

14. Letter to Rousselot, dated December 9, 1847, in Bassette, p. 135.

15. Ibid.

16. *Manuscripts Bossan* (in the Archives of the Missionaries of Our Lady of La Salette). In the course of some ten years, Father Bossan had collected a great number of documents and testimonies pertaining to the apparition. He interrogated everyone involved with the children's depositions and transcribed their every word with rare accuracy.

17. The newspaper *L'Univers*, dated February 21, 1847, quoted in Bassette, p. 34.

18. *Dossier de l'évêché*. Text reproduced by Carlier, *Histoire de l'Apparition de la Mère de Dieu sur la montagne de La Salette* (Lille: Desclée de Brouwer, 1914), p. 114.

19. For example, this weighted sentence: "If you are not converted immediately, sincerely, and seriously...."

20. Letter from Gueydan to Father Bossan, dated March 10, 1863 (in the Archives of the Missionaries of Our Lady of La Salette), *Cahiers N.-D. de La Salette*, Vol. 2, p. 164.

21. From the Guyot publishing house, Lyons.

22. *Dossier de l'évêché.* In Bassette, p. 71.

23. From a letter by Father Louis Perrin in *Nouveau récit*, by Bishop Villecourt, in Bassette, p. 81.

24. *Souvenirs intimes d'un pèlerinage* (Digne, 1848).

25. Villecourt, *Nouveau récit*, in Bassette, p. 82.

26. Carlier, *Histoire de l'apparition*, p. 92.

27. Father Louis Perrin was appointed pastor of La Salette on September 28, 1846. He replaced his namesake, Jacques Perrin, whose reassignment had been decided upon before the apparition for reasons of health. The new pastor interrogated the two children on the site of the apparition some ten days after assuming his new post, in all likelihood on October 12. His account is dated the 16th. He has no illusions about its worth as he writes Bossan on May 5, 1865: "The account I wrote, based on notes I took at the site of the apparition, was written after having heard the story only once" (Archives of the Missionaries of Our Lady of La Salette).

28. It was quite otherwise in the beginning. "The mayor of La Salette told us that the day after the apparition, the children's words were alive and fiery.... One must not judge the recital they made then with today's. Indeed, they have the same story, but the tone and the enthusiasm are no longer the same." (Bishop Villecourt, in his *Nouveau récit*, p. 102, quoted in Bassette, p. 83).

29. Lagier's more important notes were published in *Cahiers Notre-Dame de La Salette*, Vol. 3.

Chapter Three

1. This construction, slightly different from the first and stressing the imperative, would seem preferable, for reasons of textual criticism, to a simple repetition, on which traditional historians are in unanimous agreement: "Well, my children, you will make this known to all my people." The Pra and Laurent accounts, the

earliest among the so-called "privileged" relations, confirm it. Later, yet as early as Lagier, the two versions underwent a process of identification. But this is due to the children themselves or to the transcribers and is a phenomenon of "contamination" well explained by the close similarity between the two versions.

2. Mélanie to Marie des Brulais in *L'Echo de la Sainte Montagne* (Nantes, 1854), p. 158.

Chapter Four

1. A memory lapse, no doubt, but Father Louis Perrin had in his possession an account he himself wrote in mid-October, soon after his coming to the parish, which contains the thorny sentence. He might have been influenced by Pra's hesitation.

2. This does not explain the nettlesome sentence, but one can appreciate the interest that such an incidental statement can have for psychology.

3. Bassette, *Le Fait de La Salette*, p. 145.

4. Rousselot made a note of this on his own manuscript.

5. In Chapter Two we alluded to Peytard's memory lapses on this point as well as to their logical explanation.

6. Baratier, in-16 [?], (Grenoble, 1848).

7. Baratier, Grenoble.

8. *Dossier de l'évêché*, in Bassette, p. 206.

9. Rousselot, *Un nouveau sanctuaire à Marie* (Grenoble, 1853), pp. 51ff.

10. This information was communicated to Father Bossan by Mr. de Taxis in May 1862.

11. According to another opinion, the second version was written on July 4 at the bishop's residence. This opinion, dating from 1870, is incorrect, even though Mélanie's testimony is invoked in favor

of it. Mr. Dausse's papers, preserved in the Library of Grenoble, now dispel all doubt.

12. Letter dated September 11, 1856, to Bishop Ginoulhiac, in Bassette, p. 340.

13. For the story of the secrets, see Rousselot, *Un nouveau sanctuaire à Marie. Gerin's account is given by Dausse in Vie de M. Gerin*, and by Des Brulais in *L'Echo de la sainte Montagne*. See also Manuscrits Bossan.

14. The first edition of the *Nouveau récit* is dated October 1847.

15. A *Te Deum* was to be sung in all the churches of the diocese.

16. "Ejusmodi apparitiones seu revelationes neque approbatas neque damnatas ab Apostolica Sede fuisse, sed tantum permissas tanquam pie credendas fide solum humana, juxta traditionem quam ferunt, idoneis testimoniis ac monumentis confirmatam. Nihil proinde obstare quin Ordinarii pari ratione se gerant, facta desuper (si de opere typis vulgando agatur) in eodem sensu opportuna declaratione seu protestatione, ad tramiten." *Decretorum praelaudati* Urbani Papae VIII. Dated May 12, 1877, in *Collectio Authentica Decretorum S.R.C.* Vol. III, p. 79.

17. It might be well to reassure the concerned reader that what we are saying here about this canonical judgment is the shared insight of theologians and spiritual authors alike. Father Holstein, notably, explains it with nuance and clarity in an article entitled "Marian Apparitions," published by Maria, vol. V, pp.757 ff. After having shown that an apparition does not become an article of faith either by its approval or by the establishment of a feast in its honor, which feast functions as a kind of nihil obstat, he writes: "The Church insists on saying that this matter remains and must remain in the realm of opinion and of "moral certainty," always open to revision. This is why the Church never wants to impose an obligation on anyone through its approval. But it is no less certain that when authority pronounces itself in favor of a private revelation, it declares having a solidly founded opinion in its favor. By

so doing, it invites the faithful to accept its judgment (except for a serious reason), and so to commit themselves in the same way." And he quotes Father Lochet:

> We can sin by a double excess, [writes Father Lochet,] either by a rash, hasty commitment, a sentimental enthusiasm, and an excessive hunger for the spectacular, or by a distrust, a kind of arrogance and skepticism, maintained in spite of the encouragement's of the Church. Perhaps there is reason to ask whether, under the cover of this supernatural prudence supplied by the Church, we do not harbor a kind of disdain for and lack of commitment to this type of devotion—traces, perhaps, of a latent rationalism. (Nouvelle Revue Théologique [November 1954], p. 953).

There are yet more decisive references. Pope Pius XII, at the opening of the centennial year of La Salette, writing to the Superior General of the Missionaries, proclaimed the Holy See's deference to a bishop's judgment and its personal devotion to the Virgin invoked under this title:

> To our dear son Etienne Cruveiller, Superior General of the Institute of the Missionaries of Our Lady of La Salette.

> Our devotion to the Most Blessed Virgin Mary, to whose Immaculate Heart We have consecrated the Church and the world, can only rejoice before the pleasing perspective your letter allows us to see, of the coming Centenary of the Apparition of Our Lady of La Salette whose canonical proceedings instituted in their time by the Diocesan Authority proved to be favorable. It is very understandable that your religious family, grown from a seed planted by Bishop Philibert de Bruillard as a "perpetual remembrance of the merciful Apparition of Mary," should have taken especially to heart the centennial commemoration of that blessed afternoon of September 19,1846, when the Madonna in tears, as it is reported, came to beseech her children to enter resolutely into the way of conversion to her divine Son and of atonement for so many sins offending the august and eternal Majesty...."

From the Vatican, October 8, 1945. Text published in Documentation Catholique August 4, 1946, p. 858.

Chapter Five

1. Arbaud, *Souvenirs intimes d'un pèlerinage à La Salette*, le 19 septembre 1847. (Digne, 1848), p. 79.

2. Lagier, *Notes d'interrogatoire*, February 1847. From a letter written by Louis Perrin, former pastor of La Salette, to Father Bossan, May 5,1863.

3. *Le Pèlerinage à La Salette* (Angers, 1854), p. 177.

4. Marie des Brulais, *L'Echo de la Sainte Montagne* (Nantes,1854), p.164.

5. Written, as we know, by Léon Bloy.

6. *Nouveau récit de l'apparition de la Sainte Vierge*, p. 51.

7. Letter to Du Boys, dated June 11, published in *L'Ami de la Religion* April 7, 1849. The future bishop of Orléans conducted his inquiry from June 7 to 10, 1848.

8. Rousselot, *La Vérité sur l'evènement de La Salette* (Grenoble, 1848), p. 45.

9. *L'Echo de la Sainte Montagne*, p. 57.

10. Bez, *Pèlerinages à La Salette* (Lyons,1847), p. 25. He interrogated the children in May 1847.

11. *L'Echo*, p. 84.

12. Rousselot, *La Vérité sur l'événement de La Salette*, p. 51.

13. Marie des Brulais, *L'Echo*, p. 87.

14. In a letter to Du Boys.

15. Rousselot, *La Vérité*, p. 44.

16. Champon, *Récits de Maximin.*

17. *L'Echo*, p. 176.

18. *Pèlerinage à La Salette*, p. 24.

19. In a letter already quoted in note 7 above.

20. Testimony of Sister Sainte Thècle, in Rousselot, *La Vérité*, p. 43.

21. *Pèlerinage à La Salette*, p. 22.

22. Rousselot, *La Vérité*, p. 42.

23. Ibid., p. 41.

24. Arbaud, *Souvenirs intimes*, p. 63.

25. *L'Echo*, p. 71.

Chapter Six

1. Statement by Pierre Selme, drafted by Dumanoir, judge of the Tribunal of Montelimar, September 28, 1847, and appearing in *La Vérité sur l'événement de La Salette* by Rousselot.

2. Statement by Baptiste Pra, drafted by Dumanoir. Rousselot, *La Vérité.*

3. Des Brulais, *L'Echo.*—The Lagier notes.

4. *L'Echo*, p. 182.

5. Letter from Father Dupanloup to Du Boys.

Chapter Seven

1. Mademoiselle des Brulais gives us an insight into the demands and the insensitivity of the pilgrim crowds as she describes Maximin's role on the first anniversary celebration of the apparition:

The poor child was sick with fatigue. He never refused to satisfy the wishes of those who asked him to tell the wonderful story that he also was told to make known. He, like Mélanie remained unobtrusive in the crowd. As an outgoing boy, he was more at ease and open than the little girl. He had to be rescued early from the rush of the crowds. In the evening, however, he pursued his exhausting mission in the convent, carrying on as long as he had the strength. In total exhaustion, he managed to slip away from the crowd and came to sit near me and Sister Clothilde. He hid himself against me, rested his head on my shoulder, and promptly fell asleep. I smiled as I heard people asking where he had gone. Poor little one, he had begged a moment of rest with his beguiling innocence: "Excuse me, for this once, Sir, I have been hassled all day." (*L'Echo de la Sainte Montagne*).

2. Nortet, *Notre-Dame de La Salette*.

3. Mayor Peytard. See his letter to Bishop Villecourt in *Nouveau récit*.

4. According to a statement of Mélanie to Father Bossan (contained in the latter's manuscripts).

5. We correct only the spelling and the punctuation. The original text can be found in *Cahiers Notre-Dame de La Salette*, Vol. 3.

6. *Souvenirs intimes d'un pélerinage*.

7. In 1862, 1863, and 1864.

8. Letter to Du Boys.

9. See in Rousselot, *La Vérité*.

10. We have in mind especially the works of J. Piaget.

11. Doctrinal Statement of November 4, 1854.

12. Piaget, *La causalité physique chez l'enfant* (Alcan, 1927), p.213f.

13. *L'Echo de la Sainte Montagne*, pp. 91-92.

14. Ibid., p. 138.

Chapter Eight

1. Canons' report, dated December 15, 1846.

2. Rousselot, *Nouveaux Documents sur l'événement de La Salette* (Grenoble, 1850), pp.

3. *Les Miracles de La Salette*, 2 Vols. (Grenoble: Eymond, 1921).

4. From a letter dated April 12, 1847 and quoted in *Bassette*, p. 61.

5. See Father Louis Carlier, M.S., *Histoire de l'Apparition de la Mère de Dieu sur la montagne de La Salette* (Lille: Desclée de Brouwer, 1914), p. 274f. Pierre de la Gorce, an established authority, intimates that these figures as well as the social climate of the time, foreshadow the Revolution of 1848.

> *In the fall of 1846, severe flooding ravaged the Loire valley. This was followed by alarming reports on the harvest. The price of an hectoliter (about 3 bushels) of wheat rose from 29 francs in January of 1847 to 36 francs—in some areas, well past 40 francs—in April. Misery lurked everywhere. Riots were reported in Indre and Buzancais. Food shortages caused market values, notably railroad stocks, to plummet. Stricken companies even had recourse to government intervention. Rumors of corruption in government were rife.... Louis-Philippe (Plon, 1931), p. 377. Quoted in Bassette, p. 92*

6. *Nouveau récit de l'apparition*, p. 76.

7. Quoted by Father Giraud in *La Pratique de la dévotion à Notre-Dame de La Salette* and taken up again by Bloy in *Le symbolisme de l'apparition*.

8. Des Brulais, *Suite de l'Echo*, p. 44.

9. Des Brulais, *L'Echo de la Sainte Montagne*, p. 158.

10. Rousselot, *La vérité sur l'événement de La Salette*, p. 87.

11. We would do well to recall the statements of Selme, Pra, and Peytard, and a letter from Father Mélin dated October 4, 1846.

12. Quercy, *Les hallucinations*, vol. 2, p. 29. Ed. Alcan.

13. St. Thomas Aquinas, *Summa Theologica*, IIa, IIae, Q.174, art.2; Q.173, art.2.

14. Letter dated March 12, 1850, written by Mélin to Rousselot.

15. Bishop Ginoulhiac, Doctrinal Statement dated November 4,1854.

16. The Champon manuscripts. Quoted by Carlier, *Histoire de l'apparition de la Mère de Dieu*, p. 54f.

17. *Dossier de l'évêché*, No. 57.

18. Bassette, *Le Fait*, p. 133.

19. Bassette, p.138. The best witness, of course, remains Father Mélin. In his correspondence with diocesan authorities we feel the heartbeat of a quickening parish.

> *Your Excellency has kindly informed me of the Holy Father's permission to allow a single Communion to fulfill the obligation of Easter Duty as well as that of the Jubilee. I am grateful to you for this. We have encountered such good will and such an eagerness to do what is right, even among the men, that we have hardly had to use the permission. All received Communion twice. At Corps, the Jubilee was celebrated in an edifying manner. We were four confessors and all of us remarked that we had never granted absolution with such assurance as during this time. There were so many and such extraordinary graces that I am embarrassed for the future. Yesterday I placed everything into the hands of the beautiful Lady. She has been the great evangelizer, the confessor par excellence. (Letter dated April 12, 1847, in Dossier de l'évêché, No. 43).*

20. Abbé Janvier, *Vie de Soeur Saint-Pierre. Carmélite de Tours*, 2nd ed. (Tours, 1884), p. 30.

21. Ibid., p. 250.

22. Ibid., p. 256.

23. Ibid.,p. 313.

24. See in particular Thureau-Dangin, *Histoire de la Monarchie de Juillet*, and the preaching of the time.

Chapter Nine

1. Maximin's father died peacefully on February 24, 1849; his stepmother on January 24, 1848.

2. Statement made at the minor seminary of Rondeau, 1853.

3. Written by Father Nicod of the Red Cross in Lyons.

4. Azum de Bernétas, Biographie de M. Vianney, Curé d'Ars. Quoted by Giray, *Les Miracles de La Salette*, vol. 2, p. 278.

5. Letter from Verrier to Rousselot, September 1853.

6. During a hearing held on August 11, 1864. See his letters to Bishop Devie and to Cardinal de Bonald.

7. Letter dated October 3, 1852.

8. Giray, *Les Miracles*, p. 354.

9. Letter to Rousselot, dated April 24, 1851.

10. From a statement by Angélique Giraud, April 25, 1851.

11. The Count des Garets's deposition at the Bishop's proceedings, September 26, 1863.

12. Deposition entitled *Ne pereant*, dated September 27, 1876. These details were confirmed by Brother Athanasius in the presence of Father Millon, chaplain of Our Lady of La Salette, in June 1911.

13. From *Ne pereant*. Deposition of December 11, 1874.

14. *Ne pereant*, May 26, 1875.

15. Rousselot, *Un nouveau sanctuaire*, p. 128.

16. Letter from Father Bruno, Capuchin, to the Bishop of Grenoble, dated from Lyons, August 11, 1852.

17. Testimony reported by Father Reynaud in 1854 and reproduced by Father des Garets.

18. Des Garets, *Le curé d'Ars et La Salette* (Lyons, 1860), p. 42.

19. Rousselot, *Un nouveau sanctuaire à Marie*, Article 11.

20. Des Garets, *Le curé d'Ars et La Salette*, p. 19.

21. Confirmed by Father Monnin. Deposition made at the canonical proceedings, August 10, 1876.

22. Ibid., p. 20.

23. Dausse, *Souvenirs sur l'abbé J.-B. Gerin.*

24. Giray, *Les Miracles*, vol. 2, p. 279.

25. States the Countess of Cibeins at an apostolic hearing: "I know that after Maximin's visit with the Pastor, the latter declared that Maximin had told him he had not seen the Blessed Virgin but a beautiful Lady." Giray, *Les Miracles*, vol. 2, p. 274.

26. *L'Echo de la Sainte Montagne*, p. 265.

27. In clear terms? This is open to question. After eight years the Curé's memory could have betrayed him. Nicolas himself admits to dramatization and warns his readers that his dialogue is conventional. A. Nicolas, *L'Esprit de l'opposition.*

28. Des Garets, *Le Curé d'Ars et La Salette*, p. 56.

29. His deposition was made on June 7, 1864.

30. Report dated October 26, 1858.

31. Deposition dated November 4, 1874.

32. Deposition dated August 10, 1876.

33. The adjective, "badaud", has a special flavor on the lips of the

Dauphinois.

34. Father des Garets explained this reserve by the fear of saddening a few people zealously guarding their pastor's honor. They were more involved in the controversy than he would have wished, yet he did not feel that the invitation to retract should come from him.

35. Depositions of Miss des Garets, Mrs. Scipiot-Mandy, and Catherine Lassagne.

36. Letter dated November 9, 1858.

37. A. Nicolas, *L'Esprit de l'opposition*.

38. Des Garets, *Le Curé d'Ars et La Salette*, p. 65.

39. Testimony of Father Mélin. In 1911, Father Millon received a confirmation of it from Bishop Valansio, vicar general of Belley, who had accompanied Bishop de Langalerie on his pilgrimage.

40. Letter from Rousselot to Father Doyen, October 31, 1862.

41. It later became known as *La Salette des Quatre-Chemins* (*La Salette of the Crossroads*).

42. Carlier, *Un Vrai Fils de Marie, le P. Giraud*, (Grenoble, 1922), p. 383.

43. *The Cartellier manuscripts*, 1860. Grenoble library.

44. We note that only his conduct at Ars is referred to here.

45. Excerpt from a letter written by Father Eymard to Rousselot, January 29, 1851.

46. The documentation of this chapter is indebted to Bishop Giray's work, *Les Miracles de La Salette*, as well as to a research manuscript written by Father Millon, a former chaplain of the La Salette Basilica. He has the special merit of having transcribed from the originals all depositions kept at the bishop's residence at Belley in view of the beatification proceedings of the Curé of Ars.

Chapter Ten

1. Letter dated January 9, 1848, written to Bishop de Bruillard, and the first page of his Journal (fonds Chaper: Library of Grenoble).

2. Had he read it? He doesn't say. About the *Report to the Pope*, he assured Bishop Ginoulhiac that had he read it, he never would have released it.

3. *Dossier de l'évêché*, in Bassette, p. 307.

4. Letter to Rousselot, dated February 20, 1853. *Dossier de l'évêché*, in Bassette, p. 314.

5. Jacques-Marie-Achille Ginoulhiac was born in Montpellier on December 3, 1806. Before his appointment as Bishop of Grenoble on December 9, 1852, he had been a professor at the Major Seminary of Montpellier, then Vicar-General of Aix-en-Provence. His writings rank him among the best theologians of the 19th century (*Histoire du Dogme, Les Epîtres pastorales, Le Sermon sur la Montagne Les Origines du Christianisme*). His *Histoire du Dogme catholique pendant les trois premiers siècles de l'Eglise* was in Newman's library. In 1870, he succeeded Cardinal de Bonald to the See of Lyons. He died at Montpellier on November 17, 1875.

6. Circular letter dated September 19, 1857.

7. Letter dated January 19, 1855. *Dossier de l'évêché*, in Bassette, p. 387.

8. Letter to Bishop Fava, dated July 7, 1883.

9. *La Salette: Controverse épistolaire entre les abbés Bertrand et Deéléon 1889-1890* (Bar-le-Duc: Saint-Paul), p.110.

10. See his Orpheus (Picard, 1914), p. 564, a paragraph that is a veritable challenge for any reader: it is impossible to concentrate more errors in fewer words.

11. Bassette, *Le Fait de La Salette*, pp. 393-94.

12. Giray, *Les Miracles de La Salette*, vol. 1, p. 162, note.

13. Farconnet's concluding remarks in the *Affaire de La Salette* from a transcription of the debates collected and published by Sabbatier, Grenoble, 1859. The "butter in the soup" expression is the adaptation of Maximin's candid remark: "She melted away," he said, describing the disappearance of the beautiful Lady, "like a lump of butter in a pan."

14. *Manuscrits Perrin* (Archives of the Missionaries of La Salette).

15. The Month, December, 1933.

16. This text was quoted by A. Nicolas in the *Gazette du Midi* (see Bassette, *Le Fait de La Salette*, p. 389), and published in a more literary form in *La Salette devant la raison et le devoir d'un catholique* by the same author.

17. Bassette, *Le Fait*, p. 389. In note 5, he quotes a still more unchallengeable text from Giray.

Chapter Eleven

1. We refer especially to I a, II ae, Q.111, Art. 1.

2. 1 Corinthians 12.

3. Especially in *De Veritate*, Q. 12, Art. 5 and in the *Summa Theologica*, II a, II ae, Q. 172, Art. 4.

4. More precisely on March 16, 1854, from Corenc "to a La Salette Missionary" (who could only be either Father Sibillat or Father Burnoud). This letter was published by Delbreil (*Le nouveau Sinai*) and Girard, author of many partisan works.

5. *De Veritate*, Q. 9, Art. 2.

6. *L'Echo de la sainte Montagne*, p. 65.

7. *Manuscrits Bossan*. Questions addressed to Maximin; his answers. September 1871.

8. Mysterious because she herself has never published this story and because it is impossible to establish the degree of influence her directors might have had in the writing of this document.

9. Lemonnyer, O.P., *Théologie du Nouveau Testament*, p. 126.

10. From the letter addressed to Father Archier, dated August 8, 1880. (Archives of the Missionaries of La Salette).

11. *L'Apparition de la Très Sainte Vierge sur la sainte montagne de La Salette* (Société Saint-Augustin, 1922). A letter from Cardinal Pizzardo to the Reverend Procurator of the Missionaries of Our Lady of La Salette, dated January 8, 1957, points out that it is in fact the text of this booklet which is condemned by the Index and not only the objectionable additions included in some copies. See *Annales de Notre-Dame de La Salette*. 1960, No. 51.

12. Des Brulais, *L'Echo de la sainte montagne*, passim; Dupanloup, *Lettre à M. Du Boÿs*.

13. The author read this manuscript in the Archives of the Shrine at La Salette. There is no doubt as to its authenticity. The history of its transmission is assured by the following note:

This manuscript was given by Mélanie to one of her companions who has become Mrs. Dumas and who confided it to Father Fluchaire, Pastor and Archpriest of Corps. He in turn ceded it to Father Giray, Rector of the Shrine of La Salette, on Monday, July 23, 1917, in the presence of Bishop Caillot, Father Champavier, and Father Jassoud, Assistant Pastor of Bourg-d'Oisans.

In witness thereof, I have signed,

Giray, J.-B., Vicar General, Grenoble, 7/29/17.

14. *Manuscrits Bossan*, July 1871.

15. This passage is excerpted from a copybook found with the papers of Canon Annibale di Francia. We know of it only from a copy made by Father Forest, M.S. in 1929, at Messina. The copyist admits not knowing who filled this copybook. The only person to

whom it could logically belong, according to its contents, is Mrs. de Maximy (Sister Thérèse de Jesus), with whom the Canon had been acquainted. The passage harmonizes with testimony from Corenc relative to the views of the superior and the mistress of novices concerning Mélanie.

16. Father Burnoud. He left the Institute in September 1855.

17. From a letter dated April 29, 1855, to Bishop Ullathorne of Birmingham [England], in response to his own letter dated April 25. From Diocesan records.

18. *Bulletin des Missionnaires de Notre-Dame de La Salette*, March-April 1960, p. 2.

19. In *Cahiers Notre-Dame de La Salette*, vol. 1, p. 31.

20. My Profession of Faith, Part Three. Quoted by Carlier, *Histoire de l'Apparition de la Mère de Dieu sur la montagne de La Salette*, p. 212.

21. Carlier, *Histoire de l'Apparition*, p. 215.

22. *Manuscrits Bossan*, 1862.

23. *Souvenirs des Zouaves pontificaux. Recueillis par Le Chauff de Kerguenec*, (Paris, 1891), in Letter to his father, dated May 12, 1865.

24. *De Veritate*, q. 12, a. 5, ad 4m.

Chapter Twelve

1. *Mémoire au Pape*. Fifth doubt.

2. His letter to Mr. Du Boys written in 1848.

3. *Journal intime*, published by Father Branchereau, p. 335.

4. In the *Annales de Notre-Dame de La Salette*, July-August 1930.

5. In *Le voyage du Centurion*.

6. In *La Cathédrale*.

7. Letter to Bishop de Bruillard dated June 24. Cf. Giray, *Les*

Miracles.

8. L. Laplace, *La Mère de Jesus*, (Paris, 1894), pp. 150-53.

9. Letter to Father Charcosset, quoted by Henri Guitton in his *Vie de Léon Harmel*.

10. *Annales*, 1865, p. 61.

11. For more detailed information, see Father Giray's booklet, *Notre-Dame de La Salette, le P. Eymard et l'Eucharistie* (Grenoble, 1910).

12. Letter to Mère Sainte-Claire, prioress of the Capuchin Nuns of Lorgues, dated August 24, 1857.

13. Letter to Father Boulian, dated June 19, 1860.

14. *De l'Union à Notre-Seigneur dans sa vie de victime*, 8th ed., p. 325.

15. *Anthologie de la littérature spirituelle, époque contemporaine*, Ed. Louis Chaigne and Albert Garreau (Alsatia, 1941), p. 43.

16. *Pratique de la dévotion à Notre-Dame de La Salette*, pp. 28-31. Father Giraud's biography was written by Father Carlier in a work entitled *Un vrai fils de Marie* (Grenoble: Eymond, 1922). The book is lengthy, but it is a treasure trove of meaningful texts taken from his correspondence and private journals.

17. *Actes de S. S. Pie X*, vol.3 (Paris: Bonne Presse), p.174. In chapter IV we quoted the rescript of the Sacred Congregation of Rites. We can wonder why no mention is made in these documents of the bishop's approval. We believe the reason for this is that this event, judged canonically, still belongs to the realm of human faith. Similarly, we can certainly allow the same importance to the bishop's verdict as we do to other testimonies worthy of trust. In our opinion, it completes the sum of probabilities capable of justifying moral certitude.

18. Rousselot, *Un nouveau sanctuaire à Marie*, p. 60.

19. Bernard, O.P., *Le mystère de Marie*, (Paris: Desclée de Brouwer, 1933), p. 71.

20. *Bulletin des Missionnaires de La Salette*, September 1925

21. Garrigou-Lagrange, *La Mére du Sauveur et notre vie intérieure*, (Lyons: 1941), p. 264.

22. Second sermon for the season of Advent.

23. Sermon for the Sunday in the Octave of the Assumption.

24. Sermon for the Nativity of the Blessed Virgin Mary.

25. Desmarais, *Saint Albert le Grand, docteur de la médiation mariale* (Paris, Ottawa: 1935), p. 97.

26. *Discourse sur les saints*, referred to in Desmarais, *Saint Albert le Grand*, p. 106.

27. Referred to in *Desmarais*, p.108.

28. *Carmina Nisibena*, 27.

29. *Summa Aurea*, in *Migne*, vol. 1 p. 4. Here again, specialists distinguish between the texts of Saint Ephrem and texts inspired by Saint Ephrem (cf. the article by G. Jouassard, "Marie a travers la patristique," in *Maria* (Paris: Beauchesne), vol. 1, p. 88, note 3). What is important here is that both categories of writings have become part of the living tradition.

30. *La Mariologie de saint Jean Damascene* by Father Saarda, S.J., in *Bulletin de la Société francaise d'études mariales*, 1935, p. 171.

31. Ibid., p. 171.

32. *The Motherhood of the Blessed Virgin*, Hymn at Lauds.

Glossary of Proper Names

In an historical book such as this one, many names appear and the reader might find it difficult to recall who did what. The following Glossary hopes to help the reader keep track of people and places. This addition was not part of the original French edition.

A

Ablandins, Les (A hamlet of La Salette-Fallavaux)

AIX (Former diocese of Bishop Ginoulhiac)

Albert the Great, Saint (1200-1280, Doctor of the Church)

Albertin, Father (Professor at Major Seminary of Grenoble)

Annales de Notre-Dame de La Salette—see Newspapers & Magazines

Annonay (Industrial town in southeastern France)

Arbaud, Father (1815-1899, Interviewer)

Archard, Father (Canon)

Archconfraternity

> *for the Atonement of Blasphemy and the Profanation*
>
> *of the Lord's Day of Our Reconciling Lady of La Salette*
>
> *of Our Lady, Reconciler of Sinners*

Archier, Father Pierre (La Salette Missionary, first Superior General)

Ars (Town north of Lyons where St. Jean Vianney was pastor)

Athanasius, Brother (of Ars)

Augustine of Hippo, Saint (354-430, Doctor of the Church)

Auvergne, Father Alexis (Canon of Grenoble, Bishop's secretary and interviewer)

Avignon, Sacred Heart Convent at

B

Babou, Field of (Pasture where Maximin's cattle grazed)

Barnel (Publisher of Grenoble)

Bassette, Louis (La Salette author)

Beaucaire (Home of Father. Lambert)

Belley, Bishop of (Bishop Devie Diocese containing Ars)

Bernadette (Soubirous of Lourdes)

Berthier, Father (Vicar General of Grenoble, initially opposed to apparition)

Bertineaux (Hamlet near La Salette)

Bertrand, Father (Confidant of Father Déléon in later years)

Bez

> *Nicholas, Father* (Interviewer who published first book on apparition)

> *Joseph* (Name Maximin assumed at Ecully)

Blanc, Father (Interviewer, Sacristan at La Salette who later became a priest)

Bloy, Léon (1846-1917, noted French Author)

Bollenat, Antoinette (Miraculously cured)

Bonnefous, Brother (Marianist candidate, friend of Baron de Richemont)

Bossan, Antoine, Father (Interviewer)

Bourges (French town in central France)

Boutières (Present-day hamlet of Saint-Julien-Boutières, near La Salette)

Brayer, Mr. (Benefactor who went to Ars with Maximin)

Bremond, Henri (1865-1933, Catholic philosopher and theologian, French literary scholar)

Briançon (City east of La Salette, at an altitude of 4,350 feet, is the highest city in France)

Bruno, Bernard, Father, O.F.M. Cap. (Friend of Curé of Ars)

Burnoud, Father (First Superior of the La Salette Missionaries)

Butler, Father William (Anglican convert)

C

Café de l'Isère (Café in Corps near Maximin's home)

Calvat (also used Matthieu as a surname)

> *Melanie*

> *Pierre* (Melanie's father)

Cambrai, Cardinal Archbishop of

Carmel

> *of rue d'Enfer* (Paris)

> *of Tours* (Residence of Sr. Marie of Saint-Pierre)

Caron, Mother (Baptiste Pra's mother-in-law)

Cartellier, Father Jean-Pierre (Pastor of St. Joseph, Grenoble and vigorous opponent of apparition)

Cat, Father (Pastor at La Mure) — see Reports, Cat

Cathedral Chapter (Usually a diocesan-wide meeting)

Chabannerie (Hamlet near La Salette-Fallavaux)

Chalandon, Bishop (Auxiliary to Bishop Devie)

Champon

> *Father* (Maximin's tutor at Seyssins)

> *Miss* (Relative of Father Champon who lived in the rectory)

Charcosset, Father (Friend of La Salette)

Chatrousse, Bishop Pierre (1795-1857, of Valence)

Chevanas, Father (Assistant pastor at Corps)

Chiron, Father (Caretaker of Mister Antoine Gay)

Cohen, Father Hermann (Musician, Jewish convert)

Coin, Field of (Field mentioned by Our Lady in the Apparition)

Collard, Father (Director of school at Ecully)

Collet (Knoll near site of apparition)

Constitutional, Le—see Newspapers & Magazines

Corenc (Village near Grenoble, convent where Melanie was a candidate)

Corps (town in foothills of Apparition site)

Courier de l'Isère—see Newspapers & Magazines

Curé of Ars (St. Jean-Baptiste Marie Vianney)

D

Darlington (England; town where Melanie entered a Carmelite monastery)

Dausse, Mister (Close friend of Bishop de Bruillard)

Day, Mister (Questionable witness quoted by Déléon)

de Belvey, Miss (Friend of Curé of Ars)

de Bernetas, Azum (Parishioner of Ars)

de Bonald, Cardinal (1787-1870, Archbishop of Lyons, long-opposed to La Salette apparition)

de Bruillard, Philibert (1765-1860, Bishop of Grenoble, founder of Missionaries of Our Lady of La Salette)

de Certeau, Count (His castle was at Passins)

de Cissey, Count Louis (Founder of "Oeuvre dominicale de France")

de Geslin, Father (Opponent of La Salette in Rome)

de Kerguenec, Le Chauff (Friend of Maximin)

de la Bouillerie, Father François-Alexandre Roullet (1810-1882, Vicar-General of Paris, then Bishop of Carcassone, Founder of Nocturnal Adoration Society)

de Lamerlière, Miss (Resident of Corps, publicly ridiculed by Déléon Cartellier)

de la Minouna

    Mother (Rosette's mother)

    Rosette (Shepherd on mountain the day of the apparition)

de Langalerie, Bishop Pierre-Henri Gérault (1810-1886, of Belley, who replaced Bishop Alexandre-Raymond Devie, 1767-1852)

de Lemps, Father (Priest of Grenoble, opposed to the apparition)

Déléon, Father Claude-Joseph (Anti-La Salette, Editor of Union Dauphinoise, suspended by Bishop de Bruillard)

Deluil-Martiny (Family name of Mother Marie de Jésus)

Depéry, Bishop Jean-Irénée (1796-1861, of Gap)

de Richemont, Count (Pretender to the French throne)

Des Brulais, Miss Marie (1809-1896, Retired woman living at convent in Corps, interviewer)

des Garets

      Father (Canon)

      Count (Mayor of Ars)

      Mrs. (Wife of Mayor)

de Ségur, Bishop. Louis Gaston Adrien (1820-1881, Vatican official who reprimanded Déléon)

de Taxis, Canon (of Grenoble)

Devie, Bishop (of Belley, Diocese containing Ars)

Descôtes, Father (Friend of the Curé of Ars)

Desgenettes, Father Charles-Éléonore Dufriche (Pastor of Notre-Dame-des-Victoires, Paris)

Donnadieu (Pen-name used by Déléon)

Dorsières (Hamlet of La Salette-Fallavaux)

Doyen, Father (Early La Salette historian)

Dubouché, Miss Théodelinde (Co-founder of Third-Order dedicated to the Blessed Sacrament)

Du Boÿs, Albert (Lord of Combe-de-Lancey, resident of Laus and friend of Father Dupanloup)

Dumanoir, Mister (Counsel)

Dupanloup, Father (Interviewer, subsequent Bishop of Orléans)

Dupont, Father (Priest of Brittany)

Duprin, Mister (Mayor of Morestel, Isère)

E

Ecully (Suburb of Lyons, France)

Einsiedeln, Abbey of (Residence of Father Laurent Hecht)

Ephrem, Saint (306-373, a Syriac Christian deacon and a prolific Syriac-language hymnographer and theologian)

Eustelle, Marie (1814-1842, known as the "Angel of the Eucharist")

Eymard, St.-Pierre-Julien-Marie (1811-1868, born in La Mure, near La Salette, Founder of Blessed Sacrament Fathers)

Eymery, Father (Vicar of Father Maitre and visitor to La Salette)

F

Frattini, Bishop (Vatican official, Defender of the Faith)

Fallavaux (Hamlet of La Salette-Fallavaux)

Farconet, Mister (Father Cartellier's lawyer)

Fava, Bishop Armand-Joseph (1826-1899, of Grenoble, successor of Bishop Ginoulhiac)

Fonteneau, Father (Secretary to Archbishop of Bordeaux)

Fornari, Cardinal (Vatican official, former Nuncio to Paris)

Fumet, Stanislaus (1896-1983, French man of letters)

G

Gaillard, Marie (Wife of François Laurent Miraculously healed)

Gamon, Melanie (of Saint-Felicien [Ardèche], miraculously cured)

Gap (City south of Corps)

Gargas, Mount (Peak directly to north of apparition site)

Gay, Antoine Mister (Seer, sick former Trappist brother)

Genevey, Father (Priest of Grenoble opposed to apparition)

Gérente, Father (Chaplain at the convent of Corenc)

Gerin, Father (Interviewer, Pastor of the Cathedral)

Ginoulhiac, Bishop Jacques-Marie-Achille (1806-1875, Successor to Bishop de Bruillard)

Giraud

> *Angélique* (Sister of Maximin)
>
> *Monsieur* (Clerk of Corps)
>
> *Maximin* (Witness to the La Salette Apparition)
>
> *Sylvain-Marie, Father.* (La Salette Missionary)
>
> *the Wheelright* (Maximin's Father)

Giray, Bishop. Joseph-Lucien (1864-1939, of Cahors, also one-time Shrine Director)

Gousset, Cardinal Thomas-Marie-Joseph (1792-1866, Archbishop of Reims)

Grenoble (Large regional city and Diocesan See)

Gueydan, Mister (Interviewer)

Guibert, Bishop (of Viviers, later Cardinal of Paris)

Guillard (Interviewer)—see Reports & Accounts

Guillaud, Mister (Questionable witness quoted by Déléon)

Guillernain, Father (Vicar General to Bishop Devie of Belley)

Guillot, Miss Marguerite (Miraculously healed)

H

Harmel, Léon (Friend of La Salette)

Hébert, Mister (Government Minister of Justice and Worship)

Hecht, Laurent, Father (Published first German book on apparition.)

Henry, Father (Diocesan Canon from Grenoble)

Hermann, Father—see Cohen, Father Hermann

Holy See (the See of Rome, the Vatican)

Houzelot, Father (Colleague of Brother Bonnefous)

I

Irenaeus, Saint (d. 202, Doctor of the Church)

Isabelle, Mother (Prioress of Carmel on Rue d'Enfer, Paris)

Isère (French Department or area in which La Salette is located.)

J

Jesuits (of Lalouvesc, France)

John Damascene, Saint (c. 675-749, Doctor of the Church, "the golden-tongued speaker")

Jolly, Archbishop Mellon de (1795-1872, of Sens, juridical investigator)

Jourdains, The (Maximin's adoptive parents in later life)

Jayet, Father (Pastor of nearby Saint-Ismier, France)

Justin, Saint (early Christian apologist, sacred writer and martyr)

L

Lady,

> *Beautiful* (Title given to Our Lady of La Salette by the chil
> dren)
>
> *of La Salette, Our* (Official title given to apparition of the
> Virgin Mary at La Salette, France)

Lagier, Father (Interviewer, Parish priest of Saint-Pierre de
Chérennes)—see also Reports, Lagier

Lambert, Father (Interviewer from Beaucaire in southern France)

Lambruschini, Cardinal (1776-1854, Vatican Prime Minister under Pope
Pius IX)

La Mure, France (regional mining town, in the valley below La Salette)

Larivière, Miss (Target of Father Déléon)

La Salette

> *Missionaries of Our Lady of* (Chaplains and later a religious
> congregation originally founded by Bishop de Bruillard to
> take care of the pilgrims to the Shrine)

Lariviere, Miss (Target of Father Déléon)

Lassagne, Catherine (Director of Providence House at Ars)

Laurent

> *François* (Brother to Joseph)

Joseph (Haberdasher of Corps, interviewer)—see Reports, *Laurent*

Madame Marie Gaillard (Miraculously healed)

Le Mans, Diocese of (France)

Lemann brothers (Jewish converts)

Lemousin, Father (of Bleriot-Plage, France, Founder of La Salette Shrine at Baraques)

Long, Mister (Author of a deposition, Substitute Justice of the Peace at Corps)— see Reports, *Long*

Louis-Philippe I (1773-1850, King of France)

Loulou (Maximin's dog)

Lourdes, (Site of a later Marian apparition, 1858)

Lowe, Father (Commentator)

Lyons, Diocese of (Major French city and Archdiocese of which Grenoble is suffragant)

M

Madames of the Sacred Heart (Sisters at Montfleurry)

Maitre, Father (Archpriest of Mens)—see also Reports, *Maitre-Eymery*

Marche, Father (Pastor of Saint-Martin-de-la-Noue at Saint-Dizier)

Mariale (Medieval masterpiece attributed to St. Albert the Great)

Marie de la Croix, Sister (Melanie's religious name in the convent)

Marie de Saint-Pierre, Sister (Carmelite mystic)

Marie de Jesus, Mother (Founder of the Society of the Daughters of the Heart of Jesus)

Marie-Thérèse, Mother (Founder of a Third Order community)

Maron, Jean, Father (1857-1930, a La Salette Missionary)

Marseilles (City in southern France)

Mary of Egypt, Saint (c. 344- c. 421, Mystic writer, patron saint of penitents)

Matthieu — see *Calvat, Melanie*

Maximin — see *Giraud, Maximin*

Melanie — see *Calvat, Melanie*

Mélin, Father (Parish Priest of Corps)

Memin — see *Giraud, Maximin*

Minder, Doctor (Surgeon, friend of Maximin)

Monnin, Father (Commentator)

Mont-sous-les-baisses (Lower peak near site of the apparition.)

Morlot, Bishop François-Nicholas-Madeleine (1795-1862, of Tours)

Mure, La—see La Mure

N

National Shrines of France (Title of Pilgrimage movement)

Newman, John-Henry Cardinal (1801-1890, convert from Anglicanism, poet and theologian)

Newspapers & Magazines

    Annales de Notre-Dame de La Salette

    Constitutional, Le

    Courier de l'Isère

National, Le

Revue des Oeuvres Eucharistiques

Siècle, Le

Union Dauphinoise, L'

Vie Parisienne, La

Nicolas, Amédée (Friend of La Salette)

Nicoud, Father (Friend of Curé of Ars)

Nîmes (City in southern France)

Notre-Dame des Victoires (Parisian Shrine, first home of the Nocturnal Adoration Society)

Notre-Dame des Champs (Second home of the Nocturnal Adoration Society)

O

Obiou, Mount (Tallest mountain in the La Salette area)

Obier, Father (Influence on Father Sylvain-Marie Giraud, M.S.)

Orcel, Father (Interviewer, Superior of Major Seminary in Grenoble)

P

Paris (Capital city of France)

Parisis, Bishop Pierre Louis (1795-1866, of Langres, France)

Pellenc, Baron

Perrin

    Jacques, Father (Parish Priest of La Salette at time of apparition)

Louis, *Father* (Parish Priest of La Salette who followed Jacques)

Peytard, Mister (Mayor of La Salette)

Philpin, Father (Commentator)

Piguet-Chateau (Widow of Angiers with published accounts)

Pius IX, Pope (1792-1878, at time of investigations)

Planeau, Mount (small peak directly west of apparition site)

Ponton, Father (Friend of Curé of Ars)

Pra

    Baptiste (Employer of Melanie)

    Grandmother (Mother Caron)

    Jacques (Brother of Baptiste)

    Providence, Sisters of (Caretakers of the children after the apparition)

Prudhomme (Publisher)

Q

Quet-en-Beaumont (Village west of La Salette)

R

Rabilloud, Father (First Vicar of La Mure)

Rahier, M.S., Father Charles (1898-1969, Author)

Raymond, Father (Curate at Ars, enemy of La Salette)

Redon (Publishing house in Grenoble)

Reinach, Salomon (Commentator)

Renan (Commentator)

Reports & Accounts (of the apparition)

>   *Bossan*
>
>   *Cat*
>
>   *Guillard*
>
>   *Lagier*
>
>   *Lambert*
>
>   *Laurent*
>
>   *Long*
>
>   *Maitre-Eymery*
>
>   *Pra*

Rousselot-Orsel

Revue des Oeuvres Eucharistiques - see *Newspapers & Magazines*

Rigat, Father (Pastor of Vienne)

Robert, J. (Pen-name used by Déléon)

Rondeau (Grenoble's Minor Seminary where Maximin lived)

Rousselot, Joseph, Father (Professor of Theology at Major Seminary, Honorary Canon of the Grenoble Cathedral, Honorary Vicar General)

S

Sacre-Coeur de Montmartre (Permanent home of the Nocturnal Adoration Society)

Saint-Charles, Sister (of Avignon, miraculously cured)

Saint-Dizier (Home of Archconfraternity of Blasphemy...)

Saint-Gervais (in Paris, parish of Father Thévenat, who founded "National Shrines of France")

Saint-Isrnier (Home parish of Father Maron, later residence of Déléon)

Saint Jean-des-Vertus (Village and parish near La Salette)

Saint Joseph's School (Anticipated residence for Maximin)

Sainte-Luce (Village parish near La Salette)

Saint Pierre, Sister (Carmelite of Tours, France)

Sainte-Thècle, Sister (Superior at convent in Corps where the children were placed)

Seignemartin, Father (Friend of Curé of Ars)

Selme, Pierre (Farmer of La Salette who hired Maximin)

Seyssins (Town just west of Grenoble)

Sezia (brook that flows from spring at apparition site)

Sibillat, Father François (Interviewer)

Sisters of Providence - see *Providence, Sisters of*

Synodal Statutes (of Diocese of Grenoble)

T

Templier, Mister (Uncle and guardian of Maximin)

Therese de Jesus, Sister (Mistress of Novices at Corenc)

Thevenat, Father (Founder of National Shrines of France)

Thurston, Father Herbert (1856-1939, Jesuit historian)

Toccanier, Father (Confidant of Curé of Ars)

U

Ullathorne, Bishop William Bernard (1806-1889, of Birmingham, England)

Union Dauphinoise, L' — see *Newspapers & Magazines*

V

Vecchioti, Monsignor (Assistant to the Nuncio of France)

Veillard, Father (Rector of the La Salette Basilica)

Verdon, Father (Second Vicar of La Mure)

Verrier, Mister (Benefactor who went to Ars with Maximin)

Veuillot, Louis (Journalist)

Vianney, Jean-Baptiste, Father—see Curé of Ars

Villecourt, Bishop (of Larochelle)

Vintras Sect (Fringe group in Lyons area)

Viollet, Father (Pastor of Corps, under interdict)

Vonier, Dom (1875-1938, theologican and writer)

Vrau, Father Philibert (Founder of the "Revue des Oeuvres Eucharistiques [Review of Eucharistic Works]")

Biography of Fr. Jaouen

The author of the present work was a Missionary of Our Lady of La Salette. Born on March 3, 1898 in the French province of Brittany at Finistere, he died on September 15th, 1975, the feast of Our Lady of Seven Dolors. He was a humanist in the good sense of the term, possessed of a broad cultural background. Deeply interested in education, he contributed many articles on this subject to various French reviews and journals. In 1932 he published a short work entitled *La formation sociale dans l'enseignement secondaire* (Editions du Cerf, 1932 *Social Formation in Secondary Education*).

Fr. Jean Jaouen, M.S. (1898-1975)

This essay was widely acclaimed by French learned societies and he was invited to give courses at the renowned Institut Catholique de Paris. In various ways Father Jaouen brought his education competence to bear on the formation of future La Salette Missionaries.

Father Jaouen also wrote a work on the life and times of La Salette Father Sylvain Giraud whom the French *Dictionaire de Spiritualite* recognizes as "a master in the spirituality of the ministerial and lay priesthood."

But Jean Jaouen will always be known in La Salette circles for his book entitled *La Grace de La Salette au regard de l'Eglise*. It was first published in 1946, on the occasion of the 100th anniversary of the apparition of Mary at La Salette and has been reprinted in France three times since that date. It is a work that, in one manner or another, he has spent his lifetime writing. This work is the fruit of a great labor and of a love for Our Lady which typified Jaouen's life. He called the Mother of Christ the "Lady of Compassion" and always described her role in the Christian life with deep affection and sound theological sense. This work is often hailed as the best book ever written on La Salette. Indeed, it was crafted by a man fully equipped to write it.

During his last illness he wrote: "It is good for us to realize that the sufferings of this earth will eternally be the stuff of our joys in heaven. That will happen only if our tears do not remain sterile but change us and join with the grace present within us."

359

Made in the USA
Columbia, SC
10 July 2021

41625736R00205